MW00814333

Richard Rorty

20th Century Political Thinkers
Series Editors: Kenneth L. Deutsch and Jean Bethke Elshtain

Richard Rorty

Politics and Vision

Christopher J. Voparil

ROWMAN & LITTLEFIELD PUBLISHERS, INC.
Lanham • Boulder • New York • Toronto • Oxford

ROWMAN & LITTLEFIELD PUBLISHERS, INC.

Published in the United States of America
by Rowman & Littlefield Publishers, Inc.
A wholly owned subsidiary of The Rowman & Littlefield Publishing Group, Inc.
4501 Forbes Boulevard, Suite 200, Lanham, Maryland 20706
www.rowmanlittlefield.com

PO Box 317
Oxford
OX2 9RU, UK

Copyright © 2006 by Rowman & Littlefield Publishers, Inc.

All rights reserved. No part of this publication may be reproduced, stored
in a retrieval system, or transmitted in any form or by any means, electronic,
mechanical, photocopying, recording, or otherwise, without the prior permission
of the publisher.

British Library Cataloguing in Publication Information Available

Library of Congress Cataloging-in-Publication Data

Voparil, Christopher J., 1969–
  Richard Rorty : politics and vision / Christopher J. Voparil.
    p. cm. — (20th century political thinkers)
  Includes index.
  ISBN-13: 978-0-7425-5166-4 (cloth : alk. paper)
  ISBN-10: 0-7425-5166-0 (cloth : alk. paper)
  ISBN-13: 978-0-7425-5167-1 (pbk. : alk. paper)
  ISBN-10: 0-7425-5167-9 (pbk. : alk. paper)
  1. Rorty, Richard—Political and social views. 2. Political science—Philosophy.
3. Liberalism—Philosophy. I. Title. II. Twentieth-century political thinkers.

  JC251.R67V67 2006
  320.51'3092—dc22   2006004794

Printed in the United States of America

♾™ The paper used in this publication meets the minimum requirements of American
National Standard for Information Sciences—Permanence of Paper for Printed Library
Materials, ANSI/NISO Z39.48-1992.

The genius of all great political thinkers is to make public that which is of private concern, to translate into public language the more special, idiosyncratic vocabulary of inner man. . . . The great thinker suffers the malaise common to an age and possesses the courage and the craft to translate that malaise into a public vocabulary, in the hope of discovering political remedies for what had previously been thought private ills.

—Norman Jacobson, *Pride and Solace*

Without vision, the pragmatists perish.

—Lewis Mumford, *The Golden Day*

To My Parents

Contents

Acknowledgments

The book before you began as a doctoral dissertation. That some dissertations are ever finished at all is one of life's small miracles. In no small measure, a completed dissertation is a testament to the nature of the people who surround its writer. Writing a dissertation is an isolating, angst-filled process that without the support, guidance, encouragement, and admonishment of others would be impossible to survive with one's sanity intact, let alone emerge with a viable manuscript. Let me extend a heartfelt thanks to all the kind souls whose help over the years it has taken me to write this has enabled me to be here today composing these words.

Without the learned mind and incisive eye of James Miller, this book would have been an immeasurably inferior work. His continual input, advice, and challenges throughout the process have been invaluable. He often knew what I was trying to say better than I did. As a teacher, a scholar, and a mentor he has been exemplary, in the highest Emersonian sense. Sankar Muthu provided crucial insights and encouragement at various stages of the project's evolution. His skill at cutting through to key issues and his scrupulous practical advice saved me from a good deal of wasted time and frustration. His willingness to blur the lines between mentor, colleague, and friend speaks to his strengths as a person. Becoming Nancy Fraser's research assistant on that late summer day when she arrived at The New School amidst piles of boxes proved a fortuitous event. The ensuing friendship enriched my time at The New School. Her ability both to inspirit and to reprove, when needed, has improved this work. Richard Bernstein's spirited questioning during my proposal defense more years ago than I care to remember forced a pivotal rethinking of this project. The presence of his voice in my head, in addition to his body of insightful and penetrating work on Rorty, have both contributed to this project. The genesis of this dissertation may very well have been the day he arranged for Rorty himself to attend his yearlong seminar on American pragmatism.

The depth of other debts and influences defies enumeration. George Shulman's early tutelage in political theory and example of impassioned teaching left a permanent mark on me. It is difficult to imagine my own approach to political theory without, among other things, having attended his much-adored seminar on Modern European Political Thought. I am indebted to James P. Young for my introduction to political theory as an undergraduate at SUNY Binghamton. Later, during my two years in the graduate program there, the seeds of issues I am still cultivating were planted in the seminars of his I attended. For the wisdom that led him to insist that The New School was the place for me to continue my studies, I am forever grateful.

Several works pivotal to the development of my approach to the tradition of American pragmatism warrant mention. In particular, I am indebted to Cornel West's *The American Evasion of Philosophy*, Russell Goodman's *American Philosophy and the Romantic Tradition*, Richard Shusterman's *Practicing Philosophy,* John J. McDermott's *Streams of Experience,* and Stanley Cavell's work. I would also like to thank Richard Rorty himself. Though our fleeting personal contact took place before I embarked on this project, the experience of having in a sense "lived" with Rorty's thoughts over these years has greatly enriched my perspective on the world. Although frustrating and impervious at times, having to come to terms with Rorty's wide-ranging erudition and intellectual interests truly has been a horizon-expanding experience.

Finally, I wish to acknowledge the constant support of my parents, Jan and Corinne Voparil, to whom I dedicate this work. They have gallantly endured their son's vexing determination to exist for long periods as a largely unproductive member of society. Their immense generosity with their support—in all its forms—even when it went against their best instincts, has permitted me to pursue my calling and been the sine qua non of this work. Words so often are inadequate, but thank you. I also have to thank my dear grandmother, Violet Pechar. Her timely gifts kept me—and later my young family—from financial oblivion on a number of occasions. To *mis queridos suegros,* I say *muchas gracias* for allowing me to occupy their spare room and convert it to my personal study. My good friend Dave Ramos lent me his apartment one summer when I needed a place to write. I would never have finished this book if not for the tranquility afforded by these refuges. A special thanks as well to Jonathan Sisk at Rowman & Littlefield for his support of this project, and to the editors who shepherded both me and the manuscript to fruition.

I have been blessed with two wonderful young sons, Aidan and Devin. Although I might have finished this book sooner had they not wondrously appeared, the joys I owe to their presence have sustained me through this process and made my life that much richer. Lastly, I must thank my wife Mariana for enduring with saintly patience all the hardships associated with my long tenure as a graduate student and the solitude required to finish this work. I could never have done it without her love and companionship.

Abbreviations of Rorty Texts

AOC   *Achieving Our Country: Leftist Thought in Twentieth-Century America* (Cambridge, MA: Harvard University Press, 1998).

CIS   *Contingency, Irony, and Solidarity* (New York: Cambridge University Press, 1989).

CP   *Consequences of Pragmatism* (Minneapolis: University of Minneapolis Press, 1982).

EHO   *Essays on Heidegger and Others: Philosophical Papers, Vol. 2* (New York: Cambridge University Press, 1991).

ORT   *Objectivity, Relativism, and Truth: Philosophical Papers, Vol. 1* (New York: Cambridge University Press, 1991).

PMN   *Philosophy and the Mirror of Nature* (Princeton, NJ: Princeton University Press, 1979).

PSH   *Philosophy and Social Hope* (New York: Penguin Books, 1999).

TP   *Truth and Progress: Philosophical Papers, Vol. 3* (New York: Cambridge University Press, 1998).

Introduction

Reading Rorty

The recent resurgence [of pragmatism] is a confirmation of what I have long believed—that the pragmatic legacy has a richness, diversity, vitality, and power to help clarify and to provide a philosophic orientation in dealing with the tangled theoretical and practical problems that we are presently confronting.

—Richard Bernstein, "The Resurgence of Pragmatism"

Rorty's anti-epistemological radicalism and belletristic anti-academicism are refreshing and welcome in a discipline deeply entrenched in a debased and debilitating isolation. Yet, ironically, his project, though pregnant with rich possibilities, remains polemical (principally against other professional academics) and hence barren. It refuses to give birth to the offspring it conceives.

—Cornel West, *The American Evasion of Philosophy*

Reading Richard Rorty is not like reading any other philosopher. His prose is clear, cogent, and evocative. A learned expositor, he moves effortlessly from Plato to Proust to Derrida, bringing together disparate thinkers in new and refreshing ways. Witty and clever, Rorty is one of the most readable philosophers on the contemporary scene.

Yet he also can be elusive. As close examination of his texts often reveals, he can be maddeningly difficult to pin down. Apparently content to begin each work anew, Rorty shrugs off biting criticisms and sometimes his own former positions.

Rorty's elusiveness and nonchalance have frustrated more than one critic. Some have attributed his carefree attitude to his turn toward aesthetics.[1] Others

1

have denounced him as a dangerous relativist. However it is approached, Rorty's philosophy presents a host of problems for any commentator.

A standard critical approach might attempt to discern the basic coherence of his thought, lay out the framework of his argument and its assumptions in a kind of schematic, and then identify the inconsistencies or aporias that jeopardize its overall coherence.[2] But simply catching Rorty in a "performative self-contradiction," as Habermas and others have done, will not suffice to defeat his position, not least because Rorty often eschews argumentation. In recent essays, he has engaged instead in what he calls "redescription"—making his views appear more "attractive" by showing their favorable consequences and restating those of others in ways that make them "look bad."[3] As Richard Bernstein put it in an early review of *Philosophy and the Mirror of Nature*, "As one follows the nuances of [Rorty's] arguments, it begins to dawn on the reader that just when he thinks he is getting down to the hard core of these disputes, he discovers that there is no core."[4]

The problem of how to justify our most deeply held convictions and considered judgments in the absence of an ahistorical standard of truth or a universal standard of reason has always been one of pragmatism's greatest challenges. The willingness of pragmatists to forgo the certainties and assurances of fixed principles and foundational categories has long opened them to charges of self-contradiction and relativism. Yet for all the criticism they have received, pragmatists—including Richard Rorty—appear to have no problem continuing to possess deeply held convictions and making principled judgments.

For pragmatists like William James—and Rorty, too—our beliefs, our convictions, and even our philosophies express a vision, a character, and a "temperament."[5] Turning away from conceptual certainties, these pragmatists turn toward the relative constancy of the self, in a gesture of what Emerson called "self-reliance." Within this tradition, the power of ideas emanates not from their foundational or metaphysical grounding, but from their being embodied in a concrete life and *lived*.[6] I argue that it is precisely this reliance on the self as the ground of one's judgments that undergirds the pragmatist position and keeps it from the abyss of relativism. In other words, what gives our convictions weight and makes them more than randomly arrived at groundless assertions is the fact that they are *our* convictions, rooted in our personal vision of the world and its possibilities.[7]

Though superficially "relativist," I argue that Rorty's practice of redescription can be seen as rooted in his temperament or personal vision. Such a vision, understood as an imaginative reordering of the world based on one's particular perspective, also lies behind his idea of a "liberal utopia" and makes Rorty's thought of moment to political theorists who conceive of theory in terms of Sheldon Wolin's notion of vision. I contend that Rorty can be fruitfully approached as a political theorist concerned—like Wolin, among others—with promulgating a new picture of the political world. As a discourse of meaning and persuasion rather than truth and accuracy of representation, Wolin's brand of political theory, like Rorty's, values the imagination and the ability to come up with new metaphors and new angles of vision.

Framing Rorty's work in this way allows us to approach it in a spirit of hermeneutic charity and engage constructively with aspects of his writing that are sometimes given short shrift. Situating Rorty's thought in this context also enables us to better understand the turn in his recent work toward the thought of Emerson and Whitman.[8]

Stressing political effects rather than accuracy of representation, Rorty's recent thought aims at revitalizing a moribund contemporary left. Treating literature as a source for a distinctively American "sentimental education," he hopes to help his readers envision a more inclusive and more emotionally engaged democratic community. Forging a democratic community is an essential ingredient in the quest for social justice as a "larger loyalty," and a key to "achieving our country," as Rorty puts it (borrowing a phrase from James Baldwin).

In my first chapter, I lay out my argument about pragmatism and personal vision. I suggest that there is support for a Jamesian conception of the rootedness of our beliefs and philosophies in individual temperament or personal vision in Rorty's thought through a reading of Rorty's autobiographical essay "Trotsky and the Wild Orchids." In many other places, Rorty himself, ironically enough, has argued that there is *no* connection between a person's life and the philosophical beliefs the person upholds. But in this personal essay, Rorty implies that he can best account for the power of his ideas by describing how they grow out of the way he has lived his own life. Nor is this implication at all surprising, coming from someone who writes out of the pragmatic tradition: for Emerson as for James, a good way to "test" our beliefs is to put them to work in "the stream of our experience."

In the second chapter, I develop my argument about Rorty and political theory. Juxtaposing Rorty's account of redescription with a conception of political theory as vision drawn from Wolin allows us to see the shift in Rorty's work away from truth claims and accuracy of representation as foregrounding persuasiveness and the mobilization of political actors, and to better grasp the political thrust of his writing as an intervention to reinvigorate a moribund left. I also consider the fundamental assumption of Rorty's political vision that an active majoritarian politics is not possible without a sense of "romance" and forward-looking optimism, as well as the implications of giving up the idea of "getting it right" for politics.

Chapter 3 examines Rorty's turn to literature for the moral thrust of his pragmatism, in particular his claim that the novel is "the characteristic genre of democracy" and the one most suited to "the struggle for freedom and equality." Drawing on Czech novelist and critic Milan Kundera, Rorty evinces an attractive conception of novels as vehicles of an ironic sensibility consistent with the irreducible pluralism of human life. He suggests a mutually beneficial relation between irony and democratic life where novels and stories are a means of change, of both individual and collective self-criticism, for "reweaving" a community's "fabric of belief" to make it more tolerant, more inclusionary, and more just. But ultimately Rorty's appeal to irony is subordinated to his appeal to sentiment, and the pluralistic thrust of irony is subordinated to the purpose of solidifying a liberal moral identity.

This conflicting view of literature as a means of forging a moral community through ties of sympathy and affective sentiment—what Rorty calls "sentimental education"—is the subject of chapter 4. On this view, reading certain novels is a way of solidifying a common moral identity and of inculcating a particular set of values and liberal morality that rest on a shared abhorrence of suffering. Yet the cultivation of fellow feeling as a political program continually runs the risk of becoming a blueprint for imagining ourselves in the place of others and sharing their feelings of pain in lieu of actually doing something about it. Rorty's Humean conception of sympathy proves too partial to those close at hand to meet the requirements of Rorty's sense of a "larger loyalty," and the reflective process Hume proposed to "correct" this bias and to give sympathy a universal relevance can only be achieved at the cost of dulling its capacity to move us to action.

The fifth chapter takes up the aspect of Rorty's thought I find most problematic and the one that puts him most at odds with important elements of the pragmatist tradition: his argument for dividing public and private. The highest goal of liberal societies, Rorty holds, should be to "optimize the balance between leaving people's private lives alone and preventing suffering." The need for this split emerges in part from the conflicting demands of irony and a moral identity outlined in chapters 2 and 3. Revisiting the arguments of John Stuart Mill and Isaiah Berlin on which Rorty rests his case, I sketch a reading of Mill that casts private self-reform as essential to the public task of political reform and to our relations with others, rather than as corrosive of them. Drawing on the tradition of thinkers running from Emerson and Whitman to Dewey, which Rorty increasingly invokes in his recent writing, I suggest ways in which the creative energies of its citizens need not be merely corralled and tolerated by democracy, as Rorty asserts, but fully incorporated and channeled in ways that advance rather than undermine its public pursuit of justice.

Chapter 6 examines the notion of "achieving our country," an idea Rorty links to Whitman's aesthetic ideal of America as "the greatest poem." This marks the most advanced statement of his political vision. The creative tension between individual aesthetic expression and unity of collective purpose inherent in Whitman's ideal dramatizes the fundamental conflict that runs through Rorty's political thought. Tracing this conflict leads to a discussion of several key issues of interest to political theorists, including the degree of connectedness of the social critic, the kind of relation a democracy ought to have with its past, and the prerequisites of democratic collective self-transformation. The Emersonian and Whitmanian strands of the pragmatist tradition coincide with Baldwin's understanding of America's unfinished project on the point that meaningful advancement of this project involves criticism and change at the level of our very selves—the kind of change, I contend, that is exemplified by Stanley Cavell's suggestion that we ought to feel compromised by America's failures, and that Rorty's prideful public "we" consciousness works against.

A brief conclusion summarizes my central criticism of Rorty's position by situating his project of redescription alongside the eleventh of Marx's "Theses on Feuerbach." Because Rorty in theory severs redescriptions from personal visions and the selves of which they are an expression, he presents a false choice: between either changing ourselves or changing the world. Yet as poetic pragmatists like Emerson and Whitman, as well as James and Dewey, all knew, democracy is a way of life that aims to do both.

NOTES

1. See, for example, Richard J. Bernstein, "Rorty on Liberal Democracy and Philosophy," in *The New Constellation: The Ethical/Political Horizons of Modernity/Postmodernity* (Cambridge, MA: MIT Press, 1991), 233–34.

2. Several of the better accounts that go this route are Richard J. Bernstein, "Rorty's Liberal Utopia," in *The New Constellation*, 258–92; Richard Shusterman, "Pragmatism and Liberalism between Dewey and Rorty," in *Practicing Philosophy: Pragmatism and the Philosophical Life* (New York: Routledge, 1997); and Keith Topper, "Richard Rorty, Liberalism, and the Politics of Redescription," *American Political Science Review* 89, no. 4 (1995): 954–78.

3. Rorty has made this point repeatedly. Here are two representative statements from CIS: "I am not going to offer arguments against the vocabulary I want to replace. Instead, I am going to try to make the vocabulary I favor look attractive by showing how it may be used to describe a variety of topics" (9); "But 'argument' is not the right word . . . rebutting objections to one's redescriptions of some things will be largely a matter of redescribing other things, trying to outflank the objections by

enlarging the scope of one's favorite metaphors. So my strategy will be to try to make the vocabulary in which these objections are phrased look bad" (44).

4. Richard J. Bernstein, "Philosophy in the Conversation of Mankind," in *Philosophical Profiles: Essays in a Pragmatic Mode* (Philadelphia: University of Pennsylvania Press, 1986), 23.

5. On this point, see Amanda Anderson, "Pragmatism and Character," *Critical Inquiry* 29 (Winter 2003): 282–301. Richard Shusterman persuasively argues that pragmatism "is no 'evasion of philosophy,' but the revival of a tradition that saw theory as a useful instrument to a higher philosophical practice: the art of living wisely and well." See his *Practicing Philosophy: Pragmatism and the Philosophical Life* (New York: Routledge, 1997), 5.

6. On this theme in pragmatist thought more generally, see Shusterman, *Practicing Philosophy*. On Emerson's relation to pragmatism, see Cornel West, *The American Evasion of Philosophy: A Genealogy of Pragmatism* (Madison: University of Wisconsin Press, 1989); Giles Gunn, *The Culture of Criticism and the Criticism of Culture* (New York: Oxford University Press, 1987) and *Thinking Across the American Grain: Ideology, Intellect, and the New Pragmatism* (Chicago: University of Chicago Press, 1992); Russell Goodman, *American Philosophy and the Romantic Tradition* (New York: Cambridge University Press, 1990); Richard Poirier, *The Renewal of Literature* (New York: Random House, 1987) and *Poetry and Pragmatism* (Cambridge, MA: Harvard University Press, 1992); and Paul Jay, *Contingency Blues: The Search for Foundations in American Criticism* (Madison: University of Wisconsin Press, 1997).

7. Cf. Dewey's statement that "the question finally at stake in any genuinely moral situation is: what shall the agent be? What sort of character shall he assume?" Quoted in Sheldon Wolin, *Politics and Vision: Continuity and Innovation in Western Political Thought* (Boston: Little, Brown & Co., 1960), 195. Stanley Fish, like James and Dewey, has held that the ground of our judgments is nothing more than our "convictions and commitments" themselves. Writing against general principles, he argues that "when all is said and done there is nowhere to go except to the goals and desires that already possess you, and nothing to do but try as hard as you can to implement them in the world." In other words, nothing except precisely what general principles ignore: concrete matters of race, class, gender, religious affiliation, ethnic identity, sexual orientation, accomplishments, failures, values to society, moral worth, and so on. Fish's argument against principle rests on the idea that "anything one believes about a particular matter is logically independent of the account one might give of how beliefs emerge or of what underlies them or of what confirms them or calls them into question." Belief, he argues, is prior to rationality — precisely James's point about the circularity of our beliefs. See Fish, *The Trouble with Principle* (Cambridge, MA: Harvard University Press, 1999), 8–10, 280–84.

8. In PSH, Rorty characterizes the political thrust of his pragmatism as "Emersonian self-creation on a communal scale" (34). Similarly, in AOC, Whitman's idea of America as "the greatest poem," an embodiment of a forward-looking, transformative Emersonian-influenced pragmatist orientation takes center stage (22). There are more references to Emerson in PSH than the rest of Rorty's writings combined. The essay

"Ethics without Principles," included in this collection, is the best expression of Rorty's take on the Emersonian origins of pragmatism. See also his "Redemption from Egotism: James and Proust as Spiritual Exercises," *Telos* 3, no. 3 (2001): 243–63. His earlier work is peppered with references to Emerson, all positive, though mostly in passing. The most significant of these is his statement in the introduction to ORT that the papers collected there and in EHO, its companion volume, are "largely devoted to arguing" that "a sense of self-reliance is a good thing to have" (17).

Chapter One

Pragmatism and Personal Vision

Every one is nevertheless prone to claim that his conclusions are the only logical ones, that they are the necessities of universal reason, they being all the while, at bottom, accidents more or less of personal vision which had far better be avowed as such . . . .

  Let me repeat once more that a man's vision is the great fact about him. Who cares for Carlyle's reasons, or Schopenhauer's, or Spencer's? A philosophy is the expression of a man's intimate character, and all definitions of the universe are but the deliberately adopted reactions of human characters upon it.

—William James, *A Pluralistic Universe*

Taking its definition at face value, Rorty's notion of "metaphorical redescription" opposes itself to argument and to the idea that there exist single, true descriptions of the world. Rather than arguing against a view because it fails to "get it right," he would simply make it "look bad" by appealing to the indeterminacy of meaning: whether something looks good or bad will vary depending on the purpose one has in mind. Yet, as Richard Bernstein and others have shown, it is virtually impossible to eschew argumentation altogether; even Rorty himself fails his own injunction against it.[1] But perhaps his turn to redescription need not be read as supplanting argumentation tout court; Rorty is writing specifically against *rational* argumentation and against the Habermasian assumption that there exists in every context a winning argument capable of persuading all parties and ushering in a shining underlying consensus. His stance is more about "refus[ing] to talk in a certain way"—the Platonic way—than rejecting argument as such (PSH, xix).

  In what follows, I argue that redescription can be read as an alternative, more effective form of persuasion than a single-minded appeal to reasoned

9

argument.[2] As a tool for change, redescription promises transformative effects at both an individual and a social or political level: individually, as a way to "alter our self-image" in line with Rorty's effort to cast philosophy as "an aid to creating ourselves rather than to knowing ourselves," and socially or politically, as part of a discourse of meaning rather than of truth and accuracy of representation—not unlike one view of political theory—that seeks to promulgate a new picture of the political world and persuade people to adopt it (PSH, 73, 79). I take up the first level in this chapter, and the second level forms the subject of chapter 2. Interpreting Rortyan redescription as a "temperamental willingness to try out new vocabularies" foregrounds several common resonances between Rorty's pragmatism and that of William James.[3] This approach puts Rorty's stance on its strongest footing and suggests an answer to the question of why a pragmatist would be willing to die for her beliefs.

"THE POTENTEST OF ALL OUR PREMISES"

Rorty's turn to redescription rests on the idea that meaningful change in belief more often comes about through seeing things in a new light than by being won over by a better argument. Put crudely, seeing differently opens new possibilities that, to be met, require a move beyond our current selves that does not occur when we assent to a better argument. Rorty values imaginative writing over argumentative writing because of the effect of the former on the reader: "A turn of phrase in a conversation or a novel or a poem—a new way of putting things, a novel metaphor or simile—can make all the difference to the way we look at a whole range of phenomena." This view contrasts with what Rorty calls "the rationalist, Platonic, conviction that the only thing that should be allowed to change our lives is learning how something really is." This latter notion rests on a confusion between causes and reasons: the "new and strange" people we encounter in real life and in novels and plays "cause us to act differently without necessarily having given us reasons for doing so."[4]

The distinction that makes a difference between arguments and redescriptions on Rorty's view has to do with the conclusiveness of debate. Unlike arguments that rest on a claim to have gotten some aspect of reality "right," redescriptions are relative to purposes. Whether or not a particular description will have force in our lives is a function of how well it resonates with the purposes we have in mind, rather than its truth or falsity or whether it is an embodiment of reason. Agreement, then, is something that precedes argument and makes it possible rather than something that follows from it.[5] Being persuaded to adopt a competing perspective occurs more often when people change their "self-image," an event better understood as a kind of "conversion" than as the result of argument.[6] As Rorty puts it, "The phrase 'she has become a new person—you would not recognize her' typically means 'she no longer sees the point or relevance or interest of the arguments which she once deployed on the other side'" (PSH, 63). Reasons may indeed convince us. But this happens because the reasons strike our temperaments in a certain way, not because of their inherent rationality.

After all, once the rationalist presumption that there exists a winning argument that "gets it right" is jettisoned, how much persuasive or transformative force do arguments really have? We all have had arguments, to be sure. How often have we been able to convince a disagreeing party to abandon its view and adopt ours merely by arguing? How often have we been persuaded to desert our own position? One would likely argue oneself to exhaustion before convincing an antiabortion advocate to forsake her cause, or inducing a member of the Bush administration to have heeded the case against war in Iraq. Rather than possessing a more persuasive argument, the viewpoints that tend to "win" arguments are those with the most power behind them; in the real world, consensus is more often "forced" in this sense than arrived at through free assent to the better argument.

The reason arguments so often fail to spur change is because beliefs are rarely formed through rational processes in the first place. On the pragmatist account of how we come into our beliefs, arguments figure only secondarily as ex post facto justifications cited only after we have arrived at a belief.[7] Discussing nonegalitarian examples such as the belief that "dishonor brought to a woman of one's family must be paid for with blood" or that "it would be better to have no son than to have one who is homosexual," Rorty writes,

> If I am told that a controversial action which I have taken has to be defended by being subsumed under a universal, rational principle, I may be able to dream up such a principle to fit the occasion, but sometimes I may only be able to say, "Well, it seemed like the best thing to do at the time, all things considered." It is not clear that the latter defense is less rational than some universal-sounding principle which I have dreamed up *ad hoc* to justify my action. (PSH, xxx)

Things we cite as "firm moral principles" are for Rorty a function of contingent "past practices—ways of summing up the habits of the ancestors we most admire"—not "the product of a special faculty called 'reason'" (PSH, xxix). As such, making the world a more humane place is a matter of altering habits and self-images rather than of becoming more rational.

In his lively and insightful chronicle of the development of four eminent nineteenth-century American minds, Louis Menand makes the telling observation that pragmatism is, at bottom, a claim about the way we think. An account of the relation between our beliefs and principles and the concrete judgments we make, the basic pragmatist insight about thinking can be put simply: "First we decide, then we deduce." Principles, on this view, are best understood not as fixed, preexisting lights which guide deliberation and ensure right conduct, but instead as results or end products of deliberation whose meaning is not knowable prior to the process of thinking itself. "In the end, you will do what you believe is 'right,' but 'rightness' will be, in effect, the compliment you give to the outcome of your deliberations. Though it is always in view while you are thinking, 'what is right' is something that appears in its complete form at the end, not the beginning, of your deliberation."[8]

In one form or another, a similar stance can be found in virtually all pragmatist thinkers, from James to Rorty and Stanley Fish, who has made the most explicit case against principles.[9] Menand traces this view to a statement in Oliver Wendell Holmes Jr.'s first law review article of 1870: "It is the merit of the common law that it decides the case first and determines the principle afterwards." Depending on one's point of view, such contextualism represents either one of the great enabling truths of the pragmatist perspective or the site of its irretrievable collapse into relativism.[10]

The fundamental question that is begged here—perhaps *the* question for pragmatism—is, if principles do not decide cases, then what does? If we indeed decide first and only then produce the reasons behind our decision, on what basis does the original decision rest? To put it in a more general register, in the absence of fixed principles and transcendental moral norms, what is it that grounds our ethical judgments and guides moral agency? And why would anyone be willing to die for such ungrounded beliefs? As Menand notes, the implication of Holmes's remark was "not that the result was chosen randomly, but that it was dictated by something other than the formal legal rationale later adduced to support it." But what is this elusive "something"? What is it that intervenes to make pragmatist principles and judgments more than arbitrary, relativistic, spur-of-the-moment proclamations that vary according to circumstance? Menand pinpoints the crucial issue: "Pragmatism explains everything about ideas except why a person would be willing to die for one."[11]

This is significant, if only for the fact that most pragmatists have argued that giving up secure metaphysical and moral bulwarks would not spell the inevitable decline of the good of the individual and society, but rather clear the way for its improvement. James, perhaps foreseeing this doubt in the minds of his audience, addressed this question in the final pages of his *Prag-*

matism lectures and concluded that "a genuine pragmatist . . . is willing to live on a scheme of uncertified possibilities which he trusts; willing to pay with his own person, if need to, for the realization of the ideals which he frames." Rorty too holds that the "fundamental premise" of his pragmatism is that "a belief can still regulate action, can still be thought worth dying for, among people who are quite aware that this belief is caused by nothing deeper than contingent historical circumstance" (CIS, 189).[12]

The pragmatist claims for contingent beliefs only hold, I want to argue, if these beliefs are grounded in the personal commitments, the "here I stand," of the individual. For his part, James offered his defense of a detranscendentalized pragmatic attitude toward the world only after firmly establishing the primacy of temperament and personal vision. Rorty, too, as I argue below, at least implicitly recognizes the role of personal vision in grounding our commitments: for instance, when he discusses the importance of the individual's "final vocabulary"—the constellation of beliefs and values we use to describe ourselves, for which there is "no noncircular argumentative recourse," only "resort to force." Indeed, Amanda Anderson recently called Rorty "the pragmatist thinker to consider most extensively the relation between the cultivation of ethos or character and larger political goals."[13]

Conflating Rorty's philosophy with that of James would of course be a mistake. Still, if Rorty is to successfully defend his philosophy by reconciling his premise of contingency with his own clearly expressed convictions about politics and the future of America, he would do well, I believe, to follow James and embrace the origins of all our commitments—public and private alike—in personal vision. While, on the one hand, this may entail a retreat from some of his more ambitious claims—like what Bernstein has called Rorty's "logic of apartheid" between public and private—it will, on the other hand, help buttress his fundamental premise that pragmatists are willing to die for their contingent, ungrounded beliefs.[14]

It is worth recalling that James opened his *Pragmatism* lectures by arguing that philosophy "is not a technical matter" but "our more or less dumb sense of what life honestly and deeply means . . . our individual way of just seeing and feeling the total push and pressure of the cosmos." This Emersonian affirmation of the philosophy "in each of us" provides the basis for James's defense of "temperament" as the determining factor of one's philosophy. Calling the history of philosophy a "clash of human temperaments," he claims that the figures who have left their mark on philosophy—for instance, "Plato, Locke, Hegel, Spencer"—did so because of their "strong temperamental vision": "The one thing that has *counted* so far in philosophy is that a man should *see* things, see them straight in his own peculiar way, and be dissatisfied with any opposite way of seeing them."[15]

In a way that recalls the opening chapter of Nietzsche's *Beyond Good and Evil*, James charged the philosophical discussions of his day as guilty of "a certain insincerity" for failing to be up-front about this. "Of whatever temperament a professional philosopher is," James argued, "he tries, when philosophizing, to sink the fact of his temperament." As a result, "The potentest of all our premises is never mentioned." Because temperament is "no conventionally recognized reason" in the realm of philosophy, the philosopher is forced to "urge impersonal reasons only for his conclusions." Yet temperament "loads the evidence for him one way or the other, making for a more sentimental or a more hard-hearted view of the universe, just as this fact or that principle would." In what seems an echo of Nietzsche's infamous claim that "untruth is a condition of life," James asserted, "Wanting a universe that suits [the philosopher's temperament], he believes in any representation of the universe that does suit it." In other words, first we decide, then we deduce.[16]

Importantly, what distinguishes the great philosophers from everyone else is for James not attributable to superior intellect or greater creative powers but to the strength of their temperamental vision. "Most of us," James contended, "have, of course, no very definite intellectual temperament." Discerning a tendency toward unreflective conformism in intellectual matters, he continued, "We hardly know our own preferences in abstract matters; some of us are easily talked out of them, and end by following the fashion or taking up with the beliefs of the most impressive philosopher in our neighborhood, whoever he may be." James was not about to assert that everyone has a "great" philosophy inside him or her. But he did believe that "almost everyone has his own peculiar sense of a certain total character in the universe," and what is more, a sense of the "inadequacy" of the prevailing philosophies to "match" this personal vision, a sense that "they don't just cover *his* world."[17]

This context not only helps us grasp James's understanding of pragmatism; it elucidates aspects of Rorty's position sometimes given short shrift. Many are familiar with James's statement that "the pragmatic method is primarily a method of settling metaphysical disputes that otherwise might be interminable." However, it is not a method intended solely for philosophers for settling their disputes, but for everyday individuals to cut through endless philosophical debates so they can determine which view better fits their own personal vision. One goes about testing ideas for fit in this way by setting them at work "in the stream of your experience." But this can only be accomplished if one is capable of living with the "tangled, muddy, painful and perplexed" "contradictions" of real life, and not leaving them behind for the "simple, clean and noble"—but purified and contradiction-free—world of abstract speculation.[18] In the rest of this chapter, I defend this notion of living one's truths as a useful way of framing Rortyan redescription and his related idea of the ironist that highlights their value to democracy. Underlying this view is a recognition, as Stanley Cavell has eloquently put it, that there is a point in the conversation of justice when reasons and moral justifications "run out" and "something must be shown."[19]

LIVING TRUTH

James's contribution to the pragmatist legacy was to recast Peirce's "principle of pragmatism" from being a way "to grind off the arbitrary and the individualistic character of thought" to a method for enabling individuals to access philosophical debates precisely so they could use ideas for such arbitrary and individualistic purposes in their everyday lives.[20] As he put it in his *Pragmatism* lectures, "The whole function of philosophy ought to be to find out what definite difference it will make to you and me, at definite instants of our life, if this world-formula or that world-formula be the true one."[21] As we have seen, James believed that our individual "temperament"—"our more or less dumb sense of what life honestly and deeply means"—plays a constitutive role in our beliefs and commitments, rather than the abstract principles or reasons we cite when we account for them. Without some similar conception of temperament or character, the notion of a pragmatic method for aiding in the formation of one's worldview loses its meaning because there would be nothing against which to test the different beliefs one encounters.

Yet this emphasis on temperament raises a question that has dogged pragmatists for over a century: is pragmatism simply a method, a way of settling disputes, that entails no consequences and is free of value judgments and moral or ethical directives? Or does adopting a pragmatist perspective involve a certain attitude and a particular (more open, more tolerant) orientation toward the world? The horns of this fundamental tension run throughout James's writing on pragmatism and persist today, embodied, respectively, in the stances of Fish and Rorty.

The moral and political import of James's emphasis on temperament and a pragmatic "attitude of orientation" received its fullest expression in the thought of John Dewey. The attempt to cast pragmatism as inherently congenial to democratic practice, an effort which seems to drive much of Rorty's recent thought, has been assailed by pragmatist skeptics like Fish. The upshot of Fish's argument is that "if pragmatism is true, it has nothing to say to us; no politics follows from it or is blocked by it; no morality attaches to it or is enjoined by it." The moment "pragmatism becomes a program" and a particular set of consequences is articulated, on Fish's view, "It turns into the essentialism it challenges." If the pragmatist account of the world is right, "then everyone has always been a pragmatist anyway. . . . If you take the antifoundationalism of pragmatism seriously you will see that there is absolutely nothing you can do with it."[22]

Fish's counterargument poses a serious challenge to the recent pragmatist revival. Much of the current interest in pragmatism, which ranges from philosophers like Rorty and Bernstein to literary critics like Richard Poirier and Giles Gunn to cultural critics like Cornel West and historians like James Kloppenberg, among many others, resides in what is taken to be, for lack of a better word, the ethical resources of this tradition. Gunn gives voice to a common sentiment when he writes that "over the next decade or two pragmatism may well prove to be the most intellectually resilient American response to the quicksands and carapaces of cultural postmodernism."[23] Among the classical pragmatists, at least, the moral or ethical or political thrust of their pragmatism seemed to dovetail with their commitment to democracy, as Rorty himself has argued.[24] However, is it simply the case, as Fish has bluntly put it, that "if democracy has to some extent worked, it is because certain political structures are firmly in place and not because its citizens have internalized the sayings of Emerson, Dewey, and James"? On this view, not only is there "no special affinity" between pragmatism and democracy, but adopting a pragmatist stance will have no influence on your political views, which Fish argues "are more likely to be a function of whether repeal of the capital gains tax will benefit you than of your epistemology, should you be a person so odd as to have one."[25]

Finding a view more at odds with Dewey's claim that pragmatism is "the philosophy of democracy" is a difficult task. Nevertheless, Fish raises an important issue for pragmatists in general and for Rorty in particular: namely, how does one account for the consequences of ideas from a pragmatist perspective? Once the foundational and representationalist presuppositions that authorized philosophy's privileged access to the world are discarded, can one make the claim that any theoretical perspective—even a pragmatist one—has any purchase on the world? I want to argue that the Jamesian understanding of pragmatism as "an attitude of orientation," and the importance of living one's truths it entails, points to a way out of this impasse in which pragmatism, pace Fish, does not collapse into a form of essentialism.[26]

James's statements on behalf of pragmatism as "a method only" for bringing out the "practical cash-value" of our beliefs that "does not stand for any special results," for better or for worse, have always been the most well known. In the preface to his *Pragmatism* lectures, he even included the disclaimer that there is "no logical connexion" between pragmatism and the doctrine of "radical empiricism" he had set forth elsewhere.[27] Yet at the same time, only a few pages later, James famously distinguished between the "tender" and the "tough-minded," and throughout the lectures he seems to express an affinity between his pragmatism—something he describes as "uncomfortable away from facts"—and the "pluralistic" attention to facts of the tough at mind over the "monistic" and "dogmatical" tendencies of the tender minded. After all, the opening dedication of his lectures cites his indebtedness to the "pragmatic openness of mind" that he attributes to John Stuart Mill.

However, concluding the penultimate lecture, James unequivocally stated that even though he had "said so much in these lectures against the over-tender forms of rationalism," to identify pragmatism with "positivistic tough-mindedness" is to misunderstand it. The strength of the pragmatist view is that "it can remain religious like the rationalisms, but at the same time, like the empiricisms, it can preserve the richest intimacy with facts."[28]

Despite the impression created by these passages, there is an underlying consistency to James's position. In the sentence that immediately follows his assertion that pragmatism is "a method only," he announced, "But the general triumph of that method would mean an enormous change in what I called in my last lecture the 'temperament' of philosophy." This change, in short, emanates from pragmatism's antiprofessional or "anti-intellectualist" bent:

> A pragmatist turns his back resolutely and once for all upon a lot of inveterate habits dear to professional philosophers. He turns away from abstraction and insufficiency, from verbal solutions, from bad *a priori* reasons, from fixed principles, closed systems, and pretended absolutes and origins. . . . It means the open air and possibilities of nature, as against dogma, artificiality, and the pretence of finality in truth.[29]

This antiprofessional streak is of course evident in Rorty's thought. But for James, the implications of the pragmatist attitude go far beyond the professional academy. When he asserted that we must bring out the "practical cash value" of each word, it is only that one may "set it at work within the stream of your experience." Following the pragmatic method, then, involves "no particular results . . . but only an attitude of orientation." On this pragmatic orientation, when we encounter an "illuminating or power-bringing word or name" that claims to "name the universe's principle"—like "'God,' 'Matter,' 'the Absolute'"—we do not treat it as "the end of our metaphysical quest." Setting it at work in the stream of our experience—*living* it, one might say—involves treating it instead as "a program for more work, and more particularly as an indication of the ways in which existing realities may be changed."[30]

It is not so much that the pragmatic method has no consequences or results, but rather that it has no *fixed* consequences or "particular" results. As we have seen, James eschewed a facile rejection of the "over-tender forms of rationalism" that his pragmatist orientation militates against. Directly addressing his audience, he stated that he has indeed "simultaneously defended rationalistic hypotheses, *so far as these re-direct you fruitfully into experience*" (emphasis added). The point is that on a pragmatist view, if any word or hypothesis "can be shown to have any consequences whatever for our life, it has meaning." In other words, it will be true *if it works*. Whether or not something works, of course, as James put it at the close of his final lecture, is "a question that only you yourself can decide." The consequence of embracing the pragmatic method is that it sets one to the task of actively deciding.

RORTY'S TEMPERAMENT

Dewey famously claimed that "democracy is neither a form of government nor a social expediency, but a metaphysic of the relation of man and his experience in nature." As he put it more succinctly in a later essay, "Democracy is a way of life."[31] What is important to emphasize here is that Dewey, like James, grasped the importance of putting one's beliefs to the test of experience and living them. In an early essay that shows James's influence, Dewey made the point in this way: "Had Jesus Christ made an absolute, detailed and explicit statement upon all the facts of life, that statement would not have had meaning—it would have not been revelation—until men began to realize in their own action the truth that he declared—until they themselves began to *live* it."[32]

In his recent work, Rorty too has begun to recognize the importance of living one's truths. He glosses this passage of Dewey's as "saying that even if a nonhuman authority tells you something, the only way to figure out whether what you have been told is true is to see whether it gets you the sort of life you want." Merging James's pragmatic test of experience with the self-questioning that precipitated Mill's youthful crisis of belief (something which may have inspired James), he holds that we do this "by living them, trying them out in everyday life, seeing whether they make you and yours happier."[33]

The greatest support for the idea of philosophy as a way of life in Rorty's work is the figure of the ironist. Anderson has argued compellingly that the ironist may be read as "a figure who enacts antifoundationalism as a way of life or even, one might say, an art of living." This is not the place to delve into the topic of philosophy as an art of living, as interesting a topic as this is. Suffice it to say that there is evidence, as Richard Shusterman has put it, not only that "pragmatism's natural direction is the art of living" more broadly, but that such a move would be consonant with the general contours of Rorty's turn away from the truth and accuracy of representation of knowledge toward a more concrete and historicized conception of meaning.[34]

Yet although Rorty sometimes approaches the claim that the ironist's recognition of the contingent and antifoundational nature of her commitments promotes the kind of openness to other vocabularies that is beneficial to democratic life, he tends not to assert it very strongly. Part of this has to do with the objections voiced by Fish, which we will return to below.[35] However, Rorty's commitment to pragmatism and democracy occasionally gets the better of his anxiety about subjecting his liberal norms to questioning, and he makes a stronger claim for the ironist's contingent worldview. Substituting intersubjectivity for transcendence and accuracy of representation, he has argued, will not just "free philosophers from perpetual oscillation between skepticism and dogmatism." It will also "take away a few more excuses for fanaticism and intolerance," and hence strengthen the democratic spirit.[36]

The self-describing ironist recognizes the contingency of her values and is always on the lookout for candidates for new belief. Although Rorty does not put it in these terms, this process could be described as a matter of testing beliefs for fit through a Jamesian pragmatic method, which are then rewoven into her view of the world. In a way that recalls what James dubbed Mill's "pragmatic openness of mind," Rorty argues that this work of "enlarging oneself" requires one "to remain open to the possibility that the next book you read, or the next person you meet, will change your life." He contrasts the reader of imaginative writing's "desire for openness" with the "desire for completeness" of the philosophically minded. In the end, it comes down to what might be called one's temperament: those who lack this kind of openness tend to be resistant to self-enlarging change because they believe they already possess all the requisite criteria they will ever need for judging any new books or people they encounter. As a result, they are quite adept at "tucking each of them into some familiar pigeonhole." To avoid this, Rorty argues, "you must give up one of the dreams of philosophy—the dream of completeness, of the imperturbability attributed by the wise, of the mastery supposedly possessed by those who have, once and for all, achieved completion by achieving enlightenment." The temperamental desire to "go straight to the way things are" is what in Rorty's view accounts for the way "religion and philosophy have often served as shields for fanaticism and intolerance."[37]

These are precisely the kinds of claims Fish objects to. He interprets the ironist's skill at redescription as "a temperamental willingness to try out vocabularies other than our own."[38] But he rejects Rorty's belief that "if you give up on context-transcending norms, stop worrying about them, and learn to do without them—that is, if you become a Rortian—you will thereby become a better, less dogmatic, more open-minded person." Fish's contention is that "your general metaphysical position"—be it foundationalist or antifoundationalist, Platonic or pragmatic—"commits you to nothing outside of the limited sphere in which such matters are debated." Ultimately, "nothing of any consequence follows from one's philosophical positions. . . . The philosophical position someone is known to hold tells us nothing about his or her views on anything not directly philosophical and tells us nothing about his or her character or moral status."[39]

The difficulty that emerges with Rorty's position is that he tends to agree with Fish on this point. The idea that there is a linkage between our idiosyncratic, personal attachments—our temperament—and our philosophical beliefs is one of the things Rorty set out to dispel in his critique of philosophy's metaphysical presuppositions. He believes that there is seldom a relation between the philosophical views one professes and one's political beliefs, and that it is wrongheaded to think there should be. This was Plato's mistake: he attempted, in Yeats's phrase, "to hold reality and justice in a single vision" (PSH, 5, 12–3).

I now want to try and account for this discrepancy. Through a reading of his quasi-autobiographical essay, "Trotsky and the Wild Orchids," I contend that Rorty himself employed a Jamesian pragmatic method in developing his own philosophical views. He applies James's pragmatic test—what practical difference would it make if this notion were true?—to his early attachment to "the Platonic attempt to hold reality and justice in a single vision" and concludes that the longing for such a unifying vision may become an obstacle to democratic collective self-improvement and even have pernicious consequences. As a result of this self-reflection, he alters his philosophical positions, as well as transforms himself, precisely by living his truths and setting them to work in the stream of his experience.[40] While the upshot of this discussion is an affirmation of Fish's belief that someone's philosophical position tells us nothing about his or her character, it also suggests that someone's character may tell us something about the philosophical position he or she holds.

His stated intentions notwithstanding, I want to argue that the unacknowledged moral of the autobiographical story Rorty tells is that his lifelong odyssey of philosophical attachments and rejections, from Platonism to his idiosyncratic pragmatism, has been precisely about finding the philosophical worldview that best fit his own temperament or personal vision—that is, that fits what Menand calls in a Jamesian spirit, "the whole inchoate set of assumptions of our self-understanding and of the social world we inhabit, the assumptions that give the moral weight . . . to every judgment we make." At crucial moments in Rorty's story, his temperament or "individual way of just seeing and feeling the total push and pressure of the cosmos," in James's phrase, weighs in to decide issues in ways that Rorty does not acknowledge at the level of theory.[41]

The first thing that strikes one in reading Rorty's essay is the fact that he appeals to autobiographical material at all. Early on, he writes that he is turning to "a bit of autobiography" in the hope that it will shed some light on his often criticized and misunderstood views about "the relation of philosophy and politics." Quite conceivably, Rorty could have articulated a theoretical defense of his stance instead, as he had done many times before. He could also have appealed to a more obviously pragmatic justification that outlined the political consequences of holding his view versus acceding to those of his critics. Oddly, Rorty appeals to the—ostensibly private—idiosyncratic personal history of his publicly held views in order to advance the argument that the personal and the idiosyncratic have no connection to the public and political.[42]

What is at the outset of this essay framed as a question of the relation of philosophy to politics becomes one of the relation of personal aesthetic pursuits to the public quest for social justice—that is, between self-creation and politics rather than philosophy and politics. The import of Rorty's autobiography for his current beliefs emanates from two sources: first, his early obsession with knowing, finding, and cataloguing the forty different species of wild orchids, and, second, his conviction that life should involve fighting injustice, something he attributes to the Trotskyist views of his activist parents. His initial attraction to philosophy grew out of the hope that it would provide some way to reconcile these apparently contradictory impulses. He wanted to find "some intellectual or aesthetic framework" which would enable him to, in Yeats's phrase, "hold reality and justice in a single vision" and unite the "socially useless" interest in orchids and the "Wordsworthian" moments of contact with the sublime that they sparked (in Yeats's phrase, "reality") with the conviction that one's time should be spent liberating the weak from the strong ("justice"). Despite initially succumbing to the lure of Platonism—that knowledge *is* virtue—Rorty ultimately recognizes this attempt to redeem esoteric intellectual pursuits as possessed of moral virtue in themselves as both misleading and pernicious. Both reactionary fundamentalists and postmodern radicals share the misguided belief that being right about abstract philosophical matters is sufficient for right action in the world (PSH, 7–8, 19).

Rorty is surely right to decry the way philosophy has served to redeem pursuits that are either "socially useless" or politically dangerous by, as he puts it, seeking to provide "confirmation that the things you love with all your heart are central to the structure of the universe, or that your sense of moral responsibility is 'rational and objective' rather than 'just' a result of how you were brought up" (PSH, 19–20). Here he seems headed for an affirmation of James's point that our conclusions are "at bottom, accidents more or less of personal vision which had far better be avowed as such." Instead, Rorty claims that such "accidents" of personal vision are irrelevant, at least when it comes to politics and our public beliefs and commitments, and should be largely ignored in those matters.[43]

The problem is that, throughout the essay, what actually seems to exert the greatest influence on Rorty's decisions and judgments is neither the love of orchids nor his sense of injustice. For example, although "attracted by [T. S.] Eliot's suggestions that only committed Christians could overcome their un- healthy preoccupation with their private obsessions, and so to serve their fel- low humans with proper humility," Rorty tells us he rejected the path of reli- gion because of "a prideful inability to believe what I was saying when I recited the General Confession" (PSH, 9). A pivotal decision, to be sure, yet Rorty does not pause to consider the origins of this "prideful inability to be- lieve." Something similar happens when he tries to account for his "disillu- sionment with Plato":

> My reasons for turning away from the anti-Deweyan views I imbibed at Chicago are pretty much the same reasons Dewey had for turning away from evangelical Christianity and from the neo-Hegelian pantheism which he embraced in his twenties. They are also pretty much the reasons which led Hegel to turn away from Kant, and to decide that both God and the Moral Law had to be temporal- ized and historicized to be believable.

Although he never clearly spells out these reasons, he notes that talk about "the relation between subject and object" and "contextualist theories of refer- ence" are "just froth on the surface." Some other force is at work here. Ulti- mately, these reasons are apparently rooted in his "conviction that philosophy was no help in dealing with the Nazis and other bullies" (PSH, 15–16).

In my view, the operative factors behind Rorty's political and philosophi- cal positions are indeed his "convictions"—what James called his personal vision or "temperament." This is the "purpose" that lies behind his redescrip- tions. It would take George Herbert Mead to discern the social origins of the self and better account for what James referred to in a transcendentalist vein as our "individual way of just seeing and feeling the total push and pressure of the cosmos." Nevertheless, the point is that the thoughtful weighing of per- spectives Rorty undertook during his intellectual odyssey could only have been accomplished by putting them to work in the stream of his experience and testing them for fit with his own inner temperament—including his pub- lic commitments.

Rorty admits as much in his essay, noting that "our conscience and our aes- thetic taste are, equally, products of the cultural environment in which we grew up." But he also tends to obscure the contingent origins of his political orientation, stating without explication, "At twelve, I knew that the point of being human was to spend one's life fighting social injustice" (PSH, 15, 6).[44] What the entire essay implies but does not come out and say is that Rorty "knew" all these things for contingent, biographical reasons arising from the influences he was exposed to in his unconventional upbringing that constitute his Jamesian temperament.

Rorty's "socially useless" interest in wild orchids was just as much a product of this upbringing as his moral conscience. Without trying to psychoanalyze Rorty, one might speculate that the need for an escapist pursuit like his hunts for wild orchids in the northwest New Jersey mountains was a reaction to his early immersion in an environment in which everything was politicized. Like the butterfly collecting of Vladimir Nabokov, one of Rorty's favorite novelists, a lifelong resistance to the notion that the personal is political may be the result of this felt need to preserve some sphere of human activity free of political taint.[45]

In any case, there is no escaping the fact, as Rorty himself has asserted, that "socialization goes all the way down." Rorty has developed a great phrase for the process of self-articulation through which we define ourselves and our commitments by working out our relation to the social and political forces we have internalized that avoids essentialism about the self: "replacing inherited with self-made contingencies" (CIS, 98). I take this to be a good analogue for James's pragmatic test of belief, and something predicated upon living one's truths. The idea that we can somehow separate the substantive beliefs about social justice that guide us in the public realm from this process and still profess beliefs we are willing to die for seems problematic.

To recall, for James it is not only that our conclusions are, "at bottom, accidents more or less of personal vision" rather than manifestations of Logic or Reason. He also asserted that the "accidental," or we might say contingent, origins of our beliefs "had far better be avowed as such." One of Rorty's unstated motives in the essay is to prove that he does not share the politics of the postmodernists that by the early 1990s he had been lumped in with "willynilly." Specifically, he wants to establish that he, for one, does not participate in the so-called America Sucks Sweepstakes, the competition for finding "better, bitterer ways of describing the United States" (PSH, 4).[46] Taking the fact that he has been criticized with equal ardor from both the left and the right as evidence that he is on the right track, Rorty interprets the right's hostility toward him as an objection to his stance that "it is enough just to *prefer* democratic societies." With no recourse possible to either Truth or Reason, this is of course what Rorty's stance, along with that of everyone else, amounts to—a preference with no noncircular justification.

Yet, because rooted in our temperament, our preferences are, as James held, "the potentest of all our premises." On my reading, Rorty's autobiographical excursus brings home the point that there is one resource still available to the pragmatist—namely, that his views are grounded in his personal vision and are given weight by the fact that they are his views, rooted in his lived experience. When Rorty states, "Perhaps this bit of autobiography will make clear that, even if my views about the relation of philosophy and politics are odd, they were not adopted for frivolous reasons," this is precisely what he sets out to do: to offer a pragmatist justification for his views as being the result, not of any "frivolous" preference, but of a process of having lived certain truths, found them wanting, and adopted others as a result (PSH, 4–5). His reasons are not frivolous, because they are his own, and because his life both supports his beliefs and commitments and rests on them.

As I noted above, while the "Wild Orchids" essay recounts the history of Rorty's self-making, he does not describe the experiences he relates in these terms. The essay's nominal theme has more to do with an abstract account of how various philosophies treat self-creation—specifically, about how "Platonism" has sought to unite the quest for political justice and esoteric individual pursuits in a single, "self-justifying, self-sufficient synoptic vision" that morally redeems the latter.

To be clear, I believe Rorty is right to debunk this use of philosophy. But in rejecting the conceptions of philosophy that seek to justify and undergird our beliefs, Rorty reduces philosophy to a kind of verbal facility, detached from the ethical life of the individual and her "temperament." As a consequence, he has a tendency to treat philosophy as the province of a kind of sophistry rather than as an ethical way of life.

As he recounts in the essay, once he saw through the attempts of philosophers to secure access to unquestioned first principles and foundational truths, he concluded that "philosophical talent was largely a matter of proliferating as many distinctions as were needed to wriggle out of a dialectical corner . . . a matter of redescribing the nearby intellectual terrain." Philosophy, he decided, was "just a matter of out-redescribing the last philosopher." But if philosophy turned out to be of "no help in dealing with Nazis and other bullies" by yielding irrefutable arguments to defeat them, it could at least be used to make them look bad (PSH, 10–11, 16).[47]

To be sure, Rorty does not want to argue that philosophy is "socially useless." Even if philosophy is just a matter of "out-redescribing the last philosopher," the power of redescription can be used for good by "weav[ing] the conceptual fabric of a freer, better, more just society" (PSH, 19, 11). For this project, Rorty often uses Hegel's phrase of "holding one's time in thought," by which he means finding a description of all the things characteristic of your time of which you most approve, with which you unflinchingly identify, a description which will serve as a description of the end toward which the historical developments which led up to your time were means. (CIS, 55; cf. PSH, 11)

Despite the allusion to the individual self implicit in the phrase "with which you unflinchingly identify," Rorty nevertheless tends to cast this way of doing philosophy as "simply a literary skill—skill at producing gestalt switches by making smooth, rapid transitions from one terminology to another"—in other words, as divorced from individual life and personal vision (CIS, 78). By invoking Hegel's conception, he moves from the plane of the individual to that of the social and historical, which makes philosophy more a matter of capturing the essence of one's time than expressing one's temperament.[48]

A better statement of Rorty's position occurs in *Contingency, Irony, and Solidarity*, where he writes, "On my account of ironist culture, such opposites ["decency and sublimity" or justice and self-creation] can be combined in a life but not synthesized in a theory" (CIS, 120). This stance makes more intuitive sense: in our personal visions, we unite our idiosyncratic attachments and public commitments all the time. Indeed, it could be argued that such unity is a requirement for avoiding hypocrisy and perhaps for having a self at all. On this reading, Rorty's entire discourse on public and private, on his Trotsky and wild orchids, is precisely an account of how he himself united these elements in his own personal vision. Only he reconciles them in his own life by keeping them separate and rejecting any "automatic priority" of one over the other. In this way, he forestalls the temptation to ever think there is "something more important to rely on than the tolerance and decency of your fellow human beings" (PSH, 20).

After all, the pursuit of wild orchids *is* irrelevant to social justice; any theory that held otherwise would be pernicious. But wild orchids are not irrelevant to the pursuit of social justice in Rorty's own life. Even if socially useless, they sustain him as a person and permit him to fight injustice all the more vigorously in the moments when he decides to focus his energy in that direction. The political value of Rorty's individual temperament and personal vision, then, lies not in its potential as a blueprint for public solutions; Rorty is right to argue that this would not only be dangerous but would betray pragmatism's salutary opposition to single, true solutions. Rather, his temperament contributes to the democratic project by buttressing his own commitment to the cause by ensuring his commitments are something upon which he is willing to stake his entire existence, and nothing less.

REDESCRIPTION AND THE DEMOCRATIC WAY OF LIFE

One of the assumptions of the pragmatist tradition is that the democratic way of life can be, potentially, a transformative endeavor, both individually and socially. Fish rejects this assumption. Rorty, at first, did, too. But over time he has been rethinking and reformulating his position. Both of their arguments seem to founder on the same issue, which has something to do with how to account for the consequences of ideas from a pragmatist perspective. Both are convinced, rightly in my view, that virtue and knowledge are not linked in Plato's sense and that, as Rorty puts it, being right about philosophical matters is only "occasionally and incidentally" important for right action (PSH, 19). From here, Fish tends to take a more extreme position that "there is no relationship between general metaphysical accounts of human practices and the performance of human practices. There is no relationship in *any* direction." As we have seen, Rorty, too, has argued that our philosophical positions have nothing to do with our politics.[49]

I have no objection to these statements, insofar as they assert that there is no *necessary* relation between these things. Both thinkers sometimes make this qualification, but they tend to turn these premises into axioms because they are caught within the binary of our commitments either being determined by metaphysical truths or there being no relation at all. Eventually, though, they have to allow for some relationship because they cannot get around the fact that ideas *do* have consequences. Yet they seem to lack a pragmatist language to account for this. As Rorty puts it,

> Had there been no Plato, the Christians would have had a harder time selling the idea that all God really wanted from us was fraternal love. Had there been no Kant, the nineteenth-century would have had a harder time reconciling Christian ethics with Darwin's story about the descent of man. Had there been no Darwin, it would have been harder for Whitman and Dewey to detach the Americans from their belief that they were God's chosen people. Had there been no Dewey and no Sidney Hook, American leftists of the thirties would have been as buffaloed by the Marxists as were their counterparts in France and in Latin America. (PSH, 19)

Fish comes to a similar realization:

> There just is no commerce between the mundane and metaphysical levels, no bridge *except* the contingent and strategic bridges constructed by those who wish to make rhetorical use of general theories for either psychological reasons (they wish there to be a homology between their most abstract commitments and the commitments they enact in everyday life) or political reasons (they know that a certain theoretical vocabulary will have resonance with those they wish to influence).[50]

Quite a lot seems to fall under this "exception." What Fish refers to as "psychological reasons" seems to fit nicely as a description of what Rorty does in the "Wild Orchids" essay. But referring to them as narrowly psychological obscures the key point: ideas have consequences not because they are foundational or antifoundational, or moral or immoral, but because they are embodied in the lives of concrete individuals—that is to say, because they are *lived*. And the reasons why certain ideas are attractive or unattractive to certain people is a matter of how well they are perceived to fit with their individual temperaments.

That said, having a temperament of one's own is not a birthright. As Dewey in particular perceived, individuals come into being in particular times and places where established beliefs and traditions are inculcated in specific ways. To recall, James also believed that most of us have no definite temperament— hence the importance of what Dewey called "breaking the crust of convention" to facilitate seeing the world in our own way. Nor is it the case that one's temperament is defined once and for all to serve as a fixed ground against which all candidates for belief can be tested. Since the source of one's temperament is ultimately experience, the process of self-articulation is an ongoing task such that one's temperament alters as one's experience does.[51]

As he has turned more closely to the poetic precursors of his pragmatism— mostly Emerson and Whitman—in his recent work, Rorty seems increasingly drawn to the idea that pragmatism can be seen as "an attempt to alter our self-image" (PSH, 72).[52] Fish has countered that, on a pragmatist account of beliefs, what he calls "the critical space of reflection and distance from one's beliefs" that is necessary to initiate self-transformation is unavailable, citing the reason that a change in belief cannot be brought about "by an exercise of the will."[53] I have tried to argue that the Jamesian pragmatic test of living our beliefs is a conscious, self-initiated act of self-reflection that, like Rortyan redescription, entails an attitude of orientation that sets us to the task of changing ourselves, though of course not an automatic guarantee that such change will take place or of what the content of that change will be. As James put it, pragmatism is like a corridor in a hotel: "innumerable chambers open out of it."[54] Fish is right to make this point; there are no necessary consequences of holding pragmatist beliefs. Still, as Dewey held, severing our commitment to democratic values from their origins in personal vision will indeed have consequences:

> Democracy as a personal, an individual, way of life . . . signifies that powerful present enemies of democracy can be successfully met only by the creation of personal attitudes in individual human beings; that we must get over our tendency to think that its defense can be found in any external means whatever, whether military or civil, if they are separated from individual attitudes so deep-seated as to constitute personal character.[55]

Understood in a Jamesian spirit, Rorty's idea of redescription makes the circularity of our beliefs a virtue rather than a defect and puts pragmatism's historicist and contextualist assumptions in the service of democratic life by grounding them in our personal visions. Imaginative redescriptions that project future possibilities may not only spark one to see the world in a new light, but may cause one to see one's self, differently constituted, as occupying a place in that world. Such an Emersonian conception of an unattained but attainable higher self that draws us out of our current beliefs, though imperfectly realized in Rorty's own thought, may be a way of thinking that is well suited to pragmatist purposes. At the very least, it helps us understand the transformative potential inherent in the eschewal of rationalist assumptions by directing us to the self as the key locus of change.

NOTES

1. See Richard Bernstein, "Rorty's Liberal Utopia," in *The New Constellation: The Ethical-Political Horizons of Modernity/Postmodernity* (Cambridge, MA: MIT Press, 1992), 276–77. Bernstein usefully distinguishes between a strong sense of "rational justification" and "a weaker and more reasonable sense of justification." Even though we cannot give any "definitive knock-down foundational justifications," we can still offer "historically contingent fallible reasons to support our beliefs." This is what he believes Rorty offers, not merely neutral, nonargumentative redescriptions. Moreover, Bernstein asserts that whether or not Rorty's vocabulary appears attractive and alternative ones look bad "depends at least in part on his success in *arguing* that these alternative strategies fail to accomplish what they claim to prove."

2. There is support for this interpretation in Rorty's more recent work, where he is less strident in his claims against argument. In the introduction to PSH, for example, he states, "We pragmatists reply that if that were what rationality was [distinguishing between the absolute and the relative, the found and the made, object and subject, nature and convention, reality and appearance], then no doubt we are, indeed, irrationalists. But of course we go on to add that being an irrationalist in *that* sense is not to be incapable of argument. . . . Our efforts at persuasion must take the form of gradual inculcation of new ways of speaking, rather than straightforward argument within old ways of speaking" (xviii–xix). The value of redescriptions, Rorty asserts in *Contingency,* resides in its power to change minds (174).

3. This phrase is Stanley Fish's take on redescription. See his "Almost Pragmatism: The Jurisprudence of Richard Posner, Richard Rorty, and Ronald Dworkin," in *Pragmatism in Law and Society*, ed. Michael Brint and William Weaver (Boulder, CO: Westview Press, 1991), 64.

4. See "Redemption from Egotism: James and Proust as Spiritual Exercises," *Telos* 3, no. 3 (2001): 248. Rorty notes that most traditional philosophical accounts "neglect the fact people change their central projects, change those parts of their self-image which they had previously found most precious. The question is, however,

whether this ever happens as the result of *argument*. Perhaps it sometimes does, but this is surely the exception" (PSH, 63).

5. Here Rorty usefully distinguishes between communication and argument: "Communication requires no more than agreement to use the same tools to pursue shared needs. Argument requires agreement about which needs take priority over others." His point is not "that philosophy is less 'cognitive' than has been thought, but merely to point to the difference between situations in which there is sufficient agreement about ends to make possible fruitful argument about alternative means, and situations in which there is not" (PSH, 62, 70). See also PSH, xviii–xix, xxix–xxxii, 62–63, 72.

6. On the idea of conversion in Cavell's work, see Andrew Norris, "Political Revisions: Stanley Cavell and Political Philosophy," *Political Theory* 30, no. 6 (2002): 828–51.

7. Cf.: "A rational individual is always to act so that he need never blame himself no matter how things finally transpire," in John Rawls, *A Theory of Justice* (Cambridge, MA: Harvard University Press, 1971), 422. For an alternative view, see Stanley Cavell, *Conditions Handsome and Unhandsome: The Constitution of Emersonian Perfectionism* (Chicago: University of Chicago Press, 1990), 101–26.

8. Louis Menand, *The Metaphysical Club: A Story of Ideas in America* (New York: Farrar, Straus and Giroux, 2001), 351–53.

9. See Stanley Fish, *The Trouble with Principle* (Cambridge, MA: Harvard University Press, 1999).

10. Holmes, quoted in Menand, *Metaphysical Club*, 338.

11. Menand, *Metaphysical Club*, 340–41, 375.

12. William James, *Pragmatism*, in *William James: Writings, 1902–1910*, ed. Bruce Kuklick (New York: Library of America, 1987), 618. Bernstein argues that "without this 'fundamental premise' [Rorty's] entire project falls apart," in "Rorty's Liberal Utopia," 280. Cf. also Stanley Fish: "Antifoundationalism does not leave its proponents unable to assert anything strongly. It does not amount to relativism because the flip side of the unavailability of extracontextual/universal norms is the firmness of our attachment (too weak a word) to the norms of everyday practices. . . . Relativism is the name of a position in philosophy, not a possible program for living," in "Truth But No Consequences: Why Philosophy Doesn't Matter," *Critical Inquiry* 29 (Spring 2003): 414.

13. Amanda Anderson, "Pragmatism and Character," *Critical Inquiry* 29 (Winter 2003): 298. See also Jerold J. Abrams, "Aesthetics of Self-Fashioning and Cosmopolitanism: Foucault and Rorty on the Art of Living," *Philosophy Today* 28, no. 2 (Summer 2002): 185–92. For reasons in my view unrelated to his pragmatist stance, which I attempt to flesh out in subsequent chapters, Rorty tends to curtail the role of personal vision in buttressing our beliefs. When he asserts that our final vocabularies "can be and should be split into a large private and a small public sector, sectors which have no particular relation to one another," he severs our public commitments from the Jamesian personal vision or "stream of experience" in which our convictions acquire their meaning and weight for us, and with it the only basis we have for being willing to die for our beliefs (*Contingency*, 73, 100). For Rorty's interpretation of

James as helping us see the opposition between "cooperative endeavors" and "private projects," see his "Religious Faith, Intellectual Responsibility, and Romance," in PSH (148–67).

14. See Bernstein, "Rorty's Liberal Utopia," 275–76.

15. James, *Pragmatism*, 487–89.

16. James, *Pragmatism*, 488–89. For Nietzsche's views, see *Beyond Good and Evil*, aphorisms 1–9, and "On the Prejudices of Philosophers," passim. See especially 5–6, where he writes that philosophers "are not honest enough in their work. . . . They all pose as if they had discovered and reached their real opinions through the self-development of cold, pure, divinely unconcerned dialectic . . . while at bottom it is an assumption, a hunch, indeed a kind of 'inspiration'—most often a desire of the heart that has been filtered and made abstract—that they defend with reasons they have sought after the fact." Also, "Gradually it has become clear to me what every great philosophy so far has been: namely, the personal confession of its author and a kind of involuntary and unconscious memoir," trans. Walter Kaufmann.

17. James, *Pragmatism*, 502–3.

18. James, *Pragmatism*, 506, 509, 495. The greatest weakness of this view derives from what Cornel West has called James's "middle-of-the-roadism." James's claims about the power of pragmatism for "unstiffening" our beliefs are, in the name of openness and revisability, ultimately employed to unsettle merely our excessive claims and, as West puts it, "thereby preclude wholesale undermining or undergirding the status quo." See West, *The American Evasion of Philosophy*, 57, 54–68, passim.

19. Cavell, *Conditions Handsome and Unhandsome*, 112, 124.

20. Charles Sanders Peirce, quoted in Menand, *Metaphysical Club*, 366.

21. *Pragmatism*, 506–8.

22. Fish, "Truth and Toilets," in *The Trouble with Principle*, 295; "Almost Pragmatism," 63.

23. Giles Gunn, *Thinking Across the American Grain: Ideology, Intellect, and the New Pragmatism* (Chicago: University of Chicago Press, 1992), 7. Cf. also Bernstein: "The recent resurgence [of pragmatism] is a confirmation of what I have long believed—that the pragmatic legacy has a richness, diversity, vitality, and power to help clarify and to provide a philosophic orientation in dealing with the tangled theoretical and practical problems that we are presently confronting," in "The Resurgence of Pragmatism," *Social Research* 59, no. 4 (Winter 1992): 833. See also his *The New Constellation*.

24. See his "Truth without Correspondence to Reality" in PSH.

25. "Truth and Toilets," 301.

26. Part of the problem with Fish's critique is that it overlooks the common ground between pragmatism and democracy because his conceptions of both are too narrow. In contrast to Emerson, Whitman, and Dewey, he assumes pragmatism is merely the name for an epistemological stance and democracy simply an arrangement of institutions and procedures.

27. *Pragmatism*, 509, 481–82.

28. *Pragmatism*, 491, 516, 604, 500–501.

29. *Pragmatism*, 508–10.

30. *Pragmatism*, 509–10.

31. See John Dewey, "Maeterlinck's Philosophy of Life," in *The Middle Works of John Dewey*, ed. Jo Ann Boydston, vol. 6 (Carbondale: Southern Illinois University Press, 1978), 135; quoted in Richard Rorty, "Pragmatism as Romantic Polytheism," in *The Revival of Pragmatism: New Essays on Social Thought, Law, and Culture*, ed. Morris Dickstein (Durham, NC: Duke University Press, 1998), 32. The second Dewey quote is from "Creative Democracy—The Task Ahead of Us," in *The Later Works of John Dewey*, ed. Jo Ann Boydston, vol. 14 (Carbondale: Southern Illinois University Press, 1986), 226.

32. Rorty, "Pragmatism as Romantic Polytheism," 32.

33. Rorty, "Pragmatism as Romantic Polytheism," 32.

34. Anderson, "Pragmatism and Character," 296; Shusterman, *Practicing Philosophy*, 6. See also Alexander Nehamas, *The Art of Living: Socratic Reflections from Plato to Foucault* (Berkeley: University of California Press, 1998). Nehamas nicely summarizes the issues at hand: "Some philosophers want to find the answers to general and important questions, including questions about ethics and the nature of the good life, without believing their answers have much to do with the kind of person they themselves turn out to be. Others believe that general views, when organized in the right manner and adhered to in everyday life, create the right sort of person. . . . In the case of pure theory, the only issue that matters is whether the answers to one's questions are or are not correct. In the case of theory that affects life, the truth of one's views is still an issue, but what also matters is the kind of person, the sort of self, one manages to construct as a result of accepting them" (2). Rorty would seem to be moving toward the latter category, though somewhat apprehensively, while still looking for assurances.

35. I take up Rorty's rationale for keeping irony private in detail in chapters 3 and 5. See also Anderson, "Pragmatism and Character," 299–301.

36. Richard Rorty, "John Searle on Realism and Relativism," in *Truth and Progress*, 83.

37. Richard Rorty, "Redemption from Egotism: James and Proust as Spiritual Exercises," *Telos* 3, no. 3 (2001): 248–52.

38. Rorty, "Almost Pragmatism," 64.

39. Fish, "Truth But No Consequences," 390, 414, 416. Rorty agrees; see "Truth without Correspondence to Reality" in PSH.

40. There is an interesting parallel between Rorty and John Stuart Mill here. Mill puts a similar pragmatic test to the utilitarian beliefs instilled in him by his father and the idea that his object in life was to be "a reformer of the world" and found, in a moment of acute personal crisis, that their realization would leave him empty. Yet as their autobiographical writings reveal, they came to sharply divergent conclusions: even though they shared similar individual goods (Mill's idea that the object of his life was to be "a reformer of the world" and Rorty's belief that the goal in life is to struggle for human liberation), while Mill recognized the value of personal experience in the development of our substantive commitments and indeed made self-reform a critical part of his project of political reform, Rorty denies it and outlines a program for political reform in which self-creation and the personal more generally play no part. See

John Stuart Mill, "Autobiography," in *John Stuart Mill: A Selection of His Works*, ed.
J. M. Robson (New York: St. Martin's Press, 1966), esp. chap. 5.

41. Menand, *Metaphysical Club*, 353; James, *Pragmatism*, 487. This is not to say
that this set of beliefs and assumptions remains fixed; on the contrary, the point of the
pragmatist case is that beliefs are transformed in the process. Nor is it to say that there
is anything inevitable about this trajectory—this is Rorty's point about the contingency of our beliefs. It is only to say that to divorce our philosophical—or for that
matter, political—positions from the personal, ethical weight they carry in the course
of our lives is to render them little more than words.

42. Rorty's turn to autobiography can be seen as his having reached the point
Cavell describes as when "reasons" simply "run out" and "something must be
shown." See Cavell, *Conditions Handsome and Unhandsome*, 112, 124.

43. James, *A Pluralistic Universe*, in *William James: Writings, 1902–1910*, ed.
Bruce Kuklick, 634. Mill, by contrast, after having experienced his own Wordsworthian moments of private bliss, came to the opposite conclusion. He believed that the
"culture of feelings" and "sympathetic and imaginative pleasure" that was activated
in him by his reading of Wordsworth was not only "something which could be shared
in by all human beings," but something which "would be made richer by every improvement in the physical or social condition of mankind." See Mill, "Autobiography," 95–96.

44. Before making this last remark, he asserts, "I grew up knowing all decent people were, if not Trotskyites, at least socialists," and "I knew that poor people would
always be oppressed until capitalism was overcome" (PSH, 15).

45. For Rorty's reading of Nabokov, see CIS, chap. 7. There are interesting parallels between the two, which I discuss in "An Aesthetics of Immortality: Rorty's Reading of Nabokov," unpublished paper presented at the 1998 APSA (American Political
Science Association) gathering. Interestingly, such an all-consuming immersion in
politicized thought also fits the early life of Mill before his first mental or nervous
breakdown, wherein he learns of the essential importance of "the internal culture of
the individual." Mill's experience points to an alternative reading of the relation of
public and private: rather than trying to keep them separate, it could be argued that
these cases suggest that such "socially useless" individual pursuits are required to sustain the individual in the morally commendable but perhaps not always existentially
fulfilling struggle on behalf of the weak in public.

46. Rorty attributes the phrase "America Sucks Sweepstakes" to Jonathan Yardley.

47. Rorty made a similar confession in the preface to PMN, which opens with the
statement, "Almost as soon as I began to study philosophy, I was impressed by the
way in which philosophical problems appeared, disappeared, or changed shape as a
result of new assumptions or vocabularies." The earliest lesson he learned from his
philosophy teachers, he continues, was that "a 'philosophical problem' was the product of the unconscious adoption of assumptions built into the vocabulary in which the
problem was stated—assumptions which were to be questioned before the problem itself was taken seriously" (xiii). This begs the question of when it is that one does get
around to taking these problems seriously.

48. Here Rorty cites Hegel's *Phenomenology* "both as the beginning of the end of the Plato-Kant tradition and as a paradigm of the ironist's ability to exploit the possibilities of massive redescription." Rorty's best discussion of these issues is probably chapters 4 and 5 of CIS. As a general rule, Rorty tends to turn what are individual issues of personal vision and temperament in James into the collective issue of "our" vision and temperament. He does something similar to Emerson's views and reads self-reliance as a collective task of becoming more reliant on each other. I discuss this issue in the chapters that follow.

49. Fish, "Truth But No Consequences," 410–11. Like Fish, Rorty holds that "there is no reason why a fascist could not be a pragmatist" (PSH, 23).

50. "Truth But No Consequences," 411. Emphasis added.

51. This line of thought is very Emersonian and is discussed at length by Stanley Cavell in his *Conditions Handsome and Unhandsome*.

52. For Fish's view of democracy, see "Truth and Toilets," 306, passim: "Democracy (pace Bernstein) is not a program for transforming men and women into capacious and generous beings."

53. Fish, "Truth and Toilets," 306–7.

54. *Pragmatism*, 510.

55. "Creative Democracy," 226.

Chapter Two

The Mirror and the Lever

"Imaginative" writing is as it were a flank-attack upon positions that are impregnable from the front. A writer attempting anything that is not coldly "intellectual" can do very little with words in their primary meanings. He gets his effect if at all by using words in a tricky roundabout way.

—George Orwell, "New Words"

That was why *Animal Farm* was able to turn liberal opinion around. It was not its relation to reality, but its relation to the most popular alternative description of recent events, that gave it its power. It was a strategically placed lever, not a mirror.

—Richard Rorty, *Contingency*

In a move that confounded many of his readers, Rorty recently said that he will abandon the use of argumentation to support his views. Instead of appealing to a discourse of right and wrong or truth and error, he will engage in "redescription"—trying to make his views appear more attractive by restating the views of others in ways that make them look bad.[1] Arguing against the idea that our beliefs correspond to reality, he claims we would be better off without the notion of "getting something right."[2] With his characteristic combination of insouciance and incisive critique, Rorty dismisses the idea that language, knowledge, and justification are a matter of accuracy of representation, and thereby abandons a fundamental assumption of modern philosophy.

What would it mean to give up the hope of getting it right? What are the implications for the way we do theory? For politics? Rorty has been rather straightforward about his redescriptions—for instance, referring to the Dewey which appears in his texts simply as "my hypothetical Dewey."[3] Still,

I am not sure how many of his readers have taken him seriously: it is hard to form a coherent idea of what a philosophical tract without argumentation or validity claims would look like. Accepting that Rorty has completely given up argumentation is not easy, since his essays do defend certain positions and clearly express a normative point of view.[4]

These interpretive difficulties have led some to dismiss Rorty as a dangerous relativist or as hopelessly awash in "performative self-contradiction." To engage constructively with aspects of Rorty's writing sometimes given short shrift, I suggest a different tack: that we see Rorty as attempting to fundamentally alter the way we understand the relation of knowledge and language to the world. Jettisoning the "mirror" for the "lever," he casts imaginative writing as transformational rather than representational. Rather than providing "a correct depiction of how things are in themselves," we should understand words and knowledge as "instruments of change" (EHO, 152).[5]

Rorty's antirepresentationalism is more than merely an epistemological stance. The political value of "redescription," or stating things in an alternate, less familiar vocabulary, resides in its power to change minds. In *Achieving Our Country*, he argues, "You cannot urge political renewal on the basis of fact. You have to describe the country in terms of what you passionately hope it will become" (101). Seeking to reinvigorate the secular, national projects of Whitman and Dewey, redescribing America in terms that furnish a sense of "romance" becomes the sine qua non of any majoritarian political undertaking. Reenchanting the world through a secular, civic religion committed to a romance of the American experiment is, in his view, because it is an embodiment of a "concrete" fantasy, a substitute for the transcendental project of escaping time and chance common to metaphysical philosophizing and longings for unity with the divine—in short, a substitute for thinking we have gotten it right.

Highlighting parallels between Rorty's account of redescription and Sheldon Wolin's notion of political theory as a kind of "vision," I contend that Rorty can be fruitfully approached as a political theorist concerned with promulgating a new picture of the political world.[6] Rorty's recent thought is best read as a political intervention aimed at revitalizing a moribund and spectatorial contemporary left whose preoccupation with getting it right theoretically has obscured the need to act politically. It is therefore best evaluated not in terms of accuracy of representation but in terms of its political effects. As a discourse of meaning and persuasion rather than truth and accuracy of representation, political theory, like Rortyan redescription, has often disposed of competing perspectives not by pointing out the inaccuracies of their depictions of reality, but by making them look bad by portraying them in a different light. Political theory, on Wolin's conception, like Rortyan redescription, values the imagination and the ability to come up with new metaphors and new angles of vision.

Letting go of the idea of getting something right has important consequences for democratic life. It amounts to curing ourselves of what Rorty calls, following Thomas Nagel, the "ambition of transcendence" (ORT, 12). As he expressed it in *Contingency, Irony, and Solidarity*, we must "try to get to the point where we no longer worship *anything*, where we treat *nothing* as a quasi divinity, where we treat *everything*—our language, our conscience, our community—as a product of time and chance" (22). This Deweyan stance that nothing supersede the freely arrived-upon consensus of democratic citizens is the most deeply democratic sentiment to be found in Rorty's writing. Substituting intersubjectivity for transcendence and accuracy of representation, he argues, "will take away a few more excuses for fanaticism and intolerance" (TP, 83).

Yet Rorty's recent political program of reenchanting the world departs from his earlier effort to "dedivinize" it. Insofar as he constructs a false dichotomy between postmodern pessimism and romantic enthusiasm, the only alternative to joining "the School of Resentment," as Harold Bloom calls it, is for Rorty to "live in an imaginary, lightly sketched future." In the end, giving up the idea of getting it right severs Rorty's redescriptions from reality and spells a loss of critical purchase. Where Rorty seeks to alter our vocabularies, the great political theorists sought to alter the world.

POLITICAL THEORY AS REDESCRIPTION

In my view, the role of creativity and imagination in political theory parallels the creation of linguistic novelty in what Rorty calls "redescription." A key shared element is the creative or imaginative role of theoretical or "linguistic" novelty—the work of fashioning new perspectives on the world. Redescription, for Rorty, is an amalgam of a Wittgensteinian sense of language as a tool—and by extension, of imaginative writing as a "lever" rather than a "mirror"—and a Kuhnian understanding of the transformative power of conceptual revolutions. What is interesting about this is that in a series of seminal articles written in the late 1960s aimed at rescuing the practice of political theory from the behavioral and empiricist "revolution" in the social sciences, Wolin argued that political theories are best understood as Kuhnian paradigms.

On Wolin's account of "vision," it is not merely an objective act of perception or "dispassionate reportage" which most characterizes the perspective of the political theorist. Since the sixteenth and seventeenth centuries, this type of "objective" vision has been associated with scientific observation. Yet, as Wolin observes, this conception underestimates the role of imagination in the production of scientific theories. As a general rule, political theorists, unlike most scientists and most philosophers, have gone about their business without strong claims to privileged access to reality. Put another way, "polishing the mirror," to borrow one of Rorty's apt phrases, has seldom been a major preoccupation. Rather than an ability to accurately capture reality—although this surely plays some role—the stock in trade of the theorist has been the creative feat of procuring a new angle of vision or portraying some part of reality in a new light.[7]

This is the second sense of vision, as in an aesthetic or religious vision, where, not unlike Rortyan redescription, an imaginative rather than a descriptive operation dominates. This imaginative vision is, Wolin argues, "the medium for expressing the fundamental values of the theorist."[8] Why political theorists have resorted to the imagination in this way is a difficult question. As Wolin asks, "What did they hope to gain by adding an imaginative dimension to their representations?"[9] Part of it, Wolin suggests, is the result of the inability of the theorist, like the rest of the citizenry, to see the entire political world firsthand. But it also emanates from a fundamental claim about the nature of facts, and in particular, about political theory's relation to facts, especially political facts.

The relation of the vocabularies of political theory to the "facts" of political reality has always been complex. Although the practices and institutions of the political world provide the basic "data" of political theorists, Wolin argues,

> The ideas and categories we use in political analysis are not of the same order as institutional "facts," nor are they "contained," so to speak, in the facts. They represent, instead, an added element, something created by the political theorist. Concepts like "power," "authority," "consent," and so forth are not real "things," although they are intended to point to some significant aspect about political things. Their function is to render political facts significant.[10]

To be sure, accuracy of representation, if we take Plato's republic or Hobbes's social contract and state of nature, has never been a primary concern of the political theorist. On some level, the descriptions or pictures of reality the theorist presents are not "real," nor are they meant to be. Or better, as Wolin puts it, theorists saw some value in "adding" an imaginative element to their redescriptions. As theoretical constructs that do not lend themselves to easy proof or disproof by empirical tests of correspondence with reality, the vocabularies of the theorist demand a different kind of evaluative discourse.[11] The imaginative or creative element of political theory seems to thwart attempts to bind the strictures of representationalist discourse too tightly. But even its most utopian imagining remains linked to political reality as part of an effort to change it.

Wolin describes the process of "adding" something to the facts as presenting things in "a corrected fullness." Another way of putting it is that "the world must be supplemented before it can be understood and reflected upon."[12] On Wolin's view, the role of creativity and imagination in "representing" the world arises from the commitment of the theorist to "lessening the gap between the possibilities grasped through political imagination and the actualities of political existence." That is to say, it flows from a desire to transform the world through generating political action. "Precisely because political theory pictured society in an exaggerated, 'unreal' way," Wolin asserts, "it was a necessary complement to action. Precisely because action involved intervention into existing affairs, it sorely needed a perspective of tantalizing possibilities."[13] In the end, this idea of an "added" element seems to me a more attractive conception of the nature of the persuasive discourse of political theory than the free-floating quality of assertions that results from Rorty's apparently uncompromising antirepresentationalism.

This view rests on a fundamental claim about the relation of thought and action. The idea, as Wolin accounts for it, is that acting "intelligently and nobly" requires a "a perspective wider than the immediate situation for which the action was intended." This more comprehensive perspective or "vision" comes from thinking about society in its "corrected fullness," that is, from thinking about society from the perspective of the political theorist. The action-generating potential of political theory, then, is most potent when thinking about society "not as it is but as it might be."[14]

Wolin's argument that the imaginative and creative element of political theory rules out depicting the political order in terms of a "representational likeness," and, in particular, this last statement about the importance of viewing current affairs in the light of unrealized possibilities, provide a remarkable summary of Rorty's position. One of the predominant themes in Rorty's recent work is the idea that "You cannot urge political renewal on the basis of fact. You have to describe the country in terms of what you passionately hope it will become" (AOC, 101). This "imaginative reordering of political life," as Wolin puts it, echoes a major theme of the Romantic strand in American pragmatism, most visible in the thought of Emerson and Dewey, the heritage Rorty increasingly claims as his own.[15] In addition, Rorty's recent articulations of the political thrust of his project underscore its links to the generation of collective action. An optimistic, forward-looking orientation, for Rorty, is necessary for collective self-transformation. As he argues in *Achieving Our Country*, "Those who hope to persuade a nation to exert itself . . . must tell inspiring stories . . . stories about what a nation has been and should try to be" (3, 13). "Hope," he asserts categorically, is "the condition of growth" (PSH, 120).

Another way of conceptualizing the functioning of political theory as redescription, as furnishing new ways of looking at the world, is to view political theories as Kuhnian paradigms and to see the work of the theorist as the creation of new paradigms of vision. Wolin first perceived the continuities between Kuhn's account of the production of theoretical novelty in science and the functioning of political theory in the late 1960s.[16] For his part, Rorty has long been a Kuhnian convert, going as far as calling his version of pragmatism "left-wing Kuhnianism" (ORT, 38). Along with his Wittgensteinian notion of language as a tool, Kuhn's ideas about the transformative power of conceptual revolutions play an important role in Rorty's understanding of social change as essentially a linguistic phenomenon. What Kuhn's great scientific innovators, Wolin's "epic political theorists," and Rorty's "revolutionary" philosophers have in common is that they all inaugurate new ways of looking at the world, usually in times of crisis, by providing new vocabularies or terminologies that cast reality in a different light and hence open unforeseen possibilities.

The distinction between "normal" and "abnormal" discourse, modeled on Kuhn's contrast between "normal" and "revolutionary" science, plays an important role in part 3 of *Philosophy and the Mirror of Nature*. Kuhn's basic insight provides the groundwork for Rorty's overarching argument that philosophy be understood as a "cultural genre," a "voice in the conversation of mankind," rather than as a discipline which confronts permanent issues and merely requires additional polishing of its mirror to finally get things right. For the most part, though, Rorty's use of Kuhn is largely negative, a wedge he employs against several of the dominant assumptions of traditional philosophy.[17]

In *Contingency, Irony, and Solidarity*, however, a more positive use of Kuhn emerges. Kuhn is invoked whenever Rorty discusses the power of "metaphorical redescription." Here the ability to redescribe familiar phenomena in unfamiliar terms becomes a tool for providing a nonfoundational justification for liberalism. Because there are no transcendental grounds to appeal to, all we can do is show how attractive things look when stated in "our own alternative idiom." Framing the thrust of Kuhn's approach to science as the displacement of a correspondence theory of truth with intersubjective agreement helps Rorty account for his pragmatist conception of truth as whatever "we" agree upon and his reliance on a nonessentialist conception of solidarity (54–69).

Rorty also turns to Kuhn in the context of his discussion of Orwell's *Animal Farm*, one of the key passages where Rorty links the idea of redescription with a conception of imaginative writing that I have glossed as political theory. The political value of redescription, as a way of generating new perspectives on the world, not unlike political theory, resides in its ability to change minds. For Rorty, *Animal Farm* was pivotal in helping leftists let go of a way of looking at the world which insisted there was an important difference between Stalin and Hitler. Although it did not institute a new paradigm, it provided a crucial stimulus for jarring loose the old one in a time when "so many anomalies had been piling up"—not because of its relation to reality, Rorty argues, but because of its relation to other descriptions of the same events: "it was a strategically placed lever, not a mirror" (CIS, 174).

REDESCRIPTION AS POLITICAL THEORY

So what would it mean to read Rorty as doing political theory? There are at least five qualities shared by both Rorty's perspective and the conception of political theory I advance here: first, what I have called a weak representationalism—that is, a relation to the factual world where criteria other than accuracy of representation predominate; second, a primary role for the imagination and a value on novel perspectives; third, a self-consciously partial view of the world that makes no claim to objectivity; fourth, a transformative bent and orientation toward action; and fifth, a readiness to respond to perceived crises.

Reading Rorty as writing political theory helps free us from a paralyzing entanglement in questions of validity claims and the nature of discourse. It is not so much that this resolves these issues in any definitive way, but that, in a Rortyan spirit, it obviates the need to ask such questions. The benefit of this shift in approach is that it brings to the fore the political thrust of Rorty's writings. Rather than a set of universal truths about politics or about ourselves, it allows us to see Rorty's texts as political interventions, as attempts to inspire, to nudge us out of a stance of spectatorship on to the terrain of political urgency and direct engagement. Understood as the province of crafted narratives and imaginative visions rather than truth and validity, the work of political theory involves deploying perspectives designed to spark change, not to illuminate truths.[18]

To put it another way, Rorty's recent writing can be read as telling a story designed to move us to action. Not unlike Hobbes and Locke writing in the context of the English Civil War and the Glorious Revolution, Rorty wants to persuade us to adopt his perspective. To the extent that we do and we see the world through the lens he provides, we are more likely to be mobilized to his cause. Not unlike Tocqueville, Rorty is trying to revise the stories we tell ourselves by offering a new narrative.

Political theory, it can be argued, emerges in times of crisis. As Norman Jacobson once put it, "Political theory begins precisely at the moment things become, so to speak, unglued." It is not so much the urge to reflect "fixed principles," he argues, but the "impulse to meet the challenge to actually fix principles" in the midst of uncertainty, that animates the political theorist.[19]

On this perspective, the critique of foundationalism opens the door to political theory as a discourse aimed not at truth but at persuasion. The crisis Rorty addresses, as we shall see, is the absence of an animating vision to rouse and organize what he sees as an effete and ineffectual contemporary left. When he says he is "not going to offer arguments against the vocabulary I want to replace," but rather to "try to make the vocabulary I favor look attractive," he is shifting the terms of his own discourse from validity to aesthetic appeal. I want to suggest that the move to "aesthetic appeal" marks the entry into the terrain of political theory as a persuasive, politically infused discourse (CIS, 9).[20]

It should be said that the take on political theory I have sketched is a normative conception, based on the idea that political theory arises and functions in the space created by a lack of fixity or certainty. Not all political theorists accept this premise—Plato, for one—nor do all such interventions into a culture abdicate their claim on universal truth. Jeremiads and sermons, as much as political theories and novels, seek to mobilize people on the basis of their perspectives. Yet the absence of this kind of fixity seems to be precisely what Rorty is after when he makes contingency and irony the fundamental qualities of his postmetaphysical polity and asserts that we try to get to the point where there is no nonhuman authority—like God, Truth, or Scripture—able to trump democratic consensus (CIS, 22).

The political thrust of Rorty's antirepresentationalism resides in what he calls "redescriptions." Redescription—the ability to "redescribe the familiar in unfamiliar terms"—is political: describing our history, our present, and ourselves in alternate vocabularies; sketching possible scenarios, both desirable and undesirable; and offering competing narratives are all ways of altering the lens through which we view our surroundings and therefore of opening or closing different paths, different avenues of possibility. Redescription is the province of the imagination, a matter of coming up with "as yet undreamt-of metaphors" and "vocabularies still unborn," rather than of Reason or Truth. Unlike most modern philosophers, Rorty sees the fruits of the imagination in moral terms; moral progress is made by becoming more imaginative, rather than uncovering the Good or the Right. The imagination, Rorty asserts, is "the cutting edge of cultural evolution" (PSH, 87–88; EHO, 26). Our ability to imagine "new conceptions of possible communities," and new ideas of "what it is to be human" within them, can bring about greater inclusion and less hostility to difference (AOC, 18).

Rorty cites a number of historical examples to illustrate the idea of redescription and its effects:

> Such redescription was practised by the early Christians when they explained that the distinction between Jew and Greek was not as important as had been thought. It is being practised by contemporary feminists, whose descriptions of social behavior and marital arrangements seem as strange to many men (and, for that matter, many women) as St. Paul's indifference to traditional Judaic distinctions seems to the scribes and the pharisees. It is what the Founding Fathers of my country attempted when they asked people to think of themselves not so much as Pennsylvanian Quakers or Catholic Marylanders but as citizens of a tolerant, pluralistic, federal republic. (PSH, 87–88)

In short, redescriptions generate change by helping us to "alter our self-image" (PSH, 72).

Change, on a fundamental level, is for Rorty the result of altering the vocabularies or the metaphors we use to describe things. Here the linguistic premises of Rorty's pragmatism are clearly visible: his thought owes as much to analytic philosophy since the "linguistic turn" as to the Deweyan heritage of American pragmatism. The "large-scale change of belief," on this perspective, "is indistinguishable from large-scale change in the meaning of one's words." Yet the creation of linguistic novelty is not idle wordplay, of interest only to poets and etymologists: a new metaphor, Rorty asserts, is "a call to change one's language and one's life" (EHO, 13).

Moreover, this process of "liberating of culture from obsolete vocabularies through the work of weaving metaphors into our communal web of beliefs and desires" provides the central means of the "self-criticism of cultures" on Rorty's view (EHO, 15, 18). This view of change as fundamentally linguistic in nature is rooted in the assumption of the self as a center of narrative gravity, an idea Rorty attributes to analytic philosopher Daniel Dennett. For Rorty, moral progress is a matter of "self-enlargement," altering the narratives we use to describe and understand ourselves, both individually and collectively. The new metaphors produced through the process of "poetic achievement," when woven into the narratives we use to describe ourselves, can bring about changes in our behavior and in the possibilities of our world.[21]

But how are we to adjudicate between competing redescriptions or narratives if not by accuracy of representation? In a word, by their consequences. More specifically, by the extent to which they lend themselves to action—not just any kind of action, but that which is conducive to incremental, piecemeal reform. A political redescription is useful, Rorty tells us, when it suggests answers to the question, what is to be done? Choosing between different descriptions is not a matter of appealing to truth or to facts or to an underlying reality behind appearances. It is a matter of "playing off scenarios against contrasting scenarios, projects against alternative projects, descriptions against redescriptions" (CIS, 174–75). It is about understanding our current situation in terms that best lend themselves to the means for reforming it. Thus, like Wolin's "vision," it is not objectivity or impartiality or accuracy of representation which is involved here, but rather a measure of a perspective's pragmatically oriented persuasiveness or aesthetic appeal.

Rorty cites the example of Orwell's *Animal Farm* in this context. As we have noted, by retelling the political history of his century "in terms suitable for children," Orwell was able to underscore the needlessly complex nature of leftist political discussion and reveal the absurdity of attempts to distinguish between Stalin and Hitler. Rorty explains its manner of functioning by noting that "it was not its relation to reality, but its relation to the most popular alternative description of recent events, that gave it its power." This is why *Animal Farm* "turned liberal opinion around" (CIS, 174).

Let us look at two of Rorty's recent essays, "The Unpatriotic Academy" (1994) and "Back to Class Politics" (1996), both of which are collected in *Philosophy and Social Hope*. Anticipating the themes that would find expression in his 1997 Massey Lectures (published as *Achieving Our Country*), in these essays Rorty chides the academic left for having abandoned the "real" politics of labor unions in favor of the cultural politics of purging academic syllabi of dead white males—though he does acknowledge the multicultural fruits of this struggle—and urges a return to a 1950s-style, "Old Left" concern with helping the poor and achieving the goal of a classless society. With compelling imagery about "the blood-drenched history" of labor unions as a history of "heroic self-deprivation" and of "striker's skulls being broken by truncheons, decade after decade," in impassioned prose Rorty links the civil rights movement and union movement as the best examples of "Americans getting together on their own and changing society from the bottom up—forcing it to become more decent, more democratic, and more humane." Rorty repeatedly invokes the spirit of Lincoln and Thoreau and Martin Luther King Jr.—even Emerson's "Self-Reliance"—as he asserts the need for a greater, deeper identification with America on the part of its intellectuals.

These two essays are surely polemical, but they are rousing polemics. Although one could quite rightly take issue with Rorty's vague invocations of the spirit of thinkers like Emerson and King, pointing out how he elides the harsh criticisms that were inseparable from their affirmations of America's spirit, or how his one-sided view of the early labor movement neglects the fact that many of its goals were "for whites only" and that it rested on an underlying racial animus, or even that his depiction of "cultural" politics is simplistic and ignores the many important gains made in the name of diversity, this would miss the point of these essays. And what is more, that kind of enlivened engagement—even, on the most generous reading, if critical of him—is precisely what Rorty hopes to engender.

REDESCRIPTION AND SOCIAL CRITICISM

Let us pause for a moment and pose several questions. First, is anything lost by giving up claims to validity and the idea of getting it right? Habermas, for one, has argued that there is. In his view, Rorty's antirepresentationalist posture and eschewal of validity claims signifies his being mired in self-referential, aestheticized discourse. I make a different argument: the lack of social criticism in Rorty's account results not from a shortcoming in the area of reason but from an absence of reality. Yet Habermas's point, if accepted, is powerful: an absence of validity claims signals a loss of the standards of critical reason and a collapse of moral and political judgments into aesthetic ones.

Habermas distinguishes two types of discourse: "serious" and "fictive."[22] Most discourse, including everyday communication, is "serious" discourse, or language oriented toward mutual understanding. What defines discourse as serious is the implicit presence of validity claims, meaning that, if called upon, the speaker is prepared to defend her utterances with rational arguments. On Habermas's view, this is the fundamental underlying assumption of normal language and the basis of the intersubjective quality of all communicative practices. Also referred to as the "action-coordinating" dimension of language, this inherent intersubjectivity flows from the criticizable nature of validity claims—that is, their being subject, at least in principle, to universal argumentative norms. This is what allows Habermas to assert that validity claims transcend the particularity of any subject context and make intersubjective understanding possible.

Fictive discourse, by contrast, is defined by the absence or "bracketing" of claims to validity. The expectations which make intersubjective understanding possible are suspended, disengaging expression from the realm of communicative discourse. No longer tethered to the requirements of communication or intersubjectivity, poetic or "world-disclosive" language can thus be given over to innovation, creativity, and aesthetic play. This is all well and good for poetic and literary discourse. However, although empowered by the bracketing of validity claims, poetic language is "self-referential"—that is, it is "merely aesthetic," as it is sometimes called. Laden with the subjectivity and relativism of what Habermas likes to refer to pejoratively, with its Nietz-schean resonances, as *Lebensphilosophie*, such discourse can have no bind-ing force. Fictive discourse lacks the universality and basis for social inte-gration necessary to transcend particular subjective contexts.

Situating the discourse of political theory as a middle ground between these two poles provides a way out of Habermas's narrow dichotomy. The idea of a mode of discourse that eschews rational arguments and truth claims yet nonetheless wields a certain normativity seems to capture what is distinc-tive about Rortyan redescription. Although he doesn't put it in these terms, Rorty seems to be moving in this direction when he suggests that we view Habermas's distinction between different uses of language as points on a con-tinuous spectrum, thereby "blurring the line between rhetorical manipulation and genuine validity-seeking argument." It is this sort of "blurring" that char-acterizes political theory as a persuasive discourse of meaning rather than of truth or validity.

Briefly put, Rorty believes the commonality that Habermas attributes to se-rious discourse can be achieved through what he calls "sentimental education": largely through narratives—"sad, sentimental stories"—and by reading certain kinds of novels. One of the results of dropping the idea of getting something right is that what were formerly appeals to universal human nature or a shared essence become a matter of a collective moral identity rooted in the ability to extend the first person plural *we* to as many diverse others as possible.[23] Rorty turns to narratives and novels, in my view, in order to forge the kind of demo-cratic moral community that Habermas, and other pragmatist accounts that ap-peal to a Peircian notion of a community of inquirers, merely assume. In a re-mark aimed directly at Habermas, he says we must "stop asking for universal validity" and become more willing "to live with plurality" (ORT, 27).

Lastly, what of Habermas's claim about the loss of a ground for criticism? As we have noted, Rorty believes that the process of weaving the novel metaphors associated with redescription back into our belief systems fur-nishes a means for the "self-criticism of cultures." By underscoring the gap between portrayed possibilities and existing reality, redescription generates critical bite. This is the function of Rorty's emphasis on "future possibilities" and on theory as about "suggestions for future action." In other words, re-descriptions not only can change minds and inspire; they can provide a criti-cal perspective on the present by viewing it retrospectively from the vantage of a very different future.[24]

Yet juxtaposing this view to Dewey's account of the critical operation in-herent in this kind of project in *Art as Experience* reveals the limits of Rorty's scheme. This is important because Dewey ostensibly provides the model for Rorty's effort to make thought transformative rather than representational:

> A sense of possibilities that are unrealized and that might be realized are, when they are put in contrast with actual conditions, the most penetrating "criticism" of the latter that can be made. It is by a sense of possibilities opening before us that we become aware of constrictions that hem us in and of burdens that oppress.[25]

Within the distance between these portrayed possibilities and existing reality lies a potential impetus for change. This perspective provides an alternative to Habermas's notion that social criticism is predicated upon the use of reason.

Rorty's account thus suffers from an altogether different deficiency. The problem that emerges is that "actual conditions" have an uncertain place in Rorty's vision, both on a theoretical and a political level. Scenarios like that of Orwell's, or Rorty's own narrative, by his own account, are to be compared not with reality but with other alternate scenarios. Because his antirepresentationalism rules out the correspondent endeavor of comparing imaginative visions with actual reality tout court, any potential critical traction such visions might provide is lost. In other words, Rorty's approach never attempts to close the gap between imagined possibilities and actual affairs.

RORTY'S LIBERAL UTOPIA:
REDESCRIPTION AS REENCHANTMENT

For all the parallels, there are important differences between Wolin's account and Rortyan redescription. One of Wolin's statements about the functioning of political theory brings out the crucial disjuncture between this conception of political theory and Rorty's project of redescription:

> By viewing common political experience from a slightly different angle than the prevailing one, by framing an old question in a novel way, by rebelling against the conservative tendencies of thought and language, particular thinkers have helped to unfasten established ways of thought and to thrust on their contemporaries and posterity the necessity of rethinking political experience.[26]

As we have seen, Rorty too has sought to view things from a different angle and to dispose of unhelpful questions by reframing them in a new way. Yet there is little to indicate that his perspective is meant to spark a "rethinking" of political experience in any fundamental way.[27] The sense of unrealized possibility that has become so central in his recent thought never performs the critical function outlined by Wolin, or for that matter, by Dewey. Even as it authorizes the creative power of imaginative language, Rorty's antirepresentationalism thus limits the critical and transformative potential of his political project by severing his redescriptions from political reality.

To put it baldly, there seems to be little place for "reality" in Rorty's scheme. This shortcoming exists on both a theoretical and a political level. Theoretically, the key difference between Rorty's nonfoundationalist antirepresentationalism and the kind described by Wolin in the context of political theory boils down to the difference between "adding an imaginative dimension" to one's representations through imaginative, even distortive angles of vision, and doing away with representation altogether. Despite his pragmatic orientation and advocacy of contextualized and historicist thought, concrete assessments of actuality are conspicuously absent in Rorty's work. This translates into a sheer neglect of the world of "prosaic facts" that for Dewey furnished critical traction and for the political theorist, when pictured in a novel way, generate action. For the theorist, "representations," no matter how exaggerated or partial, are never "wholly severed" from the reality of existing political life.

Politically, Rorty's account diverges sharply from Wolin's in its view of the action-generating capacity of imaginative thought in two ways. First, for Rorty, this follows from a "reenchantment" of political reality that imagines it in terms of future possibilities rather than as something "added" to the facts. This is a crucial point: because Rorty believes growth or change is predicated upon a hopeful frame of mind, he believes this sort of rosy view is essential for action.

Second, Rorty has to curb the transformative power of linguistic novelty to avoid undermining the project of solidifying a democratic moral community. He views moral progress as "the expansion of the circle of beings who count as 'us,'" and he believes a strong sense of moral identification is the crucial factor in the generation of moral action on behalf of others.[28] Unlike Wolinesque political theory, his thought aims not so much to alter political reality, but simply to generate an optimistic, communitarian emotional attitude.

In a sense, this is understandable. As I shall argue, Rorty's idiosyncratic linkage of social hope, utopian imagining, and patriotism is best understood as his attempt to counteract the current mood of resigned pessimism. An emotional involvement with one's country, he claims, something sorely lacking among the postmodern left, is necessary if political deliberation is to be "imaginative and productive" (AOC, 3).[29]

But in my view, Rorty's perspective erects a false dichotomy of postmodern pessimism and "knowingness" versus romantic enthusiasm and reenchantment. He then has no choice but to choose the latter. The only alternative to joining Bloom's School of Resentment is for Rorty to "live in an imaginary, lightly sketched future" (EHO, 183). Granted, much of Rorty's motivation derives from his honest desire to generate a more active politics;

the options as he frames them are either detached spectatorship or inspired agency. Placing romance and an idealized "dream country" at the center of his political project, however, ensures that his political vision never makes contact with the actual state of affairs.

For Rorty, without "romance," the "fuzzy overlap of faith, hope and love," there can be no politics. Reinvigorating the "civic religion" of Whitman and Dewey, on his view, is an essential part of any majoritarian political project. As he argues in *Achieving Our Country*, "You have to be loyal to a dream country rather than to the one to which you wake up every morning. Unless such loyalty exists, the ideal has no chance of becoming actual" (101). It is in light of this reenchantment of the world that Rorty's depiction of "the possibility of a liberal utopia" in *Contingency, Irony, and Solidarity* and his project of "achieving our country" by reinvigorating an American "civil religion" should be understood (CIS, xv; AOC, 15; PSH, 160).

Several problems emerge for Rorty's project of "achieving our country." For one, without the contrast between a vision of transformed possibilities and the current state of affairs, appeals to a "dream country" become hollow invocations of abstract ideals—a flight from the unpleasantness of reality into a haven of idealized potential. Second, because Rorty associates a detached spectatorship with being "retrospective" and jettisons them both, his forward-looking optimism and faith in unrealized possibilities involves a refusal to face up to the unsightly realities of our past. Third, operating at such an abstract and idealized level leads to the tendency of Rorty's assertions about politics to be too vague and overgeneralized to be of much insight or practical value.

The key to understanding Rorty's rather odd and oxymoronic brand of liberal utopianism lies in recognizing that it aims not at the actual realization of the "dream country" he conjures, but at merely a widespread entertaining of the possibility of it. In other words, what matters to Rorty and to his political program is that the underlying attitude behind utopian imagining be generated, not so much the content of the utopia itself. The activation of what amounts to a nonpolitical, emotional attitude of "hopefulness" has become a cornerstone of Rorty's political theory. As a result, it is enough that such utopias merely appear attainable, for that is what inspires the greatest hope:

> Modern, literate, secular societies depend on the existence of reasonably concrete, optimistic, and plausible *political* scenarios, as opposed to scenarios about redemption beyond the grave. To retain social hope, members of such a society need to be able to tell themselves a story about how things might get better, and to see no insuperable obstacles to this story's coming true. (CIS, 86)

It is less important for Rorty that this dream come true than simply that we continue to have such dreams; his utopian longings, unlike other historical examples, are not rooted in a desire for change or driven by a deep discontent with the present. Because Rorty values the utopian imagination as merely an expression of confidence in current possibilities for reform and a manifestation of social hope, the transformative character of such imagining is curbed from the start. Turning away from such dreams toward sophisticated theories of culture is a gesture of despair, in his view, and more importantly, a prelude to political fecklessness.

The problem with Rorty's account parallels the problem of transposing a conception of scientific thought onto political thought that Wolin identified in his early essays. While both "revolutionary" scientists and great political theorists have tended to articulate their novel views in response to impending crises, political theories, by and large, have arisen not in response to crises in the community of theorists but to crises in the world.[30] Here Wolin introduces a useful distinction between "problems-in-a-theory" and "problems-in-the-world." Although they can be related, the latter have been most central to the concerns of political theorists, while the former have dominated those of scientists.[31]

With regard to Rorty, at least in his early work, he seemed to be responding to a theoretical or philosophical crisis—call it the accumulating anomalies in the Enlightenment rationalist or "Cartesian-Kantian" worldview—rather than to any kind of political breakdown. Wolin has called this Rorty's "invented crisis."[32] Yet, at least on a sympathetic reading, the underlying thrust of Rorty's project has been political in the sense that his ultimate aim is to assert the priority of democracy to philosophy rather than the other way around.

In his more recent work, Rorty does in my view respond in a more direct way to a political as opposed to a philosophical crisis—namely, the moribund state of the contemporary left. Rorty's thought since the mid-1980s can be situated as an attempt to remedy the left's crisis of political imagination. Here I differ with Wolin's diagnosis that Rorty's crisis is an "invented" one, although this element has become more pronounced since Wolin wrote. Since Laclau and Mouffe's much-discussed *Hegemony and Socialist Strategy*, this crisis has been linked to the demise of socialism, both as an intellectual position and as a practical political alternative.[33] Rorty's appeal to pride and social hope arises in response to the absence of a guiding vision to animate and unify leftist political commitment.

Although generally sympathetic to their political orientation, however, Rorty is more likely to see Laclau and Mouffe as part of the problem than the solution. He sees them as essentially self-defeating: they merely replace one set of theoretical vocabularies for conceptualizing politics with an even more sophisticated set, all in the name of being more political. Rorty's point— which is a rather powerful one—is to question the premise dear to a certain species of leftist intellectual that makes political action dependent upon a theoretical grasp of politics. The most pressing need for leftist politics for Rorty is spurring people to act, not procuring another theory or making sure we "get it right" theoretically.[34]

This comes out most vividly in an essay where he reflects upon the up-heavals of 1989 and the "end of Leninism." Considering the role the latter played in the collective imaginary of the left, Rorty raises the question,

> What events might replace the Bolshevik Revolution, and what figure might re-place Lenin, in the imaginations of the generation born around 1980, the people who will be leftist university students in the year 2000? What might irradiate the collective imaginary of leftists who take for granted that state ownership of the means of production is no longer an option? (TP, 236)

The thrust of his project is to try to retain the sense of commitment and in-spiration that socialism generated as the vague political aim in place since the Enlightenment of achieving an egalitarian, classless society, but without the Marxist theoretical underpinning which claimed to have hit the bedrock of true reality. For Rorty, it is a difference between "talking about the way things were always meant to be" and "talking about the way things never have been but might, with our help, become."[35]

This is where Rorty's call for a new "civic religion" comes in. Interestingly, Rorty attributes the importance of reenchanting the world to Dewey. He sees parallels between his own diagnosis of the current shortcomings of social democratic liberalism as a failure of collective imagination and Dewey's sug-gestion that we need to "bring back what religion gave our forefathers." How-ever, "religion" here is a detranscendentalized, pragmatic religion, a faith in the practical and concrete, if you will. Rorty describes his project of using "detailed historical narratives" to foster a "de-theoreticized sense of commu-nity" as an extension of the "Deweyan attempt to make concrete concerns with the daily problems of one's community—social engineering—the substi-tute for traditional religion" (EHO, 174–75). The key passage here, Rorty tells us, comes from the last paragraph of Dewey's *Reconstruction in Philosophy*:

> We are weak today in ideal matters because intelligence is divorced from aspi-ration. . . . When philosophy shall have cooperated with the force of events and made clear and coherent the meaning of the daily detail, science and emotion will interpenetrate, practice and imagination will embrace. Poetry and religious feeling will be the unforced flowers of life.[36]

Living in an "imaginary, lightly-sketched future" must, Rorty suggests, go hand in hand with the project of melioristic reform; the former merely provides its guiding vision. In the absence of such an imagined future, our critical insights about the present risk becoming spectatorial musings more likely to generate stagnant pessimism and disdain than hopeful activism. The problem is that Rorty never gets around to setting out the specifics of this program of reform. Despite invoking the Deweyan pragmatist project of supplanting religion with a concern for the concrete, Rorty never accomplishes this replacement; he merely exchanges a transcendental religion with a pragmatic and secular one.[37]

Ultimately, Rorty fails to recognize that disenchantment and discontent, the feeling that one's country has let one down, can also mobilize people to action, maybe even more so than enchantment and romance. It is precisely these sources which are responsible for the committed activism of people like Martin Luther King Jr. and Cornel West, and most importantly for Rorty, James Baldwin. In the end, Rorty's attempt to follow Dewey in making thought transformative rather than representative ends up making it redemptive.

CONCLUSION

Rorty's move to shift things away from a preoccupation with getting it right theoretically toward a greater political engagement is an important one. The problem is that his alternative to getting it right—a kind of reenchantment of the world—does not bring us any closer to reality. This, rather than relativism, is the more fundamental problem with Rorty's approach. The decisive difference between the political theorist and the scientific theorist, on Wolin's view, is that while the scientific theorist seeks to change only people's views of the world, the political theorist aims to change the world itself—that is, "not simply to alter the way men look at the world, but to alter the world."[38] Because it reduces social and political change to a change in vocabularies, Rorty's antirepresentationalism in my view contents itself with changes in vocabularies rather than changes in the world.

As Wolin points out, Kuhn was not always clear about what causes the theoretical innovations that characterize revolutionary science and why the challenge to an existing paradigm is ever successful. He seems to suggest that there is "an element of arbitrariness" in normal science that will lead to anomalies. For the most part, they are "produced inadvertently" and then, over time, proliferate into a more fundamental crisis.[39] Rorty tends to follow this line of thought. He holds that progress in philosophy will occur "as long as geniuses keep emerging" and that the generation of linguistic novelty is the responsibility of an elite group of "strong poets" (TP, 10). Echoing Kuhn's arbitrariness, Rorty states that "poetic, artistic, philosophical, scientific, or political progress results from the accidental coincidence of a private obsession with a public need" (CIS, 37).

But the problem is that there are fundamental differences between scientific and political innovation. For one thing, power is surely more operative in the field of politics than in science. For another, unlike scientific or poetic novelties, innovations in politics tend to come about because they are directly sought rather than accidental. That is, disenfranchised groups make direct claims upon the political apparatus, and it falls to either the *demos* or its representatives to respond to such claims in tangible ways. Simply changing vocabularies does not seem to be an adequate response here. Given Rorty's antirepresentationalism and his purely linguistic rather than experiential emphasis, it is not clear that he looks upon this crisis as "an opportunity to reorder the world," as Wolin suggests the political theorist does, and as I would argue Emerson and Dewey did, as opposed to simply a call for new metaphors.[40]

Becoming too obsessed with getting things right can distract us from the often more crucial political implications which flow from the consequences of the views we hold, regardless of whether they are right or true. Here I think Rorty is right: distinguishing better from worse, desirable from undesirable, is possible in a postfoundational world by attending to the consequences of competing perspectives. Yet we must take care not to dispense with reality altogether. To avoid the condition Wolin describes where the thinker "fabricates images without any foundation in reality," it is imperative, therefore, that while we encourage and indeed foster the creative impulse at the heart of imaginative visions and theoretical novelty, we must also ensure that our theoretical constructions make contact with reality in mulitple places.

Redescriptions do have the power to change minds: recasting the familiar in unfamiliar terms can indeed lead us to see things in a different light and perhaps even spur action. But redescriptions are partial. They distort and exclude and can do violence to reality and to the "facts." Yet by depicting society in an unreal way, as Wolin suggested, they may provide a conduit to action, but only as long as they connect with the facts of political reality.

In other words, the freedom in giving up the idea of getting something right entails more than merely "treating chance as worthy of determining our fate," as Rorty puts it, quoting Freud (CIS, 22). It also involves recognizing the extent to which we are indeed acculturated beings, constituted by forces—the past, tradition, culture, and language—outside our consent. Realizing this freedom involves more than simply acknowledging this fact on a theoretical level. Politically, we must face and confront these forces in order to make them our own if we are ever to have any hope of changing them. To quote Baldwin, "To accept one's past—one's history—is not the same thing as drowning in it; it is learning how to use it." Even more to the point, we must "cease fleeing from reality and begin to change it."[41] Unless we do, and fully embrace this freedom, to borrow one of Rorty's apt formulations, "we shall never be free of the motives which once led us to posit gods" (CIS, 67), even if these gods are secular and pragmatist.

NOTES

1. Rorty has made this point in different places. Here are two representative statements from CIS: "I am not going to offer arguments against the vocabulary I want to replace. Instead, I am going to try to make the vocabulary I favor look attractive by showing how it may be used to describe a variety of topics" (9); "But 'argument' is not the right word. . . . Rebutting objections to one's redescriptions of some things will be largely a matter of redescribing other things, trying to outflank the objections by enlarging the scope of one's favorite metaphors. So my strategy will be to try to make the vocabulary in which these objections are phrased look bad" (44).

2. Rorty makes this assertion in a footnote to "Justice as a Larger Loyalty" in *Cosmopolitics*, ed. Pheng Cheah and Bruce Robbins (Minneapolis: University of Minnesota Press, 1998), 58n22, but he develops the argument more fully in "John Searle on Realism and Relativism" in TP, 63–83. See also Rorty's introduction to ORT. Rorty's strident antirepresentationalism raises the question of whether it is possible to defend some sense of a "reality" out there while accepting pragmatist critiques of traditional philosophy. Rorty of course is not interested in defending such a notion. For a view that does, see Hilary Putnam, *Realism with a Human Face* (Cambridge, MA: Harvard University Press, 1990). Putnam, in contrast, has counseled the importance of holding on to the possibility of "getting it right."

3. For Rorty's discussion of this see "Dewey Between Hegel and Darwin" in TP, 290–306. In his most recent work, Rorty forewarns readers in the preface that his version of pragmatism "makes no pretense of being faithful to the thoughts of either James or Dewey," saying instead that it offers his own "sometimes idiosyncratic restatements of Jamesian and Deweyan themes" (PSH, xiii).

4. Richard Bernstein has observed that "Rorty desperately wants to avoid the suggestion that he is playing the old game of philosophy, that his claims about the self should be read as 'getting things right.'" In Bernstein's view, Rorty does not merely redescribe things without offering arguments. Whether or not Rorty's vocabulary appears attractive and alternative ones look bad "depends at least in part on his success in *arguing* that these alternative strategies fail to accomplish what they claim to prove." See Richard Bernstein, *The New Constellation: The Ethical-Political Horizons of Modernity/Postmodernity* (Cambridge, MA: MIT Press, 1992), 276.

5. To my knowledge, Rorty only uses the term *lever* on one occasion, in the context of his reading of Orwell. See CIS, 174. I have seized upon it for nicely capturing the nature of the major shift in Rorty's thought.

6. Rorty has always been rather skeptical, to put it mildly, about "the utility of theory." In more recent work, however, Rorty recognizes there are other uses of non-transcendental, narrative theory, and he says that "pragmatists are entirely at home

with the idea that political theory should view itself as suggestions for future action" (PSH, 272).

7. Sheldon Wolin, *Politics and Vision: Continuity and Innovation in Western Political Thought* (Boston: Little, Brown & Co., 1960), 18.

8. Wolin, *Politics and Vision*, 18–19. Here perhaps Rorty's notorious "playfulness" is more than an affectation: "Revolutionary physicists, politicians, and philosophers," he argues, have always relied on "introducing strange new senses of familiar expressions, frivolously punning, no longer playing by the rules, using rhetoric rather than logic, imagery rather than argument" (EHO, 98–99). Interestingly, Wolin, too, underlines similar qualities as "crucial to theorizing: playfulness, concern, the juxtaposition of contraries, and astonishment at the variety and subtle interconnection of things." See "Political Theory as a Vocation," *American Political Science Review* 63, no. 4 (1969): 1073.

9. Wolin, *Politics and Vision*, 18.

10. Wolin, *Politics and Vision*, 5.

11. Wolin makes this point and suggests that political theory be considered "as belonging to a different form of discourse" in Wolin, *Politics and Vision*, 14–18. The conception of political theory I rely on here is drawn largely from the first chapter of *Politics and Vision*. There are also interesting parallels—and important differences— between Wolin's efforts to defend the discourse of political theory from assaults from scientistic and behaviorist camps in the 1960s and Rorty's attempt to defend his antirepresentationalism amidst charges of relativism. Of particular interest to us here is their common effort to suggest an alternative to empiricist or representationalist discourse—for Wolin, political theory, for Rorty, redescription—and to lessen the grip of correspondence theories of truth. Interestingly, both thinkers draw on Rudolph Carnap here. See *Politics and Vision*, 14; and Rorty, PMN. See also Wolin's essays "Political Theory as a Vocation" and "Paradigms and Political Theories" in *Politics and Experience: Essays Presented to Michael Oakeshott*, ed. Preston King and B. C. Parekh (New York: Cambridge University Press, 1968).

12. Wolin, "Political Theory as a Vocation," 1073.

13. Wolin, *Politics and Vision*, 20–21.

14. Wolin, *Politics and Vision*, 20.

15. On the Romantic strand in American thought, see Russell B. Goodman, *American Philosophy and the Romantic Tradition* (New York: Cambridge University Press, 1990).

16. Wolin suggests this idea in "Paradigms and Political Theories," esp. 139–41; and "Political Theory as a Vocation," 1078–82.

17. These would include the notion of philosophy as providing a permanent neutral framework for inquiry, the objective-subjective distinction, the belief that "algorithms" for theory-choice between competing perspectives exist, and the idea that rational agreement is possible only where there is correspondence to reality. Rorty also provides an interesting addition to the Kuhnian perspective by distinguishing between two kinds of "revolutionary" philosopher: "systemic" and "edifying." Systemic philosophers are "constructive" and tend to found schools within which normal, professionalized philosophy can occur. Edifying philosophers are by contrast "reactive,"

providing satires, parodies, and aphorisms, and "dread the thought that their vocabularies should ever be institutionalized." See PMN, 368–70, passim.

18. For instance, this helps explain what strikes one as Rorty's outrageously misplaced use of the word *we* in his essays. There is no question that Rorty's use of "we liberals" or "we Deweyans" is not empirically warranted. But that is beside the point. If we see this as an effort to arouse and inspirit—even if it does so by rankling—it makes more sense. Rorty understands the invocation of a moral community in declarations like "We, the people of the United Nations" or "We, the people of the United States" as a call for an ongoing project, for a moral community yet to be forged, rather than an accurate description of the actual state of affairs. See "Who Are We? Moral Universalism and Economic Triage," *Diogenes* 173 (1996): 5–19. See also "Ethics without Principles" and "Truth without Correspondence" in PSH.

19. Norman Jacobson, *Pride and Solace: The Functions and Limits of Political Theory* (New York: Methuen, 1978), 8–10.

20. In the introduction to PMN, Rorty distinguishes Dewey from Wittgenstein and Heidegger by saying that he "wrote his polemics against traditional mirror-imagery out of a vision of a new kind of society." In Dewey's ideal society, he says, the culture is no longer dominated by the ideal of "objective cognition" but rather that of "aesthetic enhancement" (13). Though somewhat cryptic at first blush, "aesthetic enhancement" can be construed to contain all the elements—individual, social, political, critical, imaginative—embodied in the Deweyan vision of an engaged praxis which aims, in Rorty's words, to "modify our beliefs and desires and activities in ways that will bring us greater happiness than we have now" (CP 16). The problem is that the content of the phrase "aesthetic enhancement" never materialized. In my view, this is attributable to Rorty's defensive efforts of the 1980s to distinguish his "liberal" postmodernism from the more radical, aestheticized Continental versions he was initially lumped in with—as a result, he circumscribed the aesthetic by privatizing irony, individual projects of self-creation, and anything capable of jeopardizing the formation of a shared moral identity of "we liberals" in public.

21. Rorty is rather vague about how this process works. In *Contingency*, he depicts it as a matter of the "accidental coincidence of a private obsession with a public need"—that is, of new metaphors generated by "strong poets" coming to have a public resonance (37). More recently, he put it this way, echoing this elitist strain: "Philosophy will continue to make progress as long as geniuses keep emerging" (TP, 10). For a critique of this view of change, see Louis Menand, "Pragmatists and Poets: A Response to Richard Poirier," in *The Revival of Pragmatism*, 362–69. However, in other places, drawing on Phillip Rieff's idea that Freud "democratized genius by giving everyone an unconscious," Rorty seems to make the process of coming up with new metaphors something achievable by a much wider audience. See his important essay "Freud and Moral Reflection" in EHO. For Rorty's discussion of Dennett, see "Justice as a Larger Loyalty" and "Daniel Dennett on Intrinsicality" in TP.

22. Jurgen Habermas, *The Philosophical Discourse of Modernity*, trans. Frederick Lawrence (Cambridge, MA: The MIT Press, 1987), 185–210, 294–326. For an attempt to move beyond the limitations of these categories, see Frederick M. Dolan,

Allegories of America: Narratives, Metaphysics, Politics (Ithaca, NY: Cornell University Press, 1994), esp. chaps. 4 and 5.

23. One of the problems generated by Rorty's antirepresentationalism in this context is that he refers to this moral community in the terms of this vague "we" without ever taking up the complications and divisions surrounding different actual groups, communities, ethnicities, and the like.

24. Rorty takes this tack in his own contribution to the political literature of utopia, the 1996 essay "Looking Backwards from the Year 2096" in PSH.

25. John Dewey, *Art and Experience* (1934; repr., New York: Perigee Books, 1980), 346.

26. Wolin, *Politics and Vision*, 23–24.

27. Indeed, Rorty has stated that his "hunch" is that "Western social and political thought may have had the last *conceptual* revolution it needs" (CIS, 63).

28. See Rorty, "Justice as a Larger Loyalty," 57n3. Cf. also: "To believe that someone is 'one of us,' a member of our moral community, is to exhibit readiness to come to their assistance when they are in need." See "Who Are We? Moral Universalism and Economic Triage," 13. Although it has received little attention, this communitarian thrust, for lack of a better word, has become the cornerstone of Rorty's political theory: the project of forging a democratic moral community lies behind his turn to literature and is an essential ingredient in the quest for social justice understood as a "larger loyalty" and the political enterprise of "achieving our country."

29. Besides Dewey, the other source of Rorty's stance of hopeful optimism is Vaclav Havel. In his affirmations of this kind of ungrounded hope, Rorty treats Dewey and Havel as vaguely synonymous. However, Patrick Deneen has taken Rorty to task for this conflation of Dewey and Havel, arguing that Dewey articulates a form of "optimism without hope," and Havel, the position of "hope without optimism." Politically, the problem with optimism is that it entails a faith in progress that yields a complacency and lack of urgency toward change. Hope, on the other hand, being rooted in a transcendent source of something larger than ourselves, galvanizes individuals toward the necessity for struggle. See Patrick J. Deneen, "The Politics of Hope and Optimism: Rorty, Havel, and the Democratic Faith of John Dewey," *Social Research* 66, no. 2 (1999): 577–609. For Rorty's discussion of Havel, see "The End of Leninism, Havel, and Social Hope," in TP, 228–43.

30. What is often neglected by contemporary theorists of "deliberative" democracy who employ some version of the Kuhnian conception of a community upon whose agreement truth and standards of validity rest is how normal science "often suppresses fundamental novelties because they are necessarily subversive of its basic commitments." This picture has gained considerable currency among those who have made the so-called postmodern turn which foregrounds intersubjective agreement and democratic consensus in matters of knowledge, justification, and truth. See Thomas S. Kuhn, *The Structure of Scientific Revolutions*, 2nd ed. (Chicago: University of Chicago Press, 1970), 5. Successful normal science seems to require the repression of competing viewpoints and the existence of a community willing to acquiesce to the agreed-upon rules and norms. Wolin calls this the "enforcing power"

of the dominant paradigm. The nature of the process of deciding between paradigms seems more competitive than deliberative. See Wolin, "Paradigms and Political Theories," 133–38.

31. Wolin, "Political Theory as a Vocation," 1079; and "Paradigms and Political Theories," 147. In the latter work, Wolin points out that Plato, for example, was responding not to a methodological crisis but to the breakdown of the Athenian polis.

32. Wolin, "Democracy in the Discourse of Postmodernism," *Social Research* 57, no. 1 (1990): 21.

33. Ernesto Laclau and Chantal Mouffe, *Hegemony and Socialist Strategy: Towards a Radical Democratic Politics* (New York: Verso, 1985). On the idea of a "postsocialist" condition, see Nancy Fraser, *Justice Interruptus: Critical Reflections on the "Postsocialist" Condition* (New York: Routledge, 1997).

34. See "The End of Leninism" in TP, 228–43. Rorty cites Laclau and Mouffe's frequent use of the term *impossibility* as evidence of an underlying mood of politically sterile despair. See PSH, 232. It could be objected that Rorty's understanding of *theory* here is rather monolithic and that he is imputing stances to thinkers like Laclau and Mouffe which they would surely dispute.

35. See "The Intellectuals at the End of Socialism," *The Yale Review* 80 (April 1992): 1–16. However, rather than simply avoiding claims to true reality and advocating a version of perspectivism—something in keeping with his pragmatist assumptions—Rorty jettisons reality altogether. It should be pointed out that Rorty insists nothing he has to say does anything to undermine everyday facts, only philosophical facts which function as unchallengeable guarantees of the rightness of particular beliefs (TP, 73–75). I don't see the point of taking Rorty to task for occasionally appearing to deny there are any facts at all, since his views can be interpreted as directed toward the distinctive nature of political facts which we noted earlier. Nevertheless, to the extent that this antirepresentationalism leads us to lose contact with the actual world entirely, it becomes the kind of flight from reality that opens the door to dangerous political consequences itself.

36. John Dewey, *The Middle Works, 1899–1924*, ed. Jo Ann Boydston (Carbondale: Southern Illinois University Press, 1982), 12:201. Quoted by Rorty in EHO, 175. Although in these final pages Dewey's topic is indeed "the vital sources of religion and art," Rorty's reading of Dewey as wanting to reenchant the world seems misplaced, in particular given the context, which is a discussion of "the liberating of human capacity" as a "socially creative force," not to mention Dewey's more substantive treatment of these themes in *Art as Experience*. On these themes and the idea that Dewey sought a more expansive and democratic reconception of art, see Richard Shusterman, *Pragmatist Aesthetics: Living Beauty, Rethinking Art* (Cambridge: Blackwell, 1992).

37. The closest he comes to the concrete is to say we should appeal to "concrete fantasies"—a rather contradictory notion in itself—instead of grand, transcendental metafantasies. There is the occasional call for pragmatist "habits of action," but when one examines them closely, even his claims about politics—like the need to "start talking about greed and selfishness"—are vague and of no real practical value.

38. Wolin, "Political Theory as a Vocation," 1080; "Paradigms and Political Theories," 144.

39. Kuhn, *The Structure of Scientific Revolutions*, 5, 52.

40. The traditions of American pragmatism and analytic philosophy after the linguistic turn are increasingly at odds in Rorty's later work: in the more explicitly political recent writing, the insights of Sellars and Quine that fueled his influential critique of the Cartesian-Kantian foundationalism undermine the important emphasis on reality and experience endemic to the pragmatist tradition.

41. James Baldwin, *The Fire Next Time* (1963; repr., New York: Vintage Books, 1993), 10, 81.

Chapter Three

The Politics of the Novel

The novel's wisdom is different from that of philosophy. The novel is born not of the theoretical spirit but of the spirit of humor. . . . The art inspired by God's laughter does not by nature serve ideological certitudes, it contradicts them. Like Penelope, it undoes each night the tapestry that theologians, philosophers, and learned men have woven the day before.

—Milan Kundera, *The Art of the Novel*

We have the books that point out the bad conditions, that praise us for taking progressive attitudes. We have no books that raise questions in our minds not only about conditions but about ourselves.

—Lionel Trilling, *The Liberal Imagination*

One of the more provocative claims to emerge from Rorty's recent work is the idea that the novel is "the characteristic genre of democracy." Calling it the genre "most closely associated with the struggle for freedom and equality," he has argued that the novel is the primary vehicle of moral reflection in a liberal democratic culture (EHO, 68). The promise of Rorty's political thought is a way of combining a nonessentialist moral community with an ironic openness to other vocabularies—both community *and* diversity. Through "sentimental education," works like Dickens's *Bleak House*, Stowe's *Uncle Tom's Cabin*, and Nabokov's *Lolita*, his argument goes, can help forge a democratic moral community of citizens attuned to suffering and more likely to see those different from themselves as "one of us." Because it is instrumental in fostering an ability to identify with the suffering of others, literature can be linked to the pursuit of justice, understood as a form of loyalty to other human beings.[1]

Drawing on the thought of Czech novelist and critic Milan Kundera, Rorty has evinced a conception of democracy grounded in the plurality and relativity of human perspectives. Because it derives its moral thrust from novelists and poets rather than philosophers, he argues, it is able to provide the cohesion necessary for collective action while respecting diversity. Yet, in the end, the complexity and irony of great literature cannot easily be reconciled with the kinds of moral sentiments Rorty needs literature to disseminate to further the communal ends of his "liberal utopia." Despite appearances to the contrary, Rorty's appeal to literature looks not to irony but to sentiment for its political import. Kundera's subversive conception of the novel's irony undermines Rorty's bourgeois liberalism to the point where the two can coexist only by instituting a sharp division between public and private. This is the paradox of Rorty's political thought: while he intimates a conception of democracy grounded in an ironical, nonmetaphysical culture, he resists the full force of the human ambiguity and plurality of irony in public.

Even if his solution is judged inadequate, Rorty's account poses issues not easily brushed aside. His approach highlights a fundamental tension in the relation of irony to democratic politics between individual critical self-reflection and collective efforts of the *demos*, between critique and action. On Rorty's view, collective political action which aims to remedy injustice requires a shared moral identity—something that complex and ambiguous works cannot provide. In the absence of such an identity, stagnation and democratic impotence will result. It is therefore not the nuanced, introspective, highbrow novels whose "variousness, possibility, complexity, and difficulty," in Lionel Trilling's famous phrase, prompt self-reflective questioning of ourselves and our world, but the far less complex and various lessons of didactic, middlebrow, "sentimental" novels like Stowe's *Uncle Tom's Cabin* and Dickens's *Bleak House* that for Rorty are of the greatest value to democracy.

Devotees of literature as a source of human complexity and diversity capable of subverting ideological and moral certitudes must address the possibility Rorty raises: can complexity, irony, and ambiguity provide a sufficient basis for collective action? And, relatedly, are unquestioning, didactic stories capable of stimulating the emotions and sparking sympathetic identification in ways that more obviously subversive highbrow works cannot? Rorty is certainly not a believer in moral absolutes, and he does affirm a Nietzschean multiplicity of human perspective. Yet his view suggests that depicting the world in its many shades of gray may be of dubious political utility, at least when it comes to majoritarian democratic endeavors. If nothing else, Rorty's account places the burden on those given to disagreement on this last point—and I consider myself in this category—to make clear the value of ambiguity, irony, and relativity of perspective to democratic politics.

I underscore these tensions by contrasting Rorty's reading of *Uncle Tom's Cabin* with James Baldwin's. Baldwin's scathing critique of Stowe's novel, and the entire genre of the novel of moral protest that Rorty affirms, emanates from their not being complex and various enough in their presentation of African American experience and from their failing to adequately question the dominant conception of reality upon which the system of racial oppression rested. Baldwin is surely right to identify the danger inherent in reducing the complexity and ambiguity of the human world to simplified, unitary categories. Yet his critique, however justified, must be reconciled with the beneficial practical effects that novels like Stowe's and Dickens's did have in the struggles against the two greatest threats the democratic experiment has encountered: the system of chattel slavery and the unfettered practices of laissez-faire capitalism.

Ultimately, two conflicting conceptions of the role of novels, or of narratives in general, can be identified in Rorty's thought. On the one hand, narratives provide a means of collective self-criticism—the basis for "the self-criticism of cultures" and "reweaving" a community's "fabric of belief" to make it more tolerant, more inclusionary, and more just (EHO, 15–18). On the other, they serve to solidify a common moral identity and inculcate a liberal morality. As the forging of a common identity has emerged in his recent work as the central aim of his political project, the latter role increasingly overshadows the former. Yet the project of forging an inclusive, but singular, collective moral identity leaves literature's immense potential as a repository of human plurality and diversity untapped.

RORTY'S POSITION: COMMUNITY VS. IRONY

The communitarian thrust, for lack of a better word, of Rorty's work has received scant attention. Yet it has become the cornerstone of his political theory. The project of forging a democratic moral community lies behind his turn to literature. It is also an essential ingredient in the quest for social justice understood as a "larger loyalty" and the political project he has termed "achieving our country." Solidarity, as he calls it in *Contingency, Irony, and Solidarity*, is for Rorty something which is made rather than found, a commonality achieved through struggle and collective self-fashioning rather than unearthed as a shared trait within us.

This communitarian thrust was visible a decade before the publication of *Contingency*, present as early as his 1979 Presidential Address to the American Philosophical Association, which unleashed the storm on the eve of the publication of *Philosophy and the Mirror of Nature*. For those who search in

vain for the "consequences" of Rorty's pragmatism, which often appears to be
little more than a defense of the liberal status quo, if liberated from its philosophical baggage, the best candidate is this heightened, nonessentialist sense
of community. Here it is worth quoting from Rorty's 1979 address:

> Our identification with our community—our society, our political tradition, our
> intellectual heritage—is heightened when we see this community as *ours* rather
> than *nature's*, *shaped* rather than *found*, one among many which men have
> made. In the end, the pragmatists tell us, what matters is our loyalty to other hu-
> man beings clinging together against the dark, not our hope of getting things
> right. (CP, 166)

The general contours of Rorty's philosophical critique are by now fairly
well known. The point I wish to stress is that giving up the metaphysical comfort of foundations and fully accepting the radical contingency of human life
paves the way for "a renewed sense of community." With no transcendental
sources of authority to appeal to—that is, no God, Reason, History, Knowledge, or Truth—"our fellow-humans [become] our only source of guidance,"
the nonfoundational foundation of postmetaphysical politics. Here Rorty follows Dewey in bringing philosophy down from its transcendental heights into
the uncertain realm of change and contingency. But, unlike William James,
Rorty falls short of granting pragmatist philosophy a role in helping us sort
out the contingent beliefs and values that constitute us as individuals.[2]

Revisiting these early thoughts on community is useful in my view since it
is precisely this project of cultivating a broader and more inclusive sense of
solidarity, understood as a form of collective identity, that gives Rorty's appeal to literature and stories its moral thrust. The means for forging this democratic moral community is "sentimental education."[3]

In broad terms, the idea of sentimental education rests on a displacement
of reason by the imagination as the central human faculty and carves out a
role for the sentiments in ethical judgment. Indeed, the imagination, in particular the "imaginative ability to see strange people as fellow sufferers," is
for Rorty the key to creating solidarity. Solidarity, for Rorty, is achieved
through a process of coming to see other human beings as "one of us" rather
than as "them" (CIS, xvi).

In a curious and ironic way—since Rorty has always been rather dismissive
of identity politics[4]—this places a kind of identity at the center of Rorty's meliorative political endeavor. Enlarging our sense of "we," our ability to "imaginatively identify" with others, is valued for being the best means for fulfilling the fundamental political directive for late-capitalist liberal-democratic
societies: namely, the reduction of cruelty and suffering through strengthening our moral solidarity with others. If we can be brought to see our differ-

ences as less important than our shared ability to suffer and feel pain, a kind of moral progress toward a more humane social world can be made. "To believe that someone is 'one of us,' a member of our moral community," he argues, linking moral identification to moral action, "is to exhibit readiness to come to their assistance when they are in need."[5]

The goal of this kind of education, then, is to get "people of different kinds sufficiently well-acquainted with one other" to cultivate the sort of sympathy required to expand the purview of who is included in the phrase "people like us." By manipulating sentiments, as he puts it, it may be possible to train people to see differences between humans as morally insignificant, and to be able to imagine themselves in the place of the oppressed or less fortunate. For Rorty, it is literature—in particular, the novel and "sad, sentimental stories"— rather than the treatise or sermon, that is best suited to the liberal aims of increasing imaginative identification and making us more sensitive to suffering (TP, 172–79).[6]

The kind of imaginative identification with others necessary for the creation of moral solidarity involves two crucial aspects, both of them pertinent to literature and stories or narratives. If we are to identify with the details of others' lives, we must first know something about those lives, and indeed that they exist at all. Thus, what Rorty refers to as "detailed descriptions"— concrete accounts about who is being made to suffer—become paramount. Recognizing the importance of these kinds of accounts for Rorty signals a general turn "away from theory and toward narrative." As he is careful to point out, it is a task "not for theory, but for genres such as the ethnography, the journalist's report, the comic book, the docudrama, and especially the novel" (CIS, xvi). While discoveries about who is suffering can be made in general by "the workings of the free press, free universities, and enlightened public opinion," Rorty cites works like "*Germinal, Black Boy, The Road to Wigan Pier*, and *1984*" as having been responsible for such enlightening. Also paradigmatic here are the novels of Dickens and Stowe (CIS, 63–64).[7]

The second element entailed in imaginative identification, once previously unnoticed sites of suffering have been brought to our attention, involves actually "sensitizing" us to such suffering. Cultivating sensitivity or an acute awareness toward suffering is a transformative endeavor aimed at nonsufferers—those Rorty often refers to as the rich, relatively leisured members of North Atlantic democracies. Novels can "help us attend to the springs of cruelty in ourselves" and can thus compel us to in essence become better persons (CIS, 95). In *Contingency*, Rorty makes the case for reading Vladimir Nabokov and George Orwell as exemplary in this regard.[8]

Increasing our sensitivity to suffering is an integral part of the creation of fellow feeling. But it is brought about through a process of self-development, what Rorty calls "redescribing what we ourselves are like" (CIS, xvi). The way we go about redescribing ourselves is through stories. By telling different stories about ourselves, our past, and our future, we transform ourselves, both as individuals and as a community. The detailed descriptions we encounter in literature and good narrative journalism deepen and enrich these stories, pushing us toward a more tolerant, more inclusive self-understanding that is more respectful of diversity, both individually and collectively. We "reweave our webs of belief and desire in light of whatever new people and books [we] happen to encounter." Through the ceaseless endeavor of "continual redescription," of recurrently returning to the self and remaking or refashioning it in response to an expanding circle of acquaintance, we try "to make the best selves for ourselves that we can" (CIS, 80–85).

Yet while individual edification or "self-enlargement" appears to be a part of the process by which we come to imaginatively identify with others, the sort of sympathy or fellow feeling with others that allows us to see them as "one of us" is often possible without this self-transformation. That is to say, the requirement of achieving a common moral identity that Rorty makes the sine qua non of any majoritarian political project ultimately trumps the need for individuals to redescribe themselves. Rorty's sentimental education is more a program for getting the world's "rich and lucky billion" to redescribe the vocabularies they use to understand *others*, rather than for prompting them to redescribe *themselves*.

RORTY AS A MORALIST?

Despite Rorty's pragmatist eschewal of a theory of the Good and a foundationalist morality, his aims in fostering a common moral identity are essentially those of a moralist: novels for Rorty inculcate a particular set of norms as they forge a moral community. But is it even possible to be an antifoundational moralist, a didacticist who does not believe in Truth? If Freud is a moralist without a message, the first irreligious moralist, as Philip Rieff once argued, then Rorty can be seen as a moralist without a *Moralitat*.[9] As Jo Burrows observed in an insightful early essay on Rorty, the distinction between the Hegelian notions of *Sittlichkeit*, as values that are contingently shared, and *Moralitat*, as those grounded in some more fundamental, universal manner, gets blurred in Rorty's account. "Contingently held beliefs," she points out, "can display the same external features, and have the same practical political outcome, as 'grounded beliefs.'"[10] In other words, it is possible for beliefs to be contingent and nonfoundational on a philosophical level and yet still function politically as de facto "foundations."

In calling Rorty didactic, I do not mean to suggest an affiliation with the Platonic or didactic model of literature exemplified in the campaign for an education in the moral virtues championed by people like William Bennett. Arguments for literature as a kind of moral or civic education fall into a second, less didactic category, where the aim is less an education in the timeless standards of right and wrong than a program for deepening and enriching human existence. Here ahistorical moral categories play a far subtler role. Notable representatives of this tradition are nineteenth-century Victorians like Matthew Arnold and John Stuart Mill. To quote Trilling, himself rooted in this same tradition, the classic defense of literary study "holds that, from the effect which the study of literature has upon the private sentiments of a student, there results, or can be made to result, an improvement in the intelligence, and especially the intelligences as it touches the moral life."[11]

This idea of literature as "public scenes of nondidactic instruction," as David Bromwich has argued, is at home in a secular and democratic culture. A relatively recent invention which came into being near the end of the eighteenth century, Bromwich points out that the origins of this view of literature lie "in the separation of books from official doctrine, from an enforced consensus, from the patronage of ladies and gentlemen and the supervision of academies."[12] To put it another way, it coincides with the decline of nonhuman authorities—things like God, Scripture, and Truth. These are of course the very things which "stand beyond history and institutions" that Rorty no longer thinks relevant to a liberal polity where contingency and irony reign.[13] Surprisingly, though, Rorty passes over this conception of literature, as he does several others, in favor of Kundera's.

At times, Rorty seems to appeal to literature for less formal reasons, like the old platitude that reading books is a good way to get to know interesting and different people one might not otherwise meet. This view calls to mind the idea, popularized by Iris Murdoch, that the best reason for reading literature is that it can teach us about the lives of others. Prose literature in general, but especially the novel, in her view, reveals an aspect of the world which no other art can reveal: namely, that "other people exist."[14] Rorty similarly argues that a primary value of literature for democratic life is its capacity for "enlarging our acquaintance," the process by which individuals "reweave their webs of belief and desire in the light of whatever new people and books they happen to encounter." But Rorty eschews this conception too; on his view, any "enlarging" that takes place happens only in private, leaving the public commitment to liberalism unchallenged (CIS, 80, 85).

With the view of literature as a means for training the ethical imagination, of which Martha Nussbaum is the best recent example, Rorty shares the notion that literature and other forms of narrative storytelling can improve our

powers of perception. The idiom he prefers is one of increased "sensitivity"—
"sensitizing" us to the suffering of others. Still, Rorty's idea of "imaginative
identification" shares much with Nussbaum's notion of "sympathetic imagining" and the "morality of perception" that she evinces based on the hyper-
conscious, extraordinarily gifted perceivers that populate the novels of Henry
James (CIS, xvi, 94).[15] As she summarizes, echoing a Rortyan line,

> The claim seems to be that if you really vividly experience a concrete human
> life, imagine what it is like to live that life, and at the same time permit yourself
> the full range of emotional responses to that concrete life, you will (if you have
> a good moral start) be unable to do certain things to that person. Vividness leads
> to tenderness, imagination to compassion.[16]

But, as we shall see, Rorty does not believe the particular "vividness" offered
in Jamesian novels is of use in public instruction, arguing that the ambiguity
of James's novels makes them ill suited for moral inculcation.

Most surprising, however, is Rorty's neglect of Dewey's arguments on this
topic. In a discussion of Arnold's notion that "poetry is criticism of life" in
Art as Experience, Dewey criticizes all such theories that attribute a "direct
moral effect and intent to art." Characteristically, Dewey's main criticism is
that these views pry particular works from the social milieu in which they exist. As a result, they conceive their moral impact in terms of "a strictly personal relation between the selected works and a particular individual." Rather
than imputing a moral intent to the writer and postulating a moral judgment
on the part of the reader, Dewey believes art functions as a criticism of life,
not directly, but by "disclosure"—that is,

> through imaginative vision addressed to imaginative experience (not set to judg-
> ment) of possibilities that contrast with actual conditions. A sense of possibili-
> ties that are unrealized and that might be realized are, when they are put in con-
> trast with actual conditions, the most penetrating "criticism" of the latter that
> can be made. It is by a sense of possibilities opening before us that we become
> aware of constrictions that hem us in and of burdens that oppress.[17]

The view of literature as a form of social criticism expressed in this last passage is the one that meshes most seamlessly with Rorty's own presuppositions, in particular with his understanding of America in terms of a forward-
looking, as yet unrealized but ongoing project, in *Achieving Our Country*.
However, to the extent that forging a moral community displaces the portrayal of future possibilities as literature's primary purpose, on Rorty's rendering, the critical import of this conception is lost.

RORTY'S USE OF KUNDERA: WROUGHT IRONY

Despite all these common resonances, however, the conception of literature with which Rorty most explicitly aligns himself is not any of the ones just discussed, but that of Kundera. Kundera's literary criticism, in particular his reflections on the novel, appear to have deeply affected Rorty's thinking during the mid-1980s. The epigraph to Rorty's *Contingency, Irony, and Solidarity* is a long quote from Kundera's eloquent and insightful *The Art of the Novel*, and Rorty credits Kundera with suggesting the view of the novel as the characteristic genre of democracy that he defends in his recent work (EHO, 68).[18] A novelist of ideas whose erudition is wide ranging enough to rival Rorty's own and well-versed enough in philosophy to characterize the tradition of the novel in terms of a recovery of Heidegger's notion of "forgotten Being," Rorty's interest in Kundera is quite understandable. It is significant, however, that this coincides with Rorty's most ambitious attempts to think through the implications of his philosophical critique and develop a more positive vision.[19]

Initially, no doubt, Rorty was drawn to Kundera's work for its anti-Philosophical, with a capital *p*, bent. In stirring passages, Kundera rather explicitly opposes the spirit of the novel to the spirit of philosophy, the vibrant world of unmitigated relativity and multiple, conflicting perspectives to the world of one single Truth and a dictated, unquestionable Reality. Pitting Cervantes against Descartes, Sterne against Leibniz, Kundera's take on the "wisdom" of the novel is that it contradicts and subverts rather than serves ideological certitudes, "undo[ing] each night the tapestry that the theologians, philosophers, and learned men have woven the day before."[20]

This of course meshes well with Rorty's antifoundationalism and critique of the Cartesian-Kantian tradition. Yet Rorty mines Kundera's thought for more than its negative, critical thrust. He seizes upon Kundera's notion of the "imaginative world of the novel" and assimilates it to his own ideal of a democratic, liberal utopia. For Kundera, the imaginative realm of human plurality and ambiguity, where "no one owns the truth and everyone has a right to be understood," is one where tolerance and a loose fraternity reign. The highest value is "respect for the individual, for his original thought, and for his right to an inviolable private life."[21] In this picture, one perceives the broad outlines of Rorty's liberal utopia: ambiguity ("contingency" in Rorty's parlance), tolerance, diversity, fraternity ("solidarity"), and the importance of a firmly delineated and protected private realm.

The curious thing is that Kundera depicts the novel as a subversive force that "contradicts" rather than "serves" "ideological certitudes." Given, in his own words, Rorty's "plain ordinary Old Leftism" and the banal politics of labor unions and signature collection in his liberal utopia, this strikes one as an unlikely perspective for Rorty to embrace.[22] In my view, Rorty gets into trouble because he is attracted to the way Kundera sets the novel in opposition to *philosophical* certitudes. The part about undermining ideological certitudes is simply overlooked. As is the case with almost all his positive claims, Rorty's affirmations are best understood against the backdrop of the "Philosophical," conceptions he is polemicizing against.

Kundera's imaginary paradise is under constant assault from the "*agélastes*," those convinced "that the truth is obvious, that all men necessarily think the same thing, and that they themselves are exactly what they think they are."[23] For Rorty, the villains are the metaphysicians. Kundera's conflict between the novelist and the *agélaste* is mirrored by the opposition between the ironist and the metaphysician that Rorty develops in *Contingency*. The essay "Heidegger, Kundera, and Dickens," which dates to the same period, contains Rorty's strongest defense of the novel over the philosophical treatise as the characteristic genre of democracy. It is also the place where he makes most explicit his reliance on Kundera.

Yet isn't it strange, and even contradictory, for the pragmatist Rorty to appeal in his discussion of democracy and the novel to a perspective that identifies the political import of the novel as "protecting us from the forgetting of being," especially given Rorty's indictments of postmodern thinkers for theoretical oversophistication and needless abstraction and their mistaken belief that such philosophical notions are relevant to the "real" politics of ending people's suffering, not to mention his own critique of Heidegger's self-delusions about the relevance of his philosophy for politics?[24]

The lack of fit between Kundera's ethereal ideas and Rorty's prosaic liberalism, and the lengths to which Rorty has to go to make them hang together, emerge in his discussion of irony. For Kundera, the ultimate wisdom of the novel and the supreme value in his imaginary realm is "the relativity and ambiguity of things human." This is what renders the novel incompatible with totalitarianism and imbues it with subversive force in the face of all attempts to constrain and clear away this fundamental relativity and ambiguity, including those of Philosophy. It is also what Rorty seems to find most salutary in Kundera's vision.

This "relativity" is not unlike what Rorty calls the "radical contingency" of human life. It seems to evoke the values represented by his notion of irony: the figure of the ironist is defined by an awareness of the relativity and ambiguity of her beliefs. If we recall Rorty's portrait, the ironist has "radical and continuing doubts" about her most fundamental beliefs or "final vocabulary." She realizes her beliefs are only one set among many others, she does not think they are closer to reality than anyone else's, and she knows they are always potentially subject to change. In a word, ironists are aware of their "rootlessness." Or, one might say, they have a sense of the relativity and ambiguity of things human (CIS, 73–75).

Kundera too makes irony central; the novel, he states, is by definition "the ironic art." Irony irritates, he says, "not because it mocks or attacks but because it denies us our certainties by unmasking the world as an ambiguity."[25] This is why Rorty's metaphysicians, still clinging to things certain and unambiguous, fear the ironists, and why they brand them "relativists." Having repudiated the appearance-reality distinction, Rorty might object to Kundera's use of the word "unmasking" (although it does not appear to bear this strong connotation for Kundera). Yet this effect of irony is precisely why he values it in his anti-Philosophical campaign and why it must be central to his post-Philosophical liberal culture.

But it is also why Rorty insists irony must be circumscribed and carefully confined to the private sphere. Rorty gives several relatively innocuous reasons for this: For one, the idea of a public culture which is ironist would be a culture whose youth were socialized to be "continually dubious about their own process of socialization," a condition Rorty implies is unhealthy. Moreover, ironists need to have something to have doubts about—his second reason for keeping irony private. But perhaps the greatest cause for concern is that, if allowed to reign in public, irony has the potential to humiliate, for it threatens the cohesiveness of others'—presumably nonironists'— self-understandings, making them feel "futile, obsolete, powerless." However, Rorty goes to some lengths to show that there is no reason to think ironists are inherently illiberal. As long as individuals are willing to split themselves into public and private parts, there is no reason there cannot be liberal ironists (CIS, 87–91).

On the face of it, there is nothing about this that seems highly objectionable. Yet one cannot help but wonder, if we are to believe that Rorty indeed values human relativity and ambiguity as Kundera does, and if the highest value of the novel for democracy is its incompatibility with the totalitarian universe—its ability to unravel and subvert any attempt to impose singular truths or perspectives on this diversity—why circumscribe irony in this way? Won't this have the effect of neutralizing irony's most important qualities?

By Rorty's own lights, irony represents the recognition that one's "final vocabulary" is only one of many out there and the abandonment of the idea that the collective search for such vocabularies is convergent, that one true or universal final vocabulary will ever be found. Building on Kundera's powerful views about the novel, Rorty seems to make the argument that this irony or ambiguity or contingency—the lack of metaphysical certainty and universal validity—is not only central but more conducive to democratic life. But he then effectively shackles irony to the point where it becomes little more than window dressing (CIS, 73–77).

If indeed Rorty is committed to the human multiplicity that Kundera's writing on the novel so eloquently portrays, and if the novel is indeed the characteristic genre of democracy and the struggle for freedom, there is no need to limit irony, the novel's most basic characteristic. Rorty's concern for not humiliating the metaphysicians, though admirable, seems to me misplaced. If he is interested in arriving at the condition of full democracy where there is nothing which can trump the consensus of its citizens, where "nobody dreams that God, or the Truth, or the Nature of things, is on their side," as he often asserts, it would appear that undermining the certainty and transcendental appeals of the metaphysicians is a necessary aim, even at the risk of mildly offending them in the process.

It may be that irony cannot be reconciled with a demand for a singular, unified moral community in a way that promotes rather than stifles democratic pluralism. When contrasted with the truly ironic and contingent world of Kundera's, it strikes one that Rorty fails to show that there is a difference that makes a difference between the rationalist, universally grounded politics of the Enlightenment and his own "post-Philosophical" version.[26]

THE SENTIMENTAL NOVEL: MORAL INCULCATION OR ETHICAL REFLECTION?

As we have seen, at the heart of Rorty's political project is what he calls "sentimental education." This notion evokes images of Schiller and Flaubert and an ideal of human fullness attainable through aesthetic education. By "manipulating sentiments" in such a way that individuals "imagine themselves in the shoes of the despised and oppressed," Rorty thinks the kind of shared moral identity necessary for progress toward greater justice can be created. Of crucial importance here are what Rorty calls "sad, sentimental stories," but also the novel of moral protest, understood on the model of *Uncle Tom's Cabin* (TP, 176–81).[27] Although Rorty refers to Stowe's work with the radical-sounding rhetorical flourish, "novel of moral protest," Jane Tompkins characterizes it as a "sentimental novel," rooting it in a small but highly influential—at least in terms of sales figures—cadre of works that dominated the American landscape during the latter part of the nineteenth century.[28]

This is significant because Rorty briefly discusses Tompkins's original work on the sentimental novel in his account of sentimental education. What Rorty finds particularly attractive is Tompkins's characterization of the sentimental novel as "a political enterprise halfway between sermon and social theory, that both codifies and attempts to mold the values of its time" (TP, 183n). However, Tompkins goes on to point out that the sentimental novels, like *Uncle Tom's Cabin* and Susan Warner's *Wide, Wide World*, were understood by their authors and antebellum critics and readers as "stories," as opposed to "novels." Stories function more like biblical parables: they are "written for edification's sake rather than for the sake of art." In their attempts to mold public opinion, Tompkins argues, certain works are closer to propaganda than to art. It is this moral or propagandistic function elucidated by Tompkins which Rorty seems to have in mind in his assertions about the public value of middlebrow novels and when he calls for an Arnoldian "religion of literature" in *Achieving Our Country* (AOC, 136).[29]

It is important to distinguish between narratives that seek to validate a pre-existing set of abstract truths or values and those that aim at the more diffuse and subjective notion of meaning—more specifically, between those that attempt to redeem the sins of the past and those that endeavor to create a space in which those sins can be confronted.[30] *Uncle Tom's Cabin* falls into the former set of categories. Yet the rub on the power of fiction is that it is not absolute; it cannot ensure the acceptance of its perspective exactly as intended. Moreover, works of fiction seldom fail to generate multiple interpretations and to provoke argument. Even if *Uncle Tom's Cabin* did help convince a nation to go to war and free its slaves, as Abraham Lincoln believed, in terms of its own set of aims, it was a failure.[31] As Tompkins compellingly argues,

> Stowe conceived her book as an instrument for bringing about the day when the world would be ruled not by force, but by Christian love. The novel's deepest aspirations are expressed only secondarily in its devastating attack on the slave system; the true goal of Stowe's rhetorical undertaking is nothing less than the institutions of the kingdom of heaven on earth.[32]

To provide a useful vocabulary for this discussion, I suggest we draw a distinction between moral inculcation and ethical reflection to better grasp the political effects of novels. The "ethical," as literary critic Wayne Booth has argued, suggests a much broader project of "the entire range of effects on the 'character' or 'person' or 'self'" of which moral judgments are only a small part.[33] It involves individual conceptions of the good life, of how to live well, which may or may not correspond to any given set of moral norms about "right" conduct. Distinguishing between "that which is considered to be good" and "that which imposes itself as obligatory," as Paul Ricoeur puts it, allows us to clarify the difference between viewing books as capable of sparking the kind of reflection that may lead us to deepen and enrich our lives and looking to books to instruct us on how to live *morally*.[34]

It is on this basis that we may distinguish the good life from the moral life. While the moral life entails a set of minimum conditions, a constellation of constraints or codes of behavior, the good life comprises much more—the fulfilled life. This is something which may or may not, or may only to a certain degree, involve living in accordance with accepted conventions and with moral absolutes. Alexander Nehamas has argued that it is the "lesser," or popular, middlebrow works—including the dominant medium of storytelling in contemporary life, television—that function as tools of moral instruction, not the "great" works: "In acquiring the status of works of high literature, fictional writings tend to lose their role as tools of moral education."[35] In a comment directed explicitly at the literary-political projects of Rorty and Nussbaum, Nehamas perorates, "I agree that literature has much to teach us about life. But this is how to live, and that in turn is not the same as how to live morally."[36]

Rorty seems to recognize this kind of distinction when he distinguishes between two different types of books: books relevant to our duties to others and books pertaining to our duties to ourselves. This distinction runs alongside the divide between public and private, which fundamentally structures his ideal liberal polity. Rorty's case for sentimental education—that is, for the public, moral role of literature like *Uncle Tom's Cabin* and *Bleak House*—rests on the need to promote the values associated with our duties to others. Novels like James's *The Princess Casamassima*, the novel of ethical reflection par excellence for Nussbaum, on the other hand, end up in the "private" category, relevant only to our duties to ourselves.[37] These latter duties need not be actively fostered in a liberal democratic polity, but merely permitted to exist, as long as they remain private and do not impinge upon the public work of building a moral community. Such highbrow works for Rorty do edify, but in a way only of interest to those attempting to live in an original and imaginative fashion who are not concerned with their responsibilities to others.[38]

In this way, Rorty constructs an accepted public reading list for liberal democracies and severs this public sensibility from (private) self-transformation. Yet while I agree with Rorty on the point that we should not be compelled by some conception of moral duty to subordinate our private loves to our public responsibilities, distinguishing between moral rules and a larger notion of ethics along the lines I have suggested provides a better route than his rigid divide between public and private.[39]

Ultimately, Rorty's commitment to what we have called ethical reflection does not hold up. Despite a certain amount of lip service to ethical *phronesis*, Rorty appeals to literature and stories for the inculcation of moral norms. These are of course not transcendental moral norms. But his historicized conception of morality as a matter of "we-intentions" still implies a kind of universality inasmuch as it rests on collectively agreed upon and shared terms.[40]

To preserve this commonality, Rorty must insulate it from the idiosyncratic attempt to define one's character. In this way, he reproduces the traditional moral-aesthetic divide he has supposedly jettisoned along with the rest of the Kantian baggage.

On the one hand, Rorty seems to think, like Nussbaum, that reading non-didactic literature, on account of its concreteness and attention to the details of the lives of others, will help make people into better perceivers, and hence transform them such that they act in more just and more tolerant ways. Yet at the same time, Rorty concurs when Nehamas questions the idea that general moral lessons can be extracted from the concrete situations portrayed in such literature, in particular, from the rich, finely woven, detailed situations that characterize the novels of Henry James.[41] Here Rorty seems to undermine his own argument for literature making us more sensitive, conceding, in a response to Nehamas's criticisms, that

> Nehamas is surely right that it is just the specifically highbrow character of [James's] account, its extraordinary delicacy, and its consequent "incalculable specificity" that makes it relatively useless for purposes of moral instruction.[42]

Yet one can surmise from this that it is not the "incalculable specificity" that Rorty objects to, having already touted the importance of detailed descriptions, but rather the lack of clear moral norms in the Jamesian novel. In my view, Rorty attempts to have it both ways. Let me explain.

As far as I can tell, Rorty is genuinely committed to the idea that reading novels can foster the kinds of sensibilities that will not only make us better people but better citizens through individual edification, and, further, that they will promote the moral community that he sees as integral to the pursuit of social justice. But these purposes collide, given Rorty's conception of one in terms of irony, and the other, a singular moral identity. Rorty's task, then, given the logic of his commitments, is to make the normative force of literature safe for his liberal, Enlightenment politics.

What this amounts to is that Rorty must subordinate the ethical aim to the moral norm, rather than the other way around. He enlists the ethical force that literature works upon individuals in principle, but in practice its transformative power can only be allowed to function in the direction of producing better *liberal* citizens. Hence he must distinguish between works which meet this criterion and those which do not—namely, between books for public and for private purposes.

On one level, one may want to respond that Rorty may be justified in this differentiation: different novels surely do different things. But it seems to me that his stance undermines the possibility that literature will produce the enlarged, more sensitive individuals his politics require. Rorty's scheme seems to supplant one kind of narrowness with another: it is as if Rorty wants people to be free to pursue their own conceptions of the good life in private and yet still be likely to be compelled by moral compunctions to reduce the unnecessary suffering of others in their public lives, while at the same time leaving their fundamental ethical orientation unchanged.[43] Stated another way, he splits ethics off from politics, whereby the latter becomes the province of a collective moral identity and widely accepted conventions from which individual conceptions of the good life are either excluded altogether or, if admitted, required to coincide with what "we" believe.

THE NOVEL OF MORAL PROTEST: STOWE, DICKENS, AND BALDWIN

Rorty's appeal to the novel rests on a crucial linkage of stories, or narrative more generally, to the forging of an identity, specifically, to a *moral* identity. This is true whether we are speaking of personal identity or the collective identity of a community or nation. Rorty believes that it is through stories that human beings give sense to their lives. Through the larger narratives we invoke in response to the question "who are we?" we understand ourselves and our relations to others. He agrees with Alasdair MacIntyre, who says the story of one's life is always embedded in the stories of the community in which one's identity is rooted.[44]

From this premise, Rorty arrives at the fundamental insight underlying his political project: if we can alter the larger communal stories upon which we draw to craft our own narratives of self-understanding by replacing parochial and group-based stories with grand, optimistic, and inclusive tales of open vistas and possibilities unrealized, then a kind of moral progress can be made toward a more tolerant and more just world. If people revise their moral identities—what he calls their "final vocabularies"—in light of whatever new people and books they encounter, this becomes a way of achieving moral progress (CIS, 80–85).

In short, stories are for Rorty political interventions. Their political value resides in the fact that the telling of stories both about episodes in a nation's past and about the kind of future for which it can hope is for Rorty the essential prerequisite of collective self-transformation. The key premise here is that "hope is the condition of growth" (PSH, 120). In *Achieving Our Country*, Rorty likewise casts hope as the precondition of engaged action and argues that national pride is a necessary condition for collective self-improvement. His assessment of the somewhat debased and demoralized state of the contemporary left provides a case in point of the importance of stories for politics. He holds that it is the lack of "inspiring stories" which is the root cause of the predicament. Such stories are precisely what is required to "persuade the nation to exert itself" (AOC, 3–15).[45]

Distinct from his view of novels as vehicles of moral inculcation, this reading of Rorty's intentions suggests a conception closer to the broader notion of ethical reflection discussed above: the idea that we tell stories in order to change—to refashion our identities and remake ourselves by deepening or enriching our existence. Securing a place for this broader transformative role is in my view essential for an adequate account of the politics of stories. However, it is not clear that such a place really exists in Rorty's picture: his view of sentimental education as accommodating individuals to a fixed and monolithic moral identity elides this transformative potential. That is, the adoption of a common moral identity does not seem to necessarily entail self-transformation. This is the fundamental claim or assumption I want to examine. If we accept that stories or literature can foster political renewal or collective transformation, can the kind of middlebrow, "sentimental" novels, or novels of moral protest, Rorty espouses have a transformative effect if divorced from what Booth referred to as "the entire range of effects on the 'character' or 'person' or 'self'"?

Making the case that Rorty does in fact leave room for the idea that we tell stories in order to change requires something of a sympathetic reading. That the transformative role of stories is indeed part of his design rests on the idea that the moral relevance of books resides in their ability to "alter one's sense of what is possible and important" (CIS, 82). Literature fosters reflection on the possible, on what we can hope. This forward-looking orientation is a crucial ingredient of collective self-transformation. Of this, Rorty is convinced: "You cannot urge political renewal on the basis of fact. You have to describe the country in terms of what you passionately hope it will become" (AOC, 101).

Yet the exclusive focus on hope and future possibilities distances his perspective from the facts of political reality.[46] We can illustrate this point by returning to the case of *Uncle Tom's Cabin*. Although he has not devoted much space to substantive discussion of the work, Rorty repeatedly cites Stowe's novel as representative of his program of sentimental education (EHO, 80, passim; TP, 181–84). He identifies *Uncle* as exemplifying "the novel of moral protest," the genre "most closely associated with the struggle for freedom and equality," which he sees as the most enduring legacy of the West (EHO, 68).[47] To be sure, the novel contains the major qualities prized by his ideal of sentimental education: detailed descriptions of distant others' lives, a capacity to foster identificatory states of sympathy and compassion constitutive of a

democratic moral community, and the moral force necessary to compel bringing about an end to the injustice.[48]

Yet this valorization of *Uncle* as the democratic literary intervention par
excellence must be reconciled with Baldwin's scathing critique of both *Uncle*
itself and the overall genre of the novel of moral protest.[49] Insofar as Rorty
positions himself as something of a spiritual heir to Baldwin's political project of "achieving our country," the latter's take is of particular relevance.

On Baldwin's view, the sentimental novel of moral protest fails for two reasons. First, it fails to challenge the conception of reality buttressing the status
quo: in this case, the "reality" of black inferiority and the identities of privileged whiteness it makes possible. The existence of this whiteness-privileging
reality is precisely what Baldwin thinks keeps white Americans from facing
the compromised parts of their selves and from being forced either to change
or to abandon their hollow rhetoric and stated American ideals of freedom and
equality. In short, it is a recipe for lip service and the hollow invocation of
ideals that keeps us from enacting real change.

The second reason it fails is due to what Baldwin calls the sentimental
novel's "rejection of life." Taking a view which calls to mind the ugly and
frightening scenarios depicted in Arthur Miller's *The Crucible*, Baldwin argues that the mask of self-righteous sentimentality often conceals a deeper,
underlying "aversion to experience" and a "fear of life" not unlike "that spirit
of medieval times which sought to exorcise evil by burning witches" and
"that terror which activates a lynch mob."[50] Turning to *Uncle*, Baldwin con-
tends that by suppressing human complexity in its reduction of existence into
thin, stereotypical caricatures, its effect is to deny the resources—the ambiguity, paradox, and complexity of existence—necessary for changing both
ourselves, black and white, and our situation. For Baldwin, the business of the
novelist is to portray a vaster reality—namely, the "beauty, dread, and power"
of the human being—which gives the lie to fictive realities upon which such
resentment depend. In the process, it cannot avoid doing what Dewey most
highly valued in art, what makes it "more moral than moralities"—that is,
breaking the crust of convention. These complexities and ambiguities, then,
are central to Baldwin's political project of achieving our country.

I recount Baldwin's perspective here to point out that Rorty's conception
of the political relevance of literature is vulnerable to the same criticisms
Baldwin directs at *Uncle*. In the first place, Rorty makes "the fictive reality
for which we hope" ultimately more central than actual reality. Because the
notion of reality has at best an ambiguous and uncertain status for Rorty,
inasmuch as his antirepresentationalism undermines traditional categories
of truth and fact, he renders our ability to contest or criticize that reality virtually nonexistent. And, second, because of the way Rorty circumscribes

irony—something, if we recall, which Kundera identifies as crucial for highlighting the ambiguity and contingency of human existence—he sharply limits the parts of ourselves and our self-descriptions that are relevant to politics and subject to the contest of a discourse of multiple perspectives. They are instead simply affirmed by the public "we."

CONCLUSION

Stories are a double-edged sword. Unabashed advocates of a heavy-handed education in the timeless virtues, like the neo-Platonist Bennett, appeal to stories as bearers of eternal and unassailable values, while postmodern purveyors of irony and ambiguity turn to them for the critical, subversive power to undermine and expose the dictates of universalist and essentialist values as particular and subjective. If there can be no ultimate resolution of the contradictory force of stories in either direction, and if no camp can claim stories finally and inexorably as their own, the task becomes identifying in any given account in which direction the ethical force of a story cuts. The crucial issue I have tried to underscore is whether stories are employed in the name of value systems that have a monolithic or homogeneous goal at their core, or as a way of preserving and living with the fundamental ambiguity and diversity of human life.

Rorty's account of the role of novels in a democratic culture contrasts sharply with Dewey's argument about art and social criticism. If we recall from our earlier discussion, Dewey's main insight was to underscore the way imaginative projections of future possibilities perform the critical function of exposing the limitations of present conditions. In a famous passage, Dewey made the startling claim that "art is more moral than moralities." The latter, on his view, "are, or tend to become, consecrations of the *status quo*, reflections of custom, reinforcements of the established order."[51]

This seems to me a good description of the prime function of art and imaginative thought in a democratic culture. If we were to put it in the terms of our earlier discussion, we would characterize it as the "ethical" function of art—sparking critical reflection on the world and the place of our conception of the good life in it, but also on the kinds of selves we hope to be. On Rorty's rendering, however, this function is transmogrified into the moral task of bringing us in line with a common identity and shared public values in a way that leaves our selves ultimately unchanged. The kinds of novels capable of breaking the crust of convention are privatized, effectively safeguarding liberal conventions from criticism. Baldwin's pointed criticisms of the novel of moral protest also remind us that novels, or art in general, can have, apart from the moral and ideological function of "lesser" or middlebrow or sentimental art, a critical function—nay, that they *must* have such a function if they are to be of any positive social value at all toward effecting collective self-transformation and be anything more than a way of entrenching static, monolithic identities.

Yet this does not address the fundamental questions raised at the outset of this chapter. Can the types of novels that exercise a critical function promote political action? Are its readers likely to be inspired to remedy injustice? Such novels may lead to self-reflection and a thoughtful appreciation of the ambiguity and complexity of human life, but will all this self-enlarging but ponderous rumination so preoccupy us that action fails to take place? Is Rorty right when he argues that such ironic questioning must be restricted to private life because it will generate the pernicious political attitude that "there is some social goal more important than avoiding cruelty," like aesthetic purity or authenticity?

One may be tempted to respond that perhaps different novels *do* do different things and indeed serve different political purposes, both of which are beneficial to democratic life. This view suggests that there are two modes of democratic transformation, and it underscores a fundamental tension between the individual and collective levels that is as old as democracy itself: on the one hand, change brought about through collective action by a loosely organized *demos* united by a commitment to greater social justice and propelled by shared moral sentiments and emotions, and on the other, change on an individual level, where through critical reflection on ourselves and our world we transform ourselves into enlarged, more tolerant, and more virtuous citizens than we were originally socialized to be. Framed in this way, Rorty's distinction between duties to ourselves and duties to others appears quite useful. Didactic, sentimental, middlebrow novels that inspire action rather than self-reflection serve the goal of collective demotic change quite well, for what is required here is action-generating emotions, not critical questioning and potentially paralyzing ambiguity. By contrast, the more complex, highbrow repositories of ironical ambiguity we read in our spare time are very well suited to individual change through critical self-reflection.

As attractive as this bifurcated picture may appear, I want to argue that we resist it. Citizens of democracy surely do read different kinds of novels, and these different novels serve different purposes for different people, some critical and questioning, others didactic and moral. Novels, like art in general, can be put to many uses, both radical and reactionary. As long as both types exist, one is tempted to argue, democracies will be capable of generating change from within. However, to the extent that the actions we take in the public realm to collectively alter our world are severed from our efforts to transform ourselves, the power of the *demos* may end up yielding little more than a defense of the status quo.

As Dewey and others, like Sheldon Wolin, have argued, democracy is more than a form of government: it is a way of life, a "mode of being." The kind of renewal from within that democratic polities are capable of, if only sporadically and ephemerally, is only possible when it entails the transformation of individuals' self-understandings as well as change on a formal or institutional level. Although he did not do enough to link his notion of art disrupting unreflectively accepted conventions with democratic ways of living, Dewey's conception comes closest to doing justice to democracy's potential for internal criticism. It can be improved further by combining his idea of "imaginative vision" of unrealized possibilities with a conception of what Stanley Cavell has called in an Emersonian spirit, "perfectionist" change; demotic transformation can be fused with individual transformation. In the end, as Melissa Orlie has nicely put it, "the conditions of political action cannot be supplied by the individual alone. But neither can the conditions of politics be created without individual action."[52]

Rorty may be right that certain novels do less than others to further our sense of injustice and the felt need to end it. Yet this is not remedied by restricting the reading list in a democratic society but by cultivating particular ethical practices, or "habits," in pragmatist parlance. Any defense of the novel as a vehicle of democratic progress must therefore begin at the level of individual selves. Although Rorty occasionally notes the importance of the development of individual habits of action, his account of the novel's relation to democracy, skewed as it is toward forging a public moral community, divorces the transformative possibilities of books from the selves who read them and thereby runs the risk of cultivating participation in emotional states of fellow feeling—even if fueled by a sense of injustice—that result in no concrete changes where it most counts at the level of individual selves.

NOTES

1. On Rorty's notion of justice, see his essay "Justice as a Larger Loyalty," in *Cosmopolitics*, ed. Pheng Cheah and Bruce Robbins (Minneapolis: University of Minnesota Press, 1998), 45–58.

2. Many are familiar with James's statement that "the pragmatic method is primarily a method of settling metaphysical disputes that otherwise might be interminable." However, for James it is not a method intended solely for philosophers for settling their disputes, but for everyday individuals to cut through endless philosophical debates so they could determine which view better fit their own personal vision. Rorty's understanding of philosophy shares more with Peirce, who understood pragmatism as

properly philosophical in nature and as more of a collective undertaking than an individual pursuit. See William James, *Pragmatism*, in *William James: Writings, 1902–1910*, ed. Bruce Kuklick (New York: Library of America, 1987), 506–9, passim.

3. See "Human Rights, Rationality, and Sentimentality," in TP, 167–85. Here Rorty explicitly connects his antifoundationalist project and the project of strengthening community: "The best, and probably the only argument for putting foundationalism behind us is the one I have already suggested: it would be more efficient to do so, because it would let us concentrate our energies on manipulating sentiments, on sentimental education" (176).

4. See for example the essay "A Cultural Left" in AOC, 73–107.

5. Rorty, "Who Are We? Moral Universalism and Economic Triage," *Diogenes* 173 (Spring 1996): 13.

6. In general, these views are given their fullest expression in CIS, but see also "Heidegger, Kundera, and Dickens" in EHO. On the political importance of making our sense of *we* more expansive, see "Justice as a Larger Loyalty."

7. Rorty's mention of the "comic book" in this context might strike some as odd, but an excellent example of the kind of thing Rorty may have in mind is the pioneering work of Joe Sacco, a writer whose comic-strip journalism, for lack of a better description, contains the qualities exalted by Rorty: detailed descriptions and narratives that sensitize us to the suffering of others. See for example his excellent *Safe Area Gorazde: The War in Eastern Bosnia, 1992–95* (Seattle, WA: Fantagraphics Books, 2000).

8. For Rorty's discussions of Nabokov and Orwell, see chapters 7 and 8.

9. See Philip Rieff, *Freud: The Mind of the Moralist* (Garden City, NY: Doubleday, 1961), preface.

10. Jo Burrows, "Conversational Politics: Rorty's Pragmatist Apology for Liberalism," in *Reading Rorty: Critical Responses to Philosophy and the Mirror of Nature (and Beyond)*, ed. Alan R. Malachowski (Cambridge: Blackwell, 1990), 328. Burrows concludes that "despite his protests to the contrary, Rorty is peddling liberal ideology." However, noting that Rorty could simply admit to this "banal" charge and point out, a la Churchill, that liberalism, given the alternatives, is not such a bad system to be peddling, she takes a different tack and interprets Rorty's views from the perspective of a "political contender"—someone who "has good reason to contend for (say) a new political set-up"—in order to illustrate how Rorty is "surreptitiously narrowing down the options" (331–34, passim).

11. Lionel Trilling, *Beyond Culture: Essays on Literature and Learning* (New York: Harcourt Brace Jovanovich, 1965), 183–86. It is hard to find a better summary statement of this view of literature and its relevance to political life than Trilling's: "To the carrying out of the job of criticizing the liberal imagination, literature has a unique relevance, not merely because so much of modern literature has explicitly directed itself upon politics, but more importantly because literature is the human activity that takes the fullest and most precise account of variousness, possibility, complexity, and difficulty." See his *The Liberal Imagination: Essays on Literature and Society* (Garden City, NY: Anchor Books, 1950), xii–xiii. For the didactic argument, see William Bennett, ed., *The Book of Virtues: A Treasury of Great Moral Stories*

(New York: Simon & Schuster, 1993); and the companion volume, *The Moral Compass: Stories for a Life's Journey* (New York: Simon & Schuster, 1995).

12. David Bromwich, *A Choice of Inheritance: Self and Community from Edmund Burke to Robert Frost* (Cambridge, MA: Harvard University Press, 1989), viii, 2.

13. Rorty suggests that "we try to get to the point where we no longer worship *anything*, where we treat *nothing* as a quasi divinity, where we treat *everything*—our language, our conscience, our community—as a product of time and chance" (CIS, 22).

14. Iris Murdoch, "The Sublime and the Beautiful Revisited," in *Existentialists and Mystics: Writings on Philosophy and Literature*, ed. Peter Conradi (New York: Penguin Books, 1998), 281–82.

15. See Martha Nussbaum, "Finely Aware and Richly Responsible," in *Love's Knowledge: Essays on Philosophy and Literature* (New York: Oxford University Press, 1990). At the time, Nussbaum seemed to claim that the imagination itself is intrinsically ethical. However, when pressed about this issue and the question of whether good reading necessarily leads to good living, she responded in the negative and introduced a helpful distinction: she now says that she is concerned with "the morality of the *act* of reading, not the morality that is *caused* by reading." Her claims about the ethical content of the literary imagination involve what happens during the time when one is reading. There are many things, she points out, that may prevent one from acting ethically in one's life. See the interview in Richard Kearney, ed., *States of Mind: Dialogues with Contemporary Thinkers* (New York: New York University Press, 1995), 127–28. Nevertheless, her conjunction of "finely aware" and "richly responsible" seems to require such a connection if it is to have any force. By contrast, Rorty is more concerned with the latter—the common morality or solidarity of "we-ness" that may result through an indirect route from reading.

16. Nussbaum, *Love's Knowledge*, 207–9.

17. John Dewey, *Art and Experience* (1934; repr., New York: Perigee Books, 1980), 346.

18. It is not clear that Kundera has ever described the novel in these terms. Kundera undoubtedly paints the spirit of the novel as hostile to the single-Truth, absolutist views of the world that often buttress totalitarian regimes. Rorty associates this spirit with the kind of "democratic utopia" he advocates in his own work, but there is little evidence that Kundera sees it in this same light. Although obviously committed in a deep and fundamental way to individual freedom of thought, Kundera's positive claims on behalf on the novel tend to be sweeping, abstract, and ethereal, rather than a defense of the novel as supportive of democracy in practical terms. Unlike Rorty, he has no particular political program to promote. This is not to say Kundera's work is not "political"; on the contrary, as someone who lived much of his adult life in the shadow of a totalitarian regime or in exile from it and had his own works banned, the cast of his character has been forged in the fire of politics. But this is not politics in the narrow, partisan, or ideological sense. Kundera's is a politics that transcends borders, parties, and platforms, a politics that traffics in the highest human values and obtains at the most fundamental level of human existence. If there is a politics inherent in Kundera's writing—a "politics of the novel," if you will—it is first and foremost a

politics of the self, concerned with deepening and enriching human existence by overcoming and dismantling the forces that seek to limit and truncate it from the outside.

19. Ian Shapiro discerns in Rorty's work since PMN a "journey from philosophical diagnosis to political prescription" characterized by the effort to "describe a politics he thinks we should embrace once we wholeheartedly reject foundationalist presuppositions," in *Political Criticism* (Berkeley: University of California Press, 1990), 20.

20. Milan Kundera, *The Art of the Novel*, trans. Linda Asher (New York: Harper-Collins, 1988), 157–65.

21. Kundera, *The Art of the Novel*, 164–65.

22. Richard Rorty, *Against Bosses, Against Oligarchies: A Conversation with Richard Rorty*, ed. Derek Nystrom and Kent Puckett (Charlottesville, VA: Prickly Pear Pamphlets, 1998), 9.

23. Kundera, *The Art of the Novel*, 159. Kundera borrows the term *agélastes* from Rabelais for those who do not laugh. The reference is to a Jewish proverb that states, "Man thinks, God laughs," which Kundera believes inspired Rabelais' *Gargantua* and *Pantagruel*—on his view, the first great European novel. God laughs because man thinks and the truth eludes him. From this, Kundera erects his opposition between the novel's spirit of humor and the "theoretical spirit" of philosophy.

24. The raison d'etre of the novel is to keep man's concrete being, his "world of life" or *Lebenswelt*, "under permanent light and to protect us from the forgetting of being," in Kundera, *The Art of the Novel*, 17, 3–6. For Rorty's critique of Heidegger, see AOC, 73–107, and CIS, 122–40.

25. Kundera, *The Art of the Novel*, 134.

26. As Jo Burrows put it, Rorty "is concerned to drive home the difference between subscribing to liberalism simply because it is the 'best pragmatic option,' given the historical circumstances, and subscribing to it because it can somehow be shown to be 'absolutely correct' on philosophical grounds," in "Conversational Politics," 325.

27. The idea of sentimental education, of course, emerged as a reaction to the narrowness of neo-Kantian, rationalist conceptions of moral education in the early nineteenth century. This is significant, since Rorty's view of social justice rests on appeals to sentiment rather than rationality, the key component of the Kantian view. However, the more direct forebear of Rorty's politics of sentiment is David Hume.

28. Jane Tompkins, *Sensational Designs: The Cultural Work of American Fiction, 1790–1860* (New York: Oxford University Press, 1985). In this refreshing work, Tompkins attempts to recover the "sentimental novels" of Stowe, Susan Warner, Charles Brockden Brown, and James Fenimore Cooper from the subordinate status they occupy as a result of the dominant "American renaissance" perspective which cast them as overly effeminate, sensationalistic, and propagandizing. Tompkins adeptly portrays the deep moral and political force inherent in these works, characterizing the sentimental novel in general as "an act of persuasion aimed at defining social reality." In particular, she highlights the critique of American society she identifies in these novels, particularly Stowe's, as "a monumental effort to reorganize [American] culture from the woman's point a view" (124).

29. Tompkins, *Sentimental Designs*, 126, 149, 186.

30. On redemptive narratives, see George Shulman, "American Political Culture, Prophetic Narration, and Toni Morrison's *Beloved*," *Political Theory* 24, no. 2 (1996): 295–314.

31. Upon meeting Stowe in 1863, Lincoln greeted her as "the little woman who wrote the book that made this great war," quoted in Alfred Kazin in his introduction to *Uncle Tom's Cabin* (New York: Bantam Books, 1981), ix.

32. Tompkins, *Sentimental Designs*, 141.

33. Wayne C. Booth, *The Company We Keep: An Ethics of Fiction* (Berkeley: University of California Press, 1988), 8. Though sometimes used interchangeably, the idea that ethics can be distinguished from morality has gained considerable currency in the past two decades. A number of pioneering works have dissented from prevailing Kantian assumptions long dominant in moral philosophy: see, for example, Alasdair MacIntyre, *After Virtue: A Study in Moral Theory* (Notre Dame, IN: University of Notre Dame Press, 1981); Bernard Williams, *Ethics and the Limits of Philosophy* (Cambridge, MA: Harvard University Press, 1985); Charles Taylor, *Sources of the Self: The Making of Modern Identity* (Cambridge, MA: Harvard University Press, 1989). One would also have to include in this category Rorty's *Philosophy and the Mirror of Nature*, which argued that the entire edifice on which Kant's universalized morality rested was "optional." In different ways, these variegated works affirm the point that morality is a subset of ethics, one that depicts a particular constellation of values endemic to Western Christian societies. Ethics—as opposed to morality—as most of these works at some point come around to asserting, is best understood in terms of Socrates' question, "How should one live?" Similar claims have been made by literary critics interested in reviving ethical criticism, like Booth.

34. Paul Ricoeur, *Oneself as Another*, trans. Kathleen Blamey (Chicago: University of Chicago Press, 1992), 179, 169–202, passim. My thinking here has benefited from Ricoeur's distinction between the moral norm and ethical aim.

35. Alexander Nehamas, "What Should We Expect from Reading? (There Are Only Aesthetic Values)," *Salmagundi* 111 (Summer 1996): 31–32. To illustrate this argument, Nehamas recalls the lengths to which Plato went to exclude Homer and the tragic poets from the Republic. On one level, Homer and Aeschylus have survived, so perhaps Plato's efforts failed. However, the reason Plato's concerns strike us today as unnecessary and unfounded is that Homer and Aeschylus have survived as "paradigms of high culture and great art," that is, as "mere literature"; they no longer serve the direct moral and ideological roles they occupied in the fourth century BC, to which Plato reacted.

36. Nehamas, "What Should We Expect from Reading?" 56. Bernard Williams makes a similar point: "'How should I live?' does not mean 'what life morally ought I to live?,'" in *Ethics and the Limits of Philosophy*, 5.

37. In the essay where he refers to Tompkins's work, Rorty frames this distinction even more explicitly as one of "public utility" vs. "private perfection" (TP, 183–84). He sees this distinction as paralleling one drawn by Tompkins between the sentimental novelists like Stowe and Warner, on the one hand, and Thoreau, Whitman, and Melville, on the other. However, while Rorty cites this distinction approvingly, for Tompkins it is actually the pejorative differentiation her entire work is designed

to undermine. Tompkins argues that the social criticism inherent in the sentimental novelists—heretofore overlooked, largely because they are rooted in a woman's perspective debased by twentieth-century critics as overeffeminate and trivial—is far more devastating than that of the celebrated trio of Thoreau, Whitman, and Melville. Rorty, it appears, fails to see this point.

38. In his essay on Nabokov in CIS, Rorty cites Nabokov's Humbert Humbert as a representative case of this kind of aesthetic self-preoccupation. However, by taking Humbert's case of the "cruel aesthete" as exhaustive of the possibilities of aesthetic self-creation, Rorty is led to grossly overgeneralize the dangers inherent in such projects. In his zeal to protect the moral community he wants to foster in public from disruptive incursions by self-absorbed aesthetes or strong poets who refuse to remain private, Rorty elides the possibility of self-actualization in public life by democratic citizens, a possibility crucial to the effective functioning of a vibrant democracy for thinkers like Emerson and Dewey, Rorty's putative intellectual and pragmatist forebears.

39. Rorty says that it is only for those "lucky Christians from whom the love of God and of other human beings are inseparable, or revolutionaries who are moved by nothing save the thought of social justice" that duties to self and duties to others coincide—these are the two types of (potentially nonliberal) character Rorty seeks to preempt via his public-private split (PSH, 13).

40. Rorty borrows this term, and his understanding of morality and moral obligation more generally, from Wilfrid Sellars (CIS, 59, 190). In Sellars's view, the core meaning of immoral behavior is "the sort of thing *we* don't do." Rorty initially claimed that our sense of solidarity with others is strongest when we identify with them as part of some particular—that is, less than universal—community, as "one of us," whether it be as Americans, as liberals, or the like. More recently, however, he seems to have abandoned this view, suggesting that we replace the ideas of justice and universal moral obligation with the idea of—he now calls it "loyalty" rather than "solidarity" (he may be following the sometimes pragmatist Josiah Royce here)—"loyalty to a very large group—the human species." See "Justice as a Larger Loyalty," 48.

41. Nehamas lumps Nussbaum and Rorty together in his criticism of accounts that impute to literary works the capacity to teach us to live morally. However, I think this criticism applies more to Rorty than to Nussbaum—that is, more to the kind of moral instruction Rorty looks to literature for than to the agent-centered capacity for ethical deliberation that is the object of Nussbaum's thought. Nehamas raises a second concern with regard to Rorty and Nussbaum about whether the kind of sensitivity and acute powers of perception both Nussbaum and Rorty praise are in themselves sufficient to be considered moral virtues. Sensitivity and its opposite, a kind of moral obtuseness, he argues, are in themselves neither good nor evil. "Whether they are to be pursued or avoided depends on the particular use one is to make of them, the conditions under which they will function in specific circumstances, what they will produce in conjunction with other features," in Nehamas, "What Should We Expect from Reading?" 55–56.

42. Rorty, "Duties to the Self and to Others: Comments on a Paper by Alexander Nehamas," *Salmagundi* 111 (Summer 1996): 61.

43. Although it may not appear so on my rendering, Rorty's position—developed at length in CIS—is actually a very thoughtful and ingenious compromise that is not without a certain appeal. I for one have never been convinced by his claim that people can (and do) divide themselves in such a way that they can be "in alternate moments, Nietzsche and J. S. Mill" (CIS, 85). More recently he has curtailed his example somewhat to read, "There is no reason why one cannot be a revolutionary activist on weekdays and a reader of John Ashbery on weekends," in "Duties to the Self," 65. Still, it seems to me that people simply do not work this way, at least to the extent that they have any coherence to their existence. Who, after having read Nietzsche, is able to embrace liberal democratic politics as usual without, at the very least, looking askance at it?

44. See MacIntyre, *After Virtue*, 221; Rorty, "Ethics without Principles," in PSH, esp. 76–79; and "Justice as a Larger Loyalty." Rorty discusses MacIntyre's views in "Freud and Moral Reflection," in EHO, 157–62; and briefly in "Justice as a Larger Loyalty." The moral thrust and edifying force of stories arises from the fact that in our, in MacIntyre's phrase, "narrative quest" to forge a character and an identity, we draw on the narratives we know, whether encountered in literature, in stories, or in religious parables. "I can only answer the [ethical] question 'What am I to do?,'" he argues, "if I can answer the prior question 'Of what story or stories do I find myself a part?'" in *After Virtue*, 208–16. Rorty takes a similar view in the above passages.

45. Rorty has been talking about stories and narratives, largely as part of a more general shift from theory to narrative, since CIS. AOC is a good source for understanding Rorty's political use of stories. Other places he discusses the relevance of stories include "Human Rights, Rationality and Sentimentality" in TP and "Justice as a Larger Loyalty."

46. The relation of the vocabularies of political theory to the "facts" of political reality is complex. In my view, Sheldon Wolin's notion of presenting facts in a "corrected fullness" is a better conception than Rorty's notion of redescription in terms of future possibilities because the former retains its connection to the reality of the present. Cf.: "The ideas and categories we use in political analysis are not of the same order as institutional 'facts,' nor are they 'contained,' so to speak, in the facts. They represent, instead, an added element, something created by the political theorist. Concepts like 'power,' 'authority,' 'consent,' and so forth are not real 'things,' although they are intended to point to some significant aspect about political things. Their function is to render political facts significant," in Wolin, *Politics and Vision: Continuity and Innovation in Western Political Thought* (Boston: Little, Brown & Co., 1960), 5.

47. "Heidegger, Kundera, and Dickens" is a key essay for understanding Rorty's view of literature, written in the late 1980s around the time he was working on CIS. It is also noteworthy for Rorty's mind-boggling effort to read Dickens as "a sort of anti-Heidegger"—an essayistic tour de force only someone like Rorty could even attempt. See also "Human Rights" in TP.

48. Here Rorty's thinking is supported by Tompkins's claim that the novel "helped convince a nation to go to war and to free its slaves," in *Sensational Designs*, 141.

49. See James Baldwin, "Everybody's Protest Novel," in *Notes of a Native Son* (New York: Bantam Books, 1955), 9–17.

50. Baldwin, "Everybody's Protest Novel," 13.

51. Dewey, *Art as Experience*, 348.

52. Sheldon S. Wolin, "Fugitive Democracy," in *Democracy and Difference: Contesting the Boundaries of the Political*, ed. Seyla Benhabib (Princeton, NJ: Princeton University Press, 1996), 43; Melissa A. Orlie, *Living Ethically, Acting Politically* (Ithaca, NY: Cornell University Press, 1997), 4. For Cavell's conception of perfectionist change—seeing not only the world in a transformed light but also as a place for ourselves as transformed beings in it, see his *Conditions Handsome and Unhandsome: The Constitution of Emersonian Perfectionism* (Chicago: University of Chicago Press, 1990). For a picture of democracy as ongoing self-transformation like the one I have in mind, see also Fred Dallmayr, "Beyond Fugitive Democracy," in *Democracy and Vision: Sheldon Wolin and the Vicissitudes of the Political*, ed. Aryeh Botwinick and William E. Connolly (Princeton, NJ: Princeton University Press, 2001), 58–78.

Chapter Four

The Limits of Sympathy

Sympathy can be a powerful force in political life. As a motor of collective politics, it is capable of forging affective ties strong enough to bridge the divides of nation, ethnicity, race, and gender to generate inclusive concern for the well-being of others. Yet if drawn too narrowly, sympathy can initiate an exclusionary dynamic that inflames these same divides by casting those who fall outside its sphere of concern as irretrievably different and "other." Can the sentiment of sympathy ground an ongoing quest for social justice? Or will it merely spark an ephemeral state of felt concern that provokes no concrete action?

Placing our ability to imaginatively identify with others at the center of the quest for social justice, Rorty's recent work affirms the political value of sympathy. Other contemporary thinkers, such as Martha Nussbaum, have taken a similar tack.[1] Following Hume rather than Kant, these accounts look to sentiment rather than reason, sympathetic fellow feeling rather than dictates of moral law or universal duty, to account for our concern for others. By cultivating our ability to imaginatively identify with others, we can extend the reach of our sense of social injustice. A particularly attractive feature of this perspective is that it posits the nonessentialist and nonfoundational idea of sympathy as doing the work once done by rationality: identifying with others as in some way like us is more powerful than universal moral obligations or respect for human dignity when it comes to spurring political action. As Rorty puts it, "To believe that someone is 'one of us,' a member of our moral community, is to exhibit readiness to come to their assistance when they are in need."[2] Fostering such fellow feeling promises to remedy what William James once called our natural "blindness" toward others.

In this chapter, I examine Rorty's call for a politics of sentiment rooted in our capacity for sympathetic identification, and identify three problems. The first is that the conception of sympathy or fellow feeling, drawn largely from Hume, proves too partial to those close at hand to meet the requirements of Rorty's sense of justice as a "larger loyalty." Rorty does not adequately address the extent to which the thinkers who shifted the source of moral judgments from reason to moral sentiment, like Hume, Rousseau, and Adam Smith, recognized the limits of sympathy; at crucial moments, they fell back on an appeal to "nature," often quite explicitly, to pick up the slack. For Hume, the principle of "humanity" is needed to correct the natural partiality of sympathy; in the case of Smith, the intervention of the invisible hand of a benevolent Deity is required to prevent his hypothetical "man of humanity" from preferring the demise of one hundred million distant Chinese in an earthquake to the loss of his little finger; and for Rousseau, sustaining the already weak natural sentiments of pity and commiseration amidst the contrary impulses endemic to civil society is only possible if properly cultivated through the extreme rigor and solitude of Emile's training—assumptions that run counter to Rorty's pragmatist stance.[3]

The second problem with the cultivation of fellow feeling as a political program is that it continually runs the risk of becoming a blueprint for imagining ourselves in the place of others and sharing their feelings of pain in lieu of actually doing something about it. The case for sympathy must rest on a crucial link between fellow feeling and action or moral agency. Rorty adopts the reflective process Hume proposed to "correct" sympathy's natural bias and give it a universal relevance. But this extension of the circle of sympathetic concern can only be achieved at the cost of dulling its capacity to move us to action.

Third, while Rorty is able to get around the transcendental appeals by making commonality a matter of the historically contingent agreement of a community, he does not address the normative pressures inherent in making concern for others dependent upon seeing them as "one of us." Because procuring the commonality or agreement on moral issues formerly secured through reason was a central concern for the mid-eighteenth-century theorists of sentiment, their projects impose an accepted version of "right" conduct and taste to which individuals were expected (or assumed) to conform.[4] This is not the place for a historical account of liberalism's failure to adequately discern the repressive power of social conformity, but it seems to me that Rorty's politics of sentiment shares in this shortcoming.[5]

To be sure, one of Rorty's greatest contributions to the field of political theory has been his defense of contingent and historically relative forms of identification as no less weakly linked to moral or political action than universal human essences. His pragmatism rests on the fundamental premise that "a belief can still regulate action, can still be thought worth dying for, among people who are quite aware that this belief is caused by nothing deeper than contingent historical circumstance" (CIS, 189). Rorty's turn to Hume and to sentiment extends this fundamental premise. Yet because his approach relies so heavily on the category of identity—on who counts as a member of our moral community—it courts the pernicious exclusionary logic of identity formation.

Alternatively, I argue that the ability to grant full reality to the suffering of others is a better ground for a collective politics that aims to diminish suffering than the ability to imaginatively identify with others as "one of us." Not only does this route avoid the exclusionary logic of identity formation, but it provides a stronger impetus for generating action on behalf of others. Revisiting Hume reveals evidence for the view that the power of reality to affect our minds and spur action exceeds that of the moral sentiment. Understanding the suffering of others to be as real as one's own involves a use of the imagination distinct from the imagining of oneself in the place of another entailed in sympathy, and is a better check on the moral blindness that can be a barrier to the expansion of our sense of injustice toward the suffering of distant and different others.[6]

RORTY'S SENTIMENTAL EDUCATION

At work in the idea of sentimental education are two important strands of Rorty's political theory. The first concerns Rorty's depiction of an antiessentialist common moral identity—whether we call it "solidarity" or a "larger loyalty" or "fellow feeling"—as the prerequisite of any majoritarian political endeavor. This increasingly prevalent quasi-communitarian thrust in his thought has gone largely unnoticed. The unifying thread of "achieving our country," "justice as a larger loyalty," and Rorty's recent work on human rights is the notion that an inclusionary moral community is the cornerstone of an effective democratic praxis. Without the emotional involvement entailed by the creation of a self-conscious moral community, largely through sympathetic identification with the suffering of others, attempts to remedy the injustices of the world will prove feeble and hollow. This, in short, is Rorty's criticism of the detached and overtheoretical postmodern left. A kind of community of fellow feeling or "reciprocal trust" is needed for individuals to be likely to provide assistance to others. The moment one ceases to think of the other in the first person plural, the likelihood of acting on their behalf decreases dramatically.[7] The second strand is the view that imaginative literature, in particular social realist novels, but narratives and stories in general, are the primary vehicles of moral progress and the quest for social justice.

Understood as the effort to forge a democratic moral community through appeals to sentiment rather than reason, the politics of sentiment has emerged as the primary "consequence" of Rorty's antifoundational pragmatism:

> The best, and probably the only, argument for putting foundationalism behind us is the one I have already suggested: it would be more efficient to do so, because it would let us concentrate our energies on manipulating sentiments, on sentimental education. (TP, 176)

Rorty describes this kind of education as that which "gets people of different kinds sufficiently well acquainted with one another that they are less tempted to think of those different from themselves as only quasi-human." The goal here is greater inclusion: "to expand the reference of the terms 'our kind of people' and 'people like us'" (TP, 176).

Resting on a view of the imagination as the central human faculty, and seeking to carve out a role for the sentiments in moral judgment, the idea of sentimental education evokes images of Schiller and Flaubert and an ideal of human fullness attainable through aesthetic education. But Rorty reverses the priority of the relation of individual growth to the larger social goals: his version has a communal good as its end in a much more direct way. Individual edification or "enlargement" appears to be a part of the process, but the sort of sympathy with others which allows us to see them as "one of us," as we shall see, is often possible without it. The more direct intellectual forebears here are Hume and Rousseau, whose projects authorized cooperative endeavors and assumed universal agreement in matters of the communal good.

My overriding concern is whether the wellsprings of sentiment and sympathy are a sufficient engine to mobilize and drive collective efforts to reduce suffering. In other words, can sympathetic identification yield a concern for the well-being for different and often distant others that is binding enough to ground a meliorative politics of social justice? And, second, can Rorty's project of sentimental education make due on its transformative promise?

As a general rule, the positions Rorty occupies are best understood in light of the "Philosophical" arguments he is reacting against. In this context, it is a view Rorty attributes to Plato: that the way to get people to be nicer to each other is to point out what they have in common—namely, rationality. Rorty does a nice job of illustrating how beside the point rational arguments are in the face of entrenched prejudice:

> Resentful young Nazi toughs were quite aware that many Jews were clever and learned, but this only added to the pleasure they took in beating such Jews. Nor does it do much good to get such people to read Kant and agree that one should not treat rational agents simply as means. (TP, 177)

His point is that moral progress is not a matter of an increase in rationality, nor does it involve developing what Dewey called intelligence. The crucial factor is sympathy, how wide one is willing to draw the limits of one's moral community. Thus, moral progress for Rorty is a matter of increasing "sensitivity"—one's responsiveness to "the concerns of ever larger groups of people" (PSH, 81). Following contemporary moral philosopher Annette Baier, Rorty frames the goal of sentimental education as a "progress of sentiments"—that is, "an ability to see the similarities between ourselves and people very unlike us as outweighing the differences" (TP, 181).[8] This is the idea that brings Rorty to Hume. On an important level, it is a matter of "moral" or "sympathetic" identification: cultivating the "imaginative ability to see strange people as fellow sufferers" and to imagine ourselves in their place (CIS, xvi).

As examples of the kind of progress he has in mind, Rorty points to the increased sympathy manifested in "the sort of reactions Athenians had more of after seeing Aeschylus's *The Persians* than before, the sort that whites in the U.S. had more of after reading *Uncle Tom's Cabin* than before, the sort we have more of after watching television programs about the genocide in Bosnia" (TP, 180). These are the vehicles of sentimental education: "genres such as the ethnography, the journalist's report, the comic book, the docudrama, and especially the novel" (CIS, xvi). It is a task, in short, not for "theory" but for narrative:

> The fate of the women in Bosnia depends on whether television journalists manage to do for them what Harriet Beecher Stowe did for black slaves—whether these journalists can make us, the audience back in the safe countries, feel that these women are more like us, more like real human beings than we have realized. (TP, 181)

There are, thus, two dimensions to this process of sentimental education. The first is "detailed description," that is, actual accounts of what the lives of distant others are like that first bring their suffering to our attention—for instance, the work of television journalists on the condition of Bosnian women. While discoveries of who is suffering can be made in general by "the workings of the free press, free universities, and enlightened public opinion," Rorty cites works like "*Madness and Civilization* and *Discipline and Punish*, as well as those like *Germinal, Black Boy, The Road to Wigan Pier*, and *1984*" as having been responsible for such enlightening (CIS, 63–64). Also paradigmatic here, as we have seen, are the works of Stowe and Dickens. In short, social novelists and literary critics have done a lot more to advance "the struggle for freedom and equality" than have philosophers and social theorists.[9] The second dimension Rorty calls "redescribing" what we ourselves are like in such a way as to come to see these distant others as "one of us" rather than as "them"

(CIS, xvi). That is to say, it is a matter of changing the stories we tell about ourselves to make the moral identity they furnish more inclusive.

Rorty groups these operations more generally under the rubric of what he calls "sad, sentimental stories." The case he makes for their power is ultimately a pragmatic one. In response to the question, "Why should I care about a stranger, a person who is no kin to me, a person whose habits I find disgusting?" Rorty argues that the bonds of feeling and extension of moral community generated by such stories are more likely to move us to action than are invocations of a universal moral obligation rooted in our common rationality. "Because this is what it is like to be in her situation" and "Because she might become your daughter-in-law" are, pragmatically speaking, more powerful responses than "Because I am under a moral obligation to her." Sad, sentimental stories, he argues, "repeated and varied over the centuries, have induced us, the rich, safe, powerful people, to tolerate and even to cherish powerless people—people whose appearance or habits or beliefs at first seemed an insult to our own moral identity, our sense of the limits of permissible human variation" (TP, 184–85).

Rorty may be on to something here. He makes the important point that traditional moral philosophy, too often concerned with extreme cases of a misanthropic nature, is guilty of neglecting the more common case of "the person whose treatment of a rather narrow range of featherless bipeds is morally impeccable, but who remains indifferent to the suffering of those outside this range, the one he thinks of as pseudo-humans." The idea that these depreciated assessments of other humans were somehow susceptible to rational argument was wrongheaded from the start. On Rorty's view, everything turns on "who counts as a fellow human being," that is, on membership in one's moral community (TP, 177). The central task thus becomes extending this moral community through the cultivation of our capacity for sympathy.

HUME AS A PROTOPRAGMATIST

In making sentiment the primary constituent of a common moral identity, Rorty invokes the legacy of David Hume. That Hume's thought is a source of protopragmatist stirrings is nothing new; William James suggested as much in the 1898 essay credited with launching the pragmatist tradition, and Rorty's oeuvre is peppered with remarks affirming the same, although, characteristically, he does not discuss the work of Hume at any length.[10] The general direction of the Humean enterprise of turning philosophical reflection away from a preoccupation with God and transcendental matters and making it self-reflective and of a piece with human affairs, along with his inclination toward "tests" of an empirical nature, requires little reworking to see its alignment with a broadly pragmatic spirit. To be sure, "Hume is a better advisor than Kant" if you are of pragmatist leanings, and both Hume and Dewey tend to be on the same side of most philosophical arguments: namely, against Kant.

Rorty makes ample negative use of Hume against particular metaphysical assumptions like the Platonic conception of a true self and the Kantian idea that it is rational to be moral (TP, 180). Yet what he calls the "relaxed, pragmatical, Humean attitude" has come to exert a more positive influence in his recent work undergirding his understanding of morality and justice (CP, xxxii). In a brief 1987 essay, likely Rorty's first affirmative reference to sentiment, he states that he would like "the sentiments of pity and tolerance" to supplant "belief-systems (or of what Habermas calls 'the commitment to rationality') as the bond which holds liberal societies together" and suggests that his forthcoming *Contingency, Irony, and Solidarity* be read as an attempt to develop this line of thought and "follow up on Hume rather than on Kant."[11] Even if only present in broad strokes, the Humean effort, in Baier's words, "to give morality a secure basis, not in moral theory but in human active capacities for cooperation" accounts for a basic strand of the Rortyan project.[12] In particular, the idea of morality as a matter of custom and shared practices, and the displacement of conceptions of moral "obligation" and "rules" with "corrected sympathy" and a "progress of sentiments" are central.[13]

Hume opens his *Enquiry Concerning Human Understanding*, an attempt to rework the themes of his *Treatise of Human Nature* a decade after, in his words, "it fell dead-born from the press" in 1739, with the assertion that "moral philosophy," or the "science of human nature," may rest on either of two fundamental assumptions. It may either approach the human being as "chiefly born for action; and as influenced in his measures by taste and sentiment," or it may "consider man in the light of a reasonable rather than an active being." Hume, it becomes clear, adopts the former. Indeed, the linchpin of Hume's case for sentiment over reason, or impressions over ideas, is that the former "strike the mind" with a greater "degree of force and liveliness. . . . The chief spring or actuating principle of the human mind," he asserts, "is pleasure or pain; and when these sensations are remov'd, both from our thought and feeling, we are, in a great measure, incapable of passion or action, of desire or volition."[14] Whereas reason, "being cool and disengaged, is no motive to action," taste, or sentiment, becomes "a motive to action, and is the first spring or impulse to desire and volition."[15]

This all suits the antirationalist and anti-Kantian in Rorty rather well. The stress on action resonates with classic pragmatist themes, running from Peirce to Dewey. In particular, it prefigures James's claim that "our judgments concerning the worth of things, big or little, depend on the *feelings* the things arouse in us."[16] But what of sympathy as the ground for the pursuit of justice?

Hume considers the capacity for sympathy very basic to human beings, making such claims as "the minds of men are mirrors to one another" and so "similar in their feelings and operations" that no one can be actuated by any affection "of which the others are not in some degree susceptible." Of sympathy, Hume remarks that "no quality of human nature is more remarkable . . . than that propensity we have to sympathize with others, and to receive by communication their inclinations and sentiments, however different from, or even contrary to our own." Yet sympathy is first perceived by us as an idea, not an impression; it requires the power of the imagination to "convert" it into an impression which will nonetheless "acquire such a degree of force and vivacity as to become the very passion itself, and produce an equal emotion as any original affection." An "easy sympathy and correspondent emotions" are predicated upon three factors: "relation, acquaintance, and resemblance." Confirming what is intuitive about sympathy, he notes that "the stronger the relation betwixt ourselves and any object, the more easily does the imagination make the transition and convey to the related idea the vivacity of conception." The "relation of blood" produces the strongest tie; acquaintance "without relation" gives rise to "love and kindness"; and any "peculiar similarity in our manners, or character, or country, or language," especially "our country-men, our neighbors, those of the same trade," "facilitates the sympathy." Indeed, "the sentiments of others have little influence, when far remov'd from us, and require the relation of contiguity, to make them communicate themselves entirely."[17]

Interestingly, although he equivocates in a few places, Hume avoids positing an innate moral core or natural moral law to provide a way out of this partiality.[18] As is well known, Hume rooted morality in sentiment rather than reason, and he argued that morality "is more properly felt than judg'd of." The moral sentiment for Hume "can be no other than a feeling for the happiness of mankind, and a resentment of their misery." This is precisely the quality Rorty seeks to cultivate, and that which generates sympathetic identification between human beings. But for Hume, the moral sentiment is not simply equivalent to sympathy; the capacity for sympathy alone is not enough to produce the moral sentiment.[19] "Our natural uncultivated ideas of morality, instead of providing a remedy for the partiality of our affections, do rather conform themselves to that partiality, and give it an additional force and influence." Sympathy must first be *corrected*; that is, the moral sentiment—"the sentiment of humanity"—is "not deriv'd from nature but from *artifice*."[20]

In this way, Hume underscores the origins in human artifice of not only the moral sentiment but justice as well. Yet while it is never in doubt that our sense of justice and injustice is "not derived from nature, but arises artificially . . . from education, and human conventions," it remains a very weak force on Hume's account. Unable to overcome either the partiality of our affections or the "temptations" humans are prone to, the idea of justice "can never be taken for a natural principle, capable of inspiring men with an equitable conduct towards each other." Humean justice, and the civil government whose primary raison d'etre is the administration of it, arises to combat the "instability of possessions" characteristic of our uncultivated state and is largely a matter of the enforcement of property rights and the performance of promises. Offenses against one's person, the restraint of antisocial impulses—in short, anything beyond transactional wrongs—fall outside its purview.[21]

Hume's claims about the partiality of sympathy are fairly straightforward, and Rorty adopts similar views when he argues that we are most likely to help those whom we consider "one of us." Like Hume, who argues that the imagination "is more affected by what is particular, than by what is general," Rorty makes the imagination central and stresses the importance of "detailed descriptions" of the lives of others as most likely to generate imaginative identification.[22] In the chapter on solidarity in *Contingency*, he argues that "our sense of solidarity is strongest when those with whom solidarity is expressed are thought of as 'one of us,' where 'us' means something smaller and more local than the human race." The force of "us," he claims, recognizing a contemporary insight about identity formation, is "contrastive in the sense that it contrasts with a 'they' which is also made up of human beings—the wrong sort of human beings." This is his explanation of why Danes and Italians were more likely to provide a safe harbor for Jews fleeing Nazi persecution than Belgians: they used "more parochial terms" to provide a basis for their identification with Jews—"a fellow Milanese, a fellow Jutlander, a fellow bocce player" (CIS, 190–91).

More recently, however, Rorty has begun to argue that "loyalty," another variant of imaginative identification, though admittedly most powerful when narrow in purview, can be extended virtually limitlessly to cover distant others—for example, Third World victims of globalization. In this way, loyalty can assume the universal coverage reserved for Kantian justice. The latter notion, whose universality was posited largely on the basis of now untenable philosophical abstractions like "universal validity" and "Reason," can be reformulated or even replaced with the idea of a "larger loyalty" brought about through a progress of sentiments. As for the problem that every invocation of "us" entails a contrasting "they"—that identity needs difference, as it is often put—Rorty now simply requests, without further explication, that people "define their identity in nonexclusionary terms" (TP, 179).

Any sense of the limits of sympathy has thus evaporated. Through the Humean notion of a progress of sentiments, sympathetic concern can now be limitlessly extended. For Hume, the progress of sentiments refers to the road from the "rude and more *natural* condition" of our uncultivated sense of morality to the more "enlarged" moral sensibility informed by a sense of the "public interest" which is the inevitable consequence of a "civilized" collective existence,[23] or, as Baier puts it, the progress from solitary reason to sociable passions.[24] While the former is "founded on the nature of our passions, and gives the preference to ourselves and friends, above strangers," the more "cultivated" social state is achieved via the voluntary subjection to convention or artifice, the influence of "education and acquired habits," and the important lessons of experience.[25]

This is the most sympathetic reading of what Rorty is up to in broadening our capacity for loyalty: "extending the natural sentiments beyond their original bounds." In an interesting passage, Hume says of this progress, "'Tis certain, that it is here forwarded by the artifice of politicians, who, in order to govern men more easily, and preserve peace in human society, have endeavor'd to produce an esteem for justice, and an abhorrence of injustice."[26] If we expand "politicians" widely enough to include philosophers and political theorists, this provides a good description of Rorty's project of sentimental education: cultivating an "abhorrence of injustice" through the gradual enlargement of our "affections" (Hume) for others. After all, the liberal aversion to cruelty and suffering has long been the hallmark of Rorty's political *Weltanschauung*.[27]

THE CORRECTION OF SENTIMENT

So how, then, does Hume propose that the partiality of sympathy be corrected? The new wrinkle in Hume's "science" of human nature that emerges in part 3 of book 3 of the *Treatise* is that the human condition is one of "continual fluctuation. . . . In general, all sentiments of blame or praise are variable," he argues, "according to our situation of nearness or remoteness, with regard to the person blam'd or prais'd, and according to the present disposition of our mind." To correct this inherent bias and to "prevent those continual contradictions," Hume proposes a method of arriving at "a more *stable* judgment of things" by fixing on "some *steady* and *general* points of view." Through what he calls the sentiment or principle of "humanity"—namely, "some general inalterable standard . . . which may not admit of so great a variation," we are able to correct the inherent biases in our capacity for sympathy and thereby extend its domain.[28]

But there is a catch: sympathy may indeed be extended to distant others, but only via a reflective process of correction that weakens its force. As we have seen, for Hume, "Sympathy with persons remote from us is much fainter than our concern for ourselves, and a sympathy with persons remote from us much fainter than that with persons near and contiguous." The key point that now emerges is that our greatest neglect of these differences occurs "in our calm judgments concerning the characters of men." The reference to "calm judgments" reminds us that the moral sentiment, as a "calm" passion, is reflective: even though sympathy is "proportionately weaker" and our praise or blame "fainter and more doubtful" when their objects are more remote, by "correcting the appearance by reflexion, we arrive at a more constant and establish'd judgment concerning them."[29]

Hume illustrates how through reflection we can enlarge and correct our selfish passions through the example of "a rude, untaught savage" who is driven by "ideas of private utility and injury" and has "but faint conceptions of a general rule of behavior." If this man of uncultivated nature were to find himself face to face with a battlefield foe—an appropriate symbol for any kind of difference or Other—Hume explains that the attitude of the "savage" toward his opponent would be one of unmitigated hate, which would continue beyond their present context "for ever after." Not even the "most extreme punishment and vengeance" will exhaust this animus. By contrast, "we, accustomed to society, and to more enlarged reflections" consider our battle opponent in a different light: "that this man is serving his own country and community; that any man, in the same situation, would do the same; that we ourselves, in like circumstances, observe a like conduct; that, in general, human society is best supported on such maxims." By paying "this homage to general rules," we are able to correct our "ruder and narrower passions" and thereby avoid "imputing malice or injustice to [our adversary], in order to give vent to those passions, which arise from self-love and private interest."[30]

Hume goes on to tie the narrowness of the uncultivated man's perspective to a "heart full of rage"—this is what necessitates the "calmness" of reflection. Moving from the variable level of particularity to the more stable social and universal sentiment of humanity has the effect of mitigating the force of moral passion, thereby curtailing its power to motivate action. What is significant about these "general notions" is that "the *heart* does not always take part" in them. As Baier puts it, Hume's version of the moral sentiment is "derived from a sentiment so calm, so different from 'the heart's' more fiery passions" that it is ultimately quite limited in its "dependably action-producing power."[31] The passage where Hume states that "tho' the *heart* does not always take part with those general notions" ends with the qualification, "yet they are sufficient for discourse, and serve all our purposes in company, in the pulpit, on the theatre, and in the schools." Baier interprets this to mean that the actions "most dependably" produced by the moral passions amount to "expressive acts occurring in evaluative discourse"—namely, those which take place in the pulpit, in universities, and in morally instructive plays.[32] This is consistent with other statements by Hume in the *Treatise* that our sense of justice and injustice "arises artificially, tho' necessarily, from education, and human conventions" and elsewhere that morals are "the object of the most ordinary education."[33] This of course now sounds a lot like Rorty's sentimental education. However, does it remain as attractive a project if its ability to cultivate widespread sympathy comes at the cost of being unable to effectively spur action?

This problem of the limits of sympathy leads to a double bind for accounts like Rorty's which rely on its extension for a politics of remedying injustice. If left uncorrected, our capacity for sympathy, though powerful, will remain partial to those closest to us, and apply largely to those most like us, either by resemblance or relation. To extend sympathy farther, it must be corrected through reflection and the adoption of a common viewpoint of humanity. But in moving from the particular to the general level to correct its biases, the moral sentiment loses its ability to "produce or prevent actions."

Rorty's appeal to the correction of sympathy required to extend its purview runs into trouble on two counts: first, it loses its ability to generate action, and second, it must assume a degree of intersubjective agreement or consensus that is at odds with Rorty's pragmatist assumptions. That is to say, there is an enormous amount of interdependence of human sentiments assumed by Hume, and his account makes universal agreement on matters of moral sentiment a foregone conclusion.[34] It is not so much that Hume posits this sociability as an innate human quality—it is as a result of "common experience" that the solitary man is led to a communion with others—but that it is so "necessary" and "inevitable" that it might as well be.[35] This is a problem, since Rorty, in his criticisms of Habermas and elsewhere, has repudiated the assumption that human discourse is automatically convergent. Serving as a guarantee of the "rationality" of such discourse, the assumption of such an ideal endpoint of communication merely ushers a kind of de facto universalism in through the back door to secure an ahistorical grounding for our beliefs. Instead, Rorty counsels that we cultivate "an increasing willingness to live with plurality and stop asking for universal validity," and that we rest content with the "merely poetic foundations of the 'we-consciousness' which lies behind our social institutions" (CIS, 67–68).[36]

Hume, for his part, is able to get out from under this bind for two reasons: first, at the end of the day, he accepts a de facto essentialism about human nature which on some level locates a concern for others embedded inside all of us (whether it is put there by nature or customs and education, we all have it), and second, because, like fellow Scotsman Frances Hutcheson, and to a certain extent Adam Smith, Hume is more interested in moral judgment than moral action and ultimately is willing to compromise the latter. Rorty, by contrast, has neither of these two avenues open to him. His antiessentialism and contingent view of human nature close off the first route, and since his notion of sentimental education is part of a transformative political project, he cannot compromise the crucial link to action by making sentimental education into a merely literary exercise. Even if Hume's sentiment of humanity does not rise to the level of a full-blown transcendental principle like a Kantian standpoint of Reason, on its most sympathetic interpretation it still resembles the intersubjective agreement presupposed by Habermas's ideal speech situation.

IDENTITY, BLINDNESS, AND REALITY

Even if sympathy can be stretched beyond its natural partiality, sympathy, imaginative identification, and a progress of sentiments all aim at something that exists solely along the plane of feeling. While emotions and feelings certainly have a role to play here, contra rationalist or Kantian accounts of morality, Rorty's argument and others like it are vulnerable to William James's critique of participation in emotional states of fellow feeling that result in no concrete acts. Here James is worth quoting at length:

> There is no more contemptible type of human character than that of the nerveless sentimentalist and dreamer, who spends his life in a weltering sea of sensibility and emotion, but who never does a manly concrete deed. Rousseau, inflaming all the mothers of France, by his eloquence, to follow Nature and nurse their babies themselves, while he sends his own children to the foundling hospital, is the classical example of what I mean. . . . The habit of excessive novel-reading and theatre-going will produce true monsters in this line. The weeping of a Russian lady over the fictitious personages in the play, while her coachman is freezing to death on his seat outside, is the sort of thing that everywhere happens on a less glaring scale . . . . The remedy would be, never to suffer one's self to have an emotion at a concert, without expressing it afterward in *some* active way. Let the expression be the least thing in the world—speaking genially to one's aunt, or giving up one's seat in a horse-car, if nothing more heroic offers—but let it not fail to take place.[37]

This wonderful passage requires little commentary. In it James underscores the importance of connecting states of feeling with habits of action, a point we will take up in a moment. But it also suggests the line of argument I want to advance: namely, that spurring us to act is less a matter of seeing others as "one of us" than of recognizing the reality of their suffering. In other words, is the category of identity the best way to remedy James's Russian lady's blindness toward her coachman's suffering?

In a rather curious and ironic way, since Rorty has always been rather dismissive of identity politics, identity now occupies a place at the center of his meliorative project.[38] Sounding a bit like one of the contemporary theorists of identity/difference, Rorty argues that the problem is that the identity of the architects of cruelty—the "thugs"—is "bound up with their sense of who they are *not . . . not* an infidel, *not* a queer, *not* a woman, *not* an untouchable." The reason why attacking these responses with a rational arsenal fails is because they are not merely rhetorical, nor irrational; they are "heartfelt" (TP, 178), hence the project of sentimental education and Rorty's turn to Hume and away from Kant.[39] At the very least, we must recognize that identities are not static entities or neutral categories; as Rorty's own account of the narrative structure of identity makes clear, the constitution of identities occurs within the space of politics, they are not fixed but alterable, and they have implications which bear directly on political projects.

For a politics of sentiment to be effective, then, it must do more than merely extend the moral identities of "the rich and lucky billion," as Rorty calls us; it must transform them as well. To the extent that the expansion of sympathetic concern for distant and different others merely reaffirms the existing identities of the fortunate in the North Atlantic democracies, it remains a severely limited endeavor.[40] Rorty introduces a rather odd limitation on any meliorative political project by requiring that "the rich will still be able to recognize themselves" in the denouement, assuming not only that people wish to remain in their current identities, but that it is indeed desirable that they do so.[41]

This unwillingness to challenge the existing identity of the denizens of advanced capitalist democracies strikes me as one of the more problematic aspects of Rorty's thought. Rather than debate the possibilities of a nonexclusionary identity, however, I want to take a different tack here. My contention is that there is a better way to theorize the politics of sentiment than via the concept of identity. Rather than an ability to see distant others as "one of us" as the operative element in making us more likely to come to their assistance, my suggestion is that an ability to grant full reality to their suffering is the more powerful force and a better ground on which to build a politics of sentiment. Moreover, I argue that there is support for this view in Hume.

As the salient factor in social prejudice or hatred, Rorty identifies the human propensity to draw the circle of those to whom you are most loyal, of one's moral community, too narrowly. Those who fall outside this sphere obtain a depreciated status, often as subhuman, as Rorty points out in his example of "the gallant and honorable Serb who sees Muslims as circumcised dogs" (TP, 177). While I do not doubt that this is a good description of what goes on in situations of ethnic hatred and that the logic of identity formation and the creation of a subhuman category of otherness is a central force here, my point is that if our concern is what motivates people to act to end the suffering of others, perceiving the reality of their suffering is a more potent compulsion, and one more readily achievable, than coming to see them as "one of us."[42]

To a certain extent, these notions are not unrelated: coming to see another as fully human may certainly entail granting full reality to their suffering. And both involve operations of the imagination to some degree. Nevertheless, the difference in emphasis does have significant implications. For example, on my view, the impact of Stowe's *Uncle Tom's Cabin* from the perspective of a politics of sentiment was not so much that it persuaded white Americans to see blacks as "one of us," as Rorty argues—after all, given the prevalence of segregation well into the 1950s, not to mention more subtle forms of racism, it could be argued that another century was required for this identification to occur in any widespread sense—but rather that it brought home the reality of the unspeakable suffering of life under a system where, among other inhuman cruelties, children were torn from the arms of their mothers to meet the demands of a coldhearted marketplace (TP, 181). This is something, I believe, that novels are indeed good at. To ask that novel reading help achieve a moral community, however, is to make a demand of a much higher order.

Rather than seeing instances of cruelty as a failure of sympathy or of our capacity for imaginative identification, the view I am proposing identifies as the main factor a kind of moral blindness. Drawing on James's famous essay on the subject, George Kateb interprets this blindness in terms of James's contention that "almost no one grants reality to others." Suggesting that "the feeling for the human reality of others" marks a use of the imagination distinct from the cultivation of the moral imagination or "sympathetic identification" of placing oneself in the shoes of the other and generating empathy through an operation of the imagination depicted by thinkers like Rousseau, Smith, Hume, and Rorty, Kateb theorizes a new dimension of moral blindness. An important facet of moral blindness is the opposing operation of "refus[ing] to allow the present to be present." Kateb's point here is that blindness to the reality of another's feelings is not a case of an absence or a failure of the imagination, but actually an active use of it, where the other's reality is blocked from our vision. This blindness seems to provide a better account of the Russian lady's treatment toward her coachman in the Jamesian passage quoted above and of the failure of a majority of Americans to be affected by the prosaic but real suffering of the poor and underprivileged in their own backyard. Kateb also illustrates how the group feeling associated with "the self-incorporation of the I into a We," a process which involves both using the imagination and refusing to use it, can be a barrier to perceiving these others to be as real to themselves as we are to ourselves.[43]

The power of "reality" to move us to action finds support in Hume's thought as well. Hume draws a distinction between the "seeming tendencies" of objects that affect the mind and that which proceeds from the "real consequences" of objects.[44] He suggests that the strongest impulses to action come neither from sympathy, nor from the imaginative ability to share the suffering of others, nor from the reflective correction of sympathy. Instead, the most potent spur to action and acute activation of the moral passions arises from experiencing the "reality" of the suffering of others. As he put it in the *Enquiry Concerning the Principles of Morals*, "Wherever reality is found, our minds are disposed to be strongly affected by it" (223).

Hume illustrates the power of reality through the example of a man "now in safety at land" receiving pleasure from the thought of "the miserable condition of those at sea on a storm." Here he is explicating what he calls "the principle of comparison": because "we judge of objects more from comparison than from their real intrinsic merit," it follows that "according as we observe a greater or less share of happiness or misery in others, we must make an estimate of our own, and feel a consequent pain or pleasure." Thus, "the misery of another gives us a more lively idea of our happiness, and his happiness of our misery."[45]

However powerful the principle of comparison is, it will never, says Hume, "have an equal efficacy, as if I were really on the shore, and saw a ship at a distance tost by a tempest, and in danger every moment of perishing on a rock or sand-bank." In this latter case, the liveliness of the idea will ensure a sympathetic rather than comparative reaction. Making his example even more "lively," Hume then notes that if the ship were in fact close enough that the man could "perceive distinctly the horror, painted on the countenance of the seamen and passengers, hear their lamentable cries, see the dearest friends give their last adieu, or embrace with a resolution to perish in each other's arms: No man has so savage a heart as to reap any pleasure from such a spectacle, or withstand the motions of the tenderest compassion and sympathy."[46] Rather than sympathy or an imaginative identification with the shipwrecked crew as "one of us," then, the operative force in Hume's example is a perception of the inescapable reality of their suffering.

If an experience of the reality of another's suffering is the best goad to action, the implication is that the most effective program for igniting the will to improve their condition would be to physically experience their life and their suffering firsthand. But this is a rather impractical solution for the case of distant others. Hume suggests an alternate method. The "liveliness" or "vivacity" of an idea for Hume is the determining factor of the force with which it acts upon our mind. However, in his final account, this is not something our imagination is capable of generating on its own. In his work on morals, Hume suggested that it is "the business of poetry" to accomplish this task, "to bring every affection near to us by lively imagery and representation." He then added the reason why: poetry can make every affection "look like truth and reality."[47]

CONCLUSION

Rorty's turn to sentiment in his recent work has coincided with an effort to assume the mantle of the transformative projects of Emerson and Dewey. Portraying the consequences of his pragmatism as the advent of a greater plurality and openness to change, he now sees himself as continuing what Cornel West has called "the Deweyan project of an Emersonian culture of radical democracy."[48] There is a line of thought running from Emerson's "The Poet" through Whitman and James to Dewey's *Art Experience* that echoes Hume's notion of making reality more "lively" through the aesthetic enhancement provided by poets and novelists so that it will leave a deeper and more transformative impression on us. Once thus inspired, we may then return to that reality and remake it. There are occasional moments where Rorty appears to want to extend this line of thought, like his invocation of a Whitmanesque "poetic agon" in which "jarring dialectical discords would be resolved in previously unheard harmonies," and where he sounds an Emersonian call for a "new culture" (AOC, 24–25).[49]

However, if we accept that the reality of another's suffering is a more powerful force than a shared moral identity with the sufferer, given Rorty's rather stringent antirealism, there seems little room for such a notion in his account. Those familiar with Rorty's thought know that "reality" occupies a rather consistent place on the side of the metaphysical, "Philosophical" with a capital p, views he seeks to jettison. Yet at the same time, his turn to the social realism of the novels of Dickens and Stowe and the "detailed descriptions" provided by journalists as the primary vehicles of moral reflection and sentimental education, primarily because of their ability to depict the suffering of others, suggests that accounts of "reality," for lack of a better term, do in fact have a role to play here.

Some of this inconsistency may be attributable to Rorty's familiar proclivity of letting his antimetaphysical fervor get the better of him; that is, there may be room within his pragmatist assumptions to reject the idea that there is any true or ultimate reality out there and still recognize that particular versions of reality have a certain power over us and function politically.[50] Perhaps the tension in his thought can be alleviated somewhat by saying that it is not the accuracy of these accounts that matters but their "vivacity," to use Hume's term, their ability to affect us in some deep and penetrating way that activates our sentiments such that inaction or indifference becomes impossible. Still, while this may help to surmount some of the obstacles in Rorty's thought, it does not get around James's critique of feckless states of fellow feeling. Even if we accept that granting full reality to the suffering of others is more conducive to generating action than a species of identification which exists solely along the place of feeling, this does not obviate the need to cultivate habits of action.

The best account of habits and their relation to democratic practice is probably Dewey's *Human Nature and Conduct*. When juxtaposed to Rorty's, it provides a striking contrast.[51] By making moral sentiment a matter of a shared identity premised on widely accepted and unchallenged conventions, Rorty appears to follow Hume in viewing custom as "the great guide of human life."[52] Like Hume, he provides few resources for critical reflection on customs, authoring a program for the accommodation of individuals to a common standpoint that smacks of social conformity and a neglect of the plurality of human perspectives. Dewey, by contrast, set his entire philosophical and political project at odds with the uncritical acceptance of customs, which he saw as the predominant habits of a society. The commonality required by Rorty's shared moral identity, even if contingent and historicist, leaves little room for subsequent critical reflection on the customs, traditions, and institutions that form the background assumptions of Rorty's liberalism.[53]

The exclusionary effects of the constitution of a common moral identity make it a poor foundation for generating sympathetic concern for others. The inherent partiality of sympathy dooms any attempt to extend such concern to different and distant others from the start. Through an act of the imagination, the suffering of distant others can be made as real as one's own, and the threat of moral blindness can be mitigated without the undesirable (and unrealizable) requirement that we identify with everyone whose suffering we seek to diminish as "one of us." Here the role of novelists and poets resides in rendering the reality of another's suffering more "lively" rather than forging a singular moral identity. Finally, any form of felt concern for others not tied to habits of action threatens to become a hollow invocation of the spirit of social justice that provokes no real change. With less emphasis on a shared identity and more on reality and concrete practices, Rorty's politics of sentiment will better achieve its goal of moving society toward greater justice; as it now stands, his project will fall short of its aims, but, as I hope I have suggested, perhaps not irretrievably so.

NOTES

1. See Martha Nussbaum, *Poetic Justice: The Literary Imagination and Public Life* (Boston: Beacon Press, 1995).

2. Richard Rorty, "Who Are We? Moral Universalism and Economic Triage," *Diogenes* 173 (Spring 1996): 13.

3. See David Hume, *A Treatise of Human Nature*, ed. L. A. Selby-Bigge and P. H. Nidditch (Oxford: Clarendon Press, 1978), 581–82; Adam Smith, *The Theory of Moral Sentiments*, ed. D. D. Raphael and A. L. MacFie (Indianapolis, IN: Liberty Fund, 1984), 136–37; Jean-Jacques Rousseau, "Discourse on the Origin and Foundations of Inequality," in *The First and Second Discourses*, trans. Roger D. Masters and Judith R. Masters (New York: St. Martin's Press, 1964), pt. 1; and *Emile, or On Education*, trans. Allan Bloom (New York: Basic Books, 1979), pt. 4.

4. Annette Baier posits that it is not until John Stuart Mill that philosophers writing on ethics drop the supposition of a moral consensus and begin from the presumption of "a plurality of conflicting moral outlooks." See her *Postures of the Mind: Essays on Mind and Morals* (Minneapolis: University of Minneapolis Press, 1985), 228–29.

5. For one of the better critiques of liberalism in general on this point, see Sheldon Wolin, *Politics and Vision: Continuity and Innovation in Western Political Thought* (Boston: Little, Brown & Co., 1960), 331–51 and chap. 9, passim.

6. On this point, I draw on George Kateb, "The Adequacy of the Canon," *Political Theory* 30, no. 4 (2002): 482–505.

7. See Rorty, "Who Are We?"; and "Justice as a Larger Loyalty," in *Cosmopolitics*, ed. Pheng Cheah and Bruce Robbins (Minneapolis: University of Minnesota Press, 1998), 45–58.

8. See Baier, *Postures of Mind* and *A Progress of Sentiments: Reflections on Hume's Treatise* (Cambridge, MA: Harvard University Press, 1991).

9. Rorty makes this claim in several places. See, for example, "Thugs and Theorists: A Reply to Bernstein," *Political Theory* 15, no. 4 (1987): 579n26; and "Heidegger, Kundera, and Dickens," in EHO, 68, 80, passim. This essay is one of the best sources for Rorty's case for the value of novels to a democracy. This is in part because the novel, as the province of "narrative, detail, and diversity," is more suited than philosophy, given the latter's taste for "theory, abstraction, and essence," to portraying the lives of others in vibrant detail, but also because novels give us "an ability to identify imaginatively" with those distant others, and they help foster the kind of "comfortable togetherness" fitted to a politics driven by "sentimental calls for alleviation of suffering" (EHO, 81).

10. See William James, "Philosophical Conceptions and Practical Results," in *The Writings of William James*, ed. John J. McDermott (Chicago: University of Chicago Press, 1977), 360–62. For Rorty's remarks, see for instance CP, xxxii; EHO, 143–48; and PSH, 67, 153. In PMN, Rorty makes numerous passing references to Hume, the most germane being a reference to his appreciation of "the unimportance of epistemology and the importance of sentiment," but little else in the way of substantive comment (140n). Rorty's explicit turn to sentiment dates to the early 1990s and the essays collected in the third volume of his philosophical papers (TP).

11. See Rorty, "Thugs and Theorists," 578n24.

12. Baier, *Postures of Mind*, 230–31.

13. The more immediate influence on Rorty's conception of morality as a matter of "we-intentions" is Wilfrid Sellars. See CIS, 59–65, 190–98.

14. Hume, *Treatise*, 574.

15. Hume, *Enquiries: Concerning Human Understanding and Concerning the Principles of Morals*, ed. L. A. Selby-Bigge and P. H. Nidditch (Oxford: Clarendon Press, 1975), 294.

16. William James, "On a Certain Blindness in Human Beings," *The Writings of William James*, 629.

17. Hume, *Treatise*, 316–17, 318, 352, 354, 575–76.

18. While Hume is occasionally given to statements like, "There is some benevolence, however small, infused into our bosom; some spark of friendship for human kind; some particle of the dove kneaded into our frame, along with the wolf and serpent," he repeatedly stresses the influence of "custom and habit" and the influence of "education and acquired habits," in *Enquiries*, 271, 202–3. He does have something of a preoccupation with calling things "natural," but this seems to be a semantic quirk, which he addresses explicitly: while he employs *natural* in certain places as opposed to *artificial* or the product of artifice, he also retains a usage of *natural* as that which is "inseparable from the species," in *Treatise*, 485. Much of this may be rooted in his view that human beings, while not innately social in any essentialist sense, could not flourish or even survive in the absence of some social interconnection with others. Cf. also, *Enquiries*, 275.

19. Hume, *Treatise*, 470; *Enquiries*, 289; *Treatise*, 581–82. See also Baier, *Postures of Mind*, 159.

20. Hume, *Treatise*, 489.

21. Hume, *Treatise*, 483, 488. As Baier points out, unlike Locke, Hume does not include one's body within one's property. See her discussion of Humean justice, *A Progress of Sentiments*, chap. 10.

22. Hume, *Treatise*, 580.

23. Hume's arguments here, reworked and revised from the *Treatise* to the *Enquiries*, and through several editions of his *Essays*, are complex, changing, and frustratingly contradictory. His understanding of the progress of sentiments seems by turns to be that of a pragmatist, a utilitarian, and an empiricist, at times taking on a hue of Lockean convenience, at others, one of Hegelian inevitability. Hume's terminological idiosyncrasies do not help matters; it is not uncommon to encounter references to this progress variously as a matter of "early education in society" and

"experience" adjacent to descriptions of it as "natural" and "necessary." My sense is that part of the confusion traces to Hume's account of the progress of sentiments as both a onetime civilizing process which occurs in the transition from the "rude, untaught savage" to men "accustomed to society," and an ongoing process of reflection aimed at a more humane world. Baier nicely captures the spirit of the latter sense with the term "civilizing practices" in an essay by that title in *Postures of the Mind*. Perhaps it is in the nature of Hume's thought—his "protopragmatism"—that matters of moral philosophy sometimes merge with matters of political theory or justice.

24. Baier's ingenious reading of Hume's *Treatise* holds that the work's development actually "stages a thinker's dramatic development from inadequate and doubt-inviting approaches to more satisfactory reflections." Here the progress Hume himself exemplifies in the famous conclusion to book 1 becomes representative of this progress more generally. The moral of the story, as Baier tells it, is that "*all* our interpretations will 'loosen and fall of themselves' until they become cooperative and mutually corrective," in *A Progress of Sentiments*, 142, vii–ix. See esp. chap. 1.

25. Hume, *Treatise*, 483–500.

26. Hume, *Treatise*, 500.

27. Rorty cites his definition of *liberal*, which he borrows from Judith Shklar: "liberals are the people who think that cruelty is the worst thing we do" (CIS, xv).

28. Hume, *Treatise*, 581–82.

29. Hume, *Treatise*, 583, 603.

30. Hume, *Enquiries*, 274n. This is a telling passage, with manifold implications. The idea of "enlarged reflections" seems to suggest a kind of Nietzschean perspectivism, seeing a situation from multiple angles. But there is only one perspective operative here, that of the sentiment of humanity. Despite the passing reference to rules, it should be pointed out that the notion of moral rules or Kantian obligation is quite foreign to Hume's thought. Rather than any kind of transcendent law, these principles represent "the party of humankind" (275).

31. Hume, *Treatise*, 603; Baier, *A Progress of Sentiments*, 184. This interpretation goes against the grain of many of Hume's more famous claims that "morals excite passions, and produce or prevent actions," in *Treatise*, 457. Baier accounts for this with the explanation that in the earlier sections Hume is "appealing to the rationalist moralists' own presuppositions, and trying to reduce their positions *ad absurdum*, just as he did in Part IV of Book I." See *A Progress of Sentiments*, 184–86, 174–97, passim.

32. Hume, *Treatise*, 603; Baier, *A Progress of Sentiments*, 183–84.

33. Hume, *Treatise*, 483; Baier, *Postures of Mind*, 132. As we pointed out above, Hume's conception of justice is relatively weak, concerned only with restraining the "love of gain" and securing a "stability of possessions," making no reference to wrongs against persons. See Baier, *A Progress of Sentiments*, chap. 10.

34. Baier, *Postures of Mind*, 163–65.

35. Hume, *Treatise*, 332, 363.

36. The main difference between Rorty and Habermas on this count is that while Rorty does assume a kind of fixed "background" of "shared descriptions, assumptions, and hopes," this is a fluid notion, with no preestablished harmony or ideal end—that is, a "true" or "genuine" consensus—presupposed (EHO, 164–76).

37. William James, *The Principles of Psychology*, vol. 1 (New York: Dover Publications, 1950), 125–26.

38. See, for example, his criticisms of identity politics in "A Cultural Left" (AOC, 73–107).

39. Cf.: "Identity categories are never merely descriptive, but always normative, and as such, exclusionary," in Judith Butler, "Contingent Foundations: Feminism and the Question of 'Postmodernism,'" in *Feminists Theorize the Political*, ed. Judith Butler and Joan W. Scott (New York: Routledge, 1992), 16. William Connolly puts it this way, "If difference requires identity and identity requires difference, then politics, in some sense of that protean word, pervades social life." Attempts to protect the purity of an identity are what lead to "the constitution of an other against which that identity may define itself." Although "identity requires difference in order to be," Connolly seems to suggest that not all identities need "to convert difference into otherness." See William Connolly, *Identity/Difference: Democratic Negotiations of Political Paradox* (Ithaca, NY: Cornell University Press, 1991), ix–x, 64–65, passim.

40. On this point, see Bruce Robbins, "Sad Stories in the International Public Sphere: Richard Rorty on Culture and Human Rights," *Public Culture* 9 (1997): 221–22.

41. Rorty, "Justice as a Larger Loyalty," 51.

42. Nussbaum makes the point, "We have compassion for nonhuman animals, without basing it on any imagined similarity." She adds, "Although of course we need somehow to make sense of the predicament as serious and bad." See Martha Nussbaum, "Compassion and Terror," *Daedalus*, Winter 2003, 15. I argue that imagining the suffering of others to be as real as one's own suffices for the latter.

43. Kateb, "The Adequacy of the Canon," 496–97.

44. Hume, *Treatise*, 586.

45. Hume, *Treatise*, 291, 375. This inherent threat to sympathy from comparison was more keenly perceived by the eighteenth-century authors of this perspective than by its contemporary devotees, like Rorty and Nussbaum. However, in a recent article, Nussbaum provides a more nuanced conception of the concept of sympathy or "compassion," identifying four problems that work against compassion: a judgment of the seriousness of their situation, a judgment of nondesert of their plight, a judgment of similar possibilities, and what she calls a eudaimonistic judgment. See Nussbaum, "Compassion and Terror." While comparison, which is most powerful when its objects are close to us, seems less of an issue for Rorty's attempt to extend sympathy toward distant others, I believe it represents a more widespread negative force than either Hume or Baier allows, particularly in an egalitarian society, where the kinds of hierarchies which create distance between individuals are absent. To the extent that comparison is most active amongst those nearest and most alike one another, it could quite possibly become the source of the kind of seething but concealed resentment between fellow citizens that manifests itself in the frightening ways Arthur Miller portrayed in *The Crucible*. But that is another topic.

46. Hume, *Treatise*, 594.

47. Hume, *Enquiries*, 222–23.

48. Cornel West, *The American Evasion of Philosophy: A Genealogy of Pragmatism* (Madison: University of Wisconsin Press, 1989), 128. See Rorty's "Pragmatism, Pluralism, and Postmodernism" for this argument (PSH, 262–77). Rorty's own phrase for his project is "Emersonian self-creation on a communal scale" (PSH, 34).

49. On the "aesthetics of communication" common to Whitman and James, see Raphael C. Allison, "Walt Whitman, William James, and Pragmatist Aesthetics," *Walt Whitman Quarterly Review* 20, no. 1 (2002): 19–29.

50. The traditions of American pragmatism and analytic philosophy after the linguistic turn are increasingly at odds in Rorty's later work: in the more explicitly political recent writing, the insights of Sellars and Quine that fueled his influential critique of the Cartesian-Kantian foundationalism undermine the important emphasis on reality and experience endemic to the pragmatist tradition. Rorty's welcome leveling of epistemological privileges must not lead us to adopt the erroneous view that inequalities between different perspectives or knowledges—inequalities of power, not epistemology—are thus automatically leveled, too. The fact that certain viewpoints still have the power of the dominant behind them remains.

51. See John Dewey, *Human Nature and Conduct: An Introduction to Social Psychology* (1922; New York: The Modern Library, 1950). I have benefited from Robert Westbrook's lucid discussion of habit in his *John Dewey and American Democracy* (Ithaca, NY: Cornell University Press, 1991), 286–93. The following passage from Dewey encapsulates the difference between his approach and Rorty's: "We may desire abolition of war, industrial justice, greater equality of opportunity for all. But no amount of preaching good will or the golden rule or cultivation of sentiments of love and equity will accomplish the results. There must be change in objective arrangements and institutions. We must work on the environment not merely on the hearts of men," in *Human Nature and Conduct*, 21–22.

52. Hume, *Enquiries*, 44.

53. In fairness to Rorty, it should be pointed out that there is one passage where he does in fact suggest the necessity of yoking moral identification to action: "Moral identification is empty when it is no longer tied to habits of action." See "Who Are We?" 15. Cryptic, if suggestive, remarks of Rorty's, like, "James's claim that thinking is 'only there for behavior's sake' is his improved version of Hume's claim that 'reason is, and ought to be, the slave of the passions,'" are the closest we come to an account of habits of action (PSH, 153).

Chapter Five

Public Pragmatism
and Private Narcissism

At the present time, the frontier is moral, not physical. The period of free lands that seemed boundless in extent has vanished. Unused resources are now human rather than material. They are found in the waste of grown men and women who are without the chance to work, and in the young men and young women who find doors closed where there was once opportunity. The crisis that one hundred and fifty years ago called out social and political inventiveness is with us in a form which puts a heavier demand on human creativeness.

. . . We can escape from this external way of thinking only as we realize in thought and act that democracy is a *personal* way of individual life; that it signifies the possession and continual use of certain attitudes, forming personal character and determining desire and purpose in all the relations of life. Instead of thinking of our own dispositions and habits as accommodated to certain institutions we have to learn to think of the latter as expressions, projections and extensions of habitually dominant personal attitudes.

—John Dewey, "Creative Democracy"

One of democracy's greatest justifications, to paraphrase Walt Whitman, lies in its encouragement of individuality. Yet, as Whitman well knew, the functioning of democratic politics may neither enlist nor require the individual's highest energies. Embodying "the unyielding principle of the average," the temper of democratic public life more often threatens to crush individuality through the force of the "en masse." Protecting individual life, both from these collective pressures and from invasive governmental authority, has long recommended to liberals the need for a firm boundary between public and private.[1]

Despite its enduring commitment to the individual, however, liberalism is often criticized for producing flattened or "thin" selves, amenable to social control and unlikely to resist the dictates of the mob. Its loftiest ideal of individuality is impugned as little more than an unimpeded bearer of abstract rights and liberties. Typically, criticism of this kind emanates from communitarians who believe correcting liberal shortcomings requires anchoring the individual in the traditions and values of their communities. These solutions merely usher in a new set of dictates where the individual fares no better: moral and political projects grounded in a strong communal good have even less use for the creative energies of the individual.

In recent years, Rorty's emergent liberalism has suggested a way out of this democratic problematic. Premised on the priority of democracy over philosophy and on treating "the demands of self-creation and of human solidarity as equally valid," the promise of Rorty's political theory is a way of combining self-development with social justice that overcomes historic liberal shortcomings.[2] Taking cues from John Stuart Mill, Rorty argues that the highest goal of liberal societies should be to "optimize the balance between leaving people's private lives alone and preventing suffering." Liberal individuals, he holds, more provocatively, should divide themselves into "private self-creators" and "public liberals," ideally being in alternate moments "Nietzsche and J. S. Mill." Instituting a public-private divide along these lines will not only enrich liberal individuality, creating the space necessary for Nietzschean projects of becoming what one is, but at the same time will galvanize the public's resolve to diminish suffering (CIS, 63, 85).

In this chapter, I consider Rorty's liberalism and this bifurcated conception of the self. Assessing his views involves addressing fundamental issues about democratic self-realization: If democratic politics does not require fully developed selves, does a fully realized existence require participation in public life? What of the relation of individual flourishing to democratic politics? If one indeed affirms the value of demarcated public and private realms, does the individual need to be protected from the operations and effects of the public sphere, or is it the public sphere that needs protecting from effects of robust individuals? To put it in terms closer to the perspective of Mill, does genuine democracy require more than mere negative liberty?

The central aim of this chapter is twofold: first, to demonstrate that Rorty's severing of individual self-cultivation from the pursuit of social justice undermines his larger reformist project, but also to suggest how relaxing his strictures on these self-creative energies will reanimate the political goals of his pragmatism. I take greatest issue with Rorty's appropriation of Mill, whom he reads through Isaiah Berlin. Rather than suggesting that we "leave people's private lives alone," Mill viewed inner self-reform as a crucial concomitant to the reform of society and institutions. Indeed, this is the crucial insight that he derives from his youthful mental or psychological crisis—namely, that institutional reform pursued independently of self-cultivation and to the neglect of "the internal culture of the individual" and "the cultivation of the feelings" runs the risk of becoming a hollow invocation of ideals that results in indifference and stagnation, or worse, a paralyzing disenchantment.

The cultivation of character for Mill is also needed to remedy the lack of self-reliance that leads citizens to look to the majority rather than to forge their own views.[3] This is significant because Rorty has come to see the pragmatist rejection of representationalism and the move away from seeing human beings as answerable to either God, Truth, or Reality as a movement toward increasing self-reliance.[4] Yet while Mill, like other precursors of the pragmatist tradition including Emerson, Thoreau, and Whitman, offers a *public* defense of the private, where self-cultivation is understood as a means of strengthening the democratic public, Rorty defends his sharply delineated realms as a way of isolating individual creative energies from public life and the quest for justice.

As more than one critic has noted, Rorty's "firm distinction" between public and private seems to occupy a privileged, almost ahistorical status at odds with his antifoundationalist and contingent assumptions. Richard Bernstein has observed that this divide functions to insulate Rorty's liberal convictions from the ironical self-doubt he champions. Protecting these liberal values from questioning is essential for Rorty to defend the "fundamental premise" of his pragmatism, namely that "a belief can still regulate action, can still be thought worth dying for, among people who are quite aware that this belief is caused by nothing deeper than contingent historical circumstance" (CIS, 189). As Bernstein puts it, "Without this 'fundamental premise' his entire project falls apart."[5] The wall between public and private also serves to cordon off the transcendental or foundationalist "sources" used to justify our beliefs, which are not amenable to democratic debate and compromise, from our (contingent) beliefs themselves. Only in this way, Rorty argues, can we attain a detranscendentalized public sphere where nothing can trump the fruits of a democratic consensus, "where we no long worship *anything*, where we treat *nothing* as a quasi divinity, where we treat *everything*—our language, our conscience, our community—as a product of time and chance" (CIS, 22). The question is whether a public thus constituted will contain individuals who are indeed willing to die for their beliefs.

William James, whom it should be recalled dedicated his *Pragmatism* lectures to the memory of Mill, argued that our individual "temperament"—"our more or less dumb sense of what life honestly and deeply means"—plays a constitutive role in our beliefs and commitments, rather than the abstract principles or reasons we cite when we account for them.[6] Some cognate of this "temperament" or personal vision would seem necessary for Rorty to defend his "fundamental premise." Yet when he asserts that our final vocabularies "can be and should be split into a large private and a small public sectors, sectors which have no particular relation to one another," Rorty severs our public commitments from this Jamesian personal vision or "stream of experience" in which our convictions acquire their meaning and weight for us, and with it the only basis we have for being willing to die for our beliefs (CIS, 73, 100, 189).[7]

The notion of a public defense of privacy rests on an assumption about the relation between the internal culture of the individual and outside cultural forces, and a claim about the value of a certain kind of inner reform for political life. It comports rather well with a conception of intermittent citizenship understood as an episodic expression of democratic individuality. This is not the same thing as Rorty's divided self. It also differs from the participatory tradition of civic republicanism. My claim is not that democracy requires "the participation of all of the people in at least some aspects of self-government" or a firm boundary between public and private.[8] Nor is it that democratic politics *requires* publicly realized selves. What democracy does require, in my view, is something more than self-interest or an altruistic concern for others to adequately motivate the quest for social justice. Democracy need not fear individual creative energies; it may indeed even derive some benefit from them. That liberalism can be nudged out of its anxiety-rooted frame and be made to see individual creative energies as less of a threat to its coherence and continued existence, and to weave them into its underlying fabric, is the underlying hope of this chapter.[9]

At times, Rorty seems drawn toward such a view. For instance, in *Achieving Our Country*, he affirms the ideal of a "poetic agon, in which jarring dialectical discords would be resolved in previously unheard harmonies," and he invokes Whitman's vision of "a truly grand nationality" that would allow expression of "a large variety of character" and "full play for human nature to expand itself in numberless and even conflicting directions" (24). Yet more often, Rorty's privatization of our individual complexity tends to fetishize Mill's Humboldtian commitment to "the absolute and essential importance of human development in its richest diversity." In so doing, he elides the greatest insights of these thinkers—especially Whitman, who began his *Democratic Vistas* with a paean to Mill—about the value of such diversity of character in *public* and, as Mill put it, the importance of "social support for nonconformity" for the health of a democracy.[10]

THE RATIONALES FOR BOUNDED REALMS

The idea that human existence can be divided into distinct spheres of political and nonpolitical activity is as old as the ancient polis. In the two millennia since, the rationales and impulses behind such divisions have been many. Indeed, the tradition of political thought, as Sheldon Wolin and others have eloquently argued, has been in important measure an ongoing debate about what the political is and where the boundaries between the political and the nonpolitical lie. What must be recalled about these attempts to constitute the political is that, in all cases, they are substantive political interventions borne of particular interests and specific designs.[11]

As a way of clearing a path through the thicket of arguments surrounding the public-private issue, let us set out several broad types. For classical liberals, the idea of carving out a sphere of "private" activity was driven by a political logic: it was first and foremost a way of limiting the power of government. As such, its rationale was largely negative, but one nonetheless motivated by political concerns. One could therefore call it a *public* rationale for private life.[12] Here the distinction between public and private does not seek to protect a private realm of individual freedom from public intrusion, but merely to circumscribe the governmental realm as distinct from civil society. Private life is not simply the life of the individual, but life in civil society, including secondary associations and other "political" commitments. The central concern, then, is to limit government, not to assert a positive claim on behalf of the individual.

For the most part, these assumptions hold from Locke onward, until the first generation of "Romantic" liberals, including Wilhelm von Humboldt and Benjamin Constant, emerges in the late eighteenth century. Their resulting stress on individuality and concern for the inner life of the individual led to a shift in the meaning of public and private. For these later thinkers, the public-private boundary is justified as a way of securing a private, nonpolitical realm insulated not only from the encroachments of state authority but also from the social pressures of collective life. Recalling Humboldt's dictum about the supreme importance of "human development in its richest diversity," the arguments of these romantic liberals can be seen as a *private* rationale for private life.

What is common to both these visions is a rather paltry conception of political life and a surprising lack of interest in active citizens. Part of this is attributable to the general fear or distrust of democracy as "mob rule" that existed until the generation of Emerson, Thoreau, and Whitman. But it also relates to the implicitly antipolitical bent of liberal assumptions.[13] In demarcating the world into the dual realms of government and civil society, and by identifying the former with coercion and the latter with its absence, classical liberals, beginning with Locke, succeeded in creating what is largely a nonpolitical conception of society. As the development of liberal theory runs its course through the eighteenth century, absorbing the influences of David Hume and Adam Smith, the erosion of political space set in motion by Locke's articulation of the aim of government as the protection of property gains momentum. Economic pursuits come to displace political involvement as the primary feature of civil society, and the "public" rationale for privacy evolves into a defense of unfettered economic rather than political activity.

In a similar fashion, the romantic liberals' preoccupation with unfettered individual self-realization contributed to an understanding of the aim of government as providing a protective framework for the free pursuit of various nonpolitical activities. At its extreme, the valorization of individuality combined with an indifference, even distaste, toward democratic institutions, as it tended to for Humboldt, who believed a monarchical or aristocratic political system would better protect individual liberty than a democratic one. On his view, which was shared by others of his time, the cultivation of individuality is the highest end of human life. The "en masse" character, to use Whitman's phrase, of democratic life makes it a greater threat to the development of individuality or *Bildung* than more authoritarian political forms that could be counted on to leave the individual to her own devices, beyond a veneer of allegiance in public.[14]

In neither of these two rationales is the divide between public and private life invoked in the name of a fuller or more active politics. For such an understanding, we must look outside liberalism to the participatory tradition of civic republicanism. Hannah Arendt's stance toward the issue of distinct public and private realms provides a representative example.[15] Modeled on the ancient division between the polis and the *oikia*, or household, Arendt's view of public and private rests on a crucial circumscription of the prepolitical sphere of necessity, inequality, and domination. Only in this way can the political realm of freedom and genuine public citizenship—speech and action among true equals—be preserved.

The emergence in the seventeenth century with Locke of a third category, the "social" realm, from this vantage is the bane of politics, blurring as it does the clear delineation of spheres and thereby allowing the freedom and equality cultivated in public to be contaminated with baser material claims of want and need. Despite the attractiveness of this lofty conception of active participation among equals, as it is frequently pointed out, and as Arendt herself freely acknowledged, it is predicated upon the vigilant maintenance of the lower, private sphere and of the "gulf" which separates it from the political one, where the activities of the household—reproduction, labor, command-ing, and the mastering of necessity—could be carried out at a safe distance from affairs of the polis, even if this meant the continued presence of an over-whelming majority of society's members—the "unequals" (slaves, women, workers, etc.)—confined to a depreciated, private existence.[16]

BETWEEN POSITIVE AND NEGATIVE LIBERTY

None of the accounts we have considered thus far enacts the law of separate spheres in the name of expanding the political—at least none that are tenable from an egalitarian position. The question this raises is whether negative lib-erty suffices to found a genuinely democratic politics. The contrast between the degree of individual participation in public life required for politics in the liberal and republican theories is often portrayed as the difference between positive and negative conceptions of liberty. Rorty's own conception, mod-eled largely on the views of Mill and Isaiah Berlin, is decidedly negative and can be usefully contrasted with a positive conception like Dewey's (CIS, 45–46).[17] However, I want to argue that in his readings of these thinkers, Rorty doesn't tell the whole story; their arguments are more complex than a defense of negative liberty pure and simple.

Rorty's understanding of negative liberty rests on a view that he attributes to Berlin: namely that liberal societies need only create room for individual self-creation, not ensure its use (CIS, 63). All that liberal democratic politics requires, on Rorty's reading, vis-à-vis individual liberty, is simply to leave people alone, "to let them try out their private visions of perfection in peace," with the Millean proviso that they not encroach upon the liberties of others— in other words, to "equalize opportunities for self-creation and then leave people alone to use, or neglect, their opportunities" (ORT, 194; CIS, 85).

The indebtedness of the position Rorty develops in *Contingency, Irony, and Solidarity* to Berlin has gone largely unnoticed. In the final paragraph of his classic tract "Two Concepts of Liberty," Berlin concluded his essay with a quote from Joseph Schumpeter: "To realize the relative validity of one's convictions and yet stand for them unflinchingly, is what distinguishes a civ-ilized man from a barbarian."[18] Rorty seizes upon Schumpeter's affirmation of the "relative validity" of our convictions and marshals it against the strong philosophic claims to Truth that he rejects. More positively, this translates into Rorty's embrace of the "contingent" nature of our deepest beliefs and most cherished values that provides the cornerstone of his post-Philosophical liberal utopia. Echoing the sentiment of Schumpeter's passage, Rorty says that the "fundamental premise" of the stance articulated in *Contingency*, as we have seen, is that "a belief can still regulate action, can still be thought worth dying for, among people who are quite aware that this belief is caused by nothing deeper than contingent historical circumstance" (CIS, 189). Though I agree with Rorty that it can, the question I wish to pursue is whether beliefs can still regulate action if severed from what Mill called "character" or what James called our individual "temperament."

In "Two Concepts," Berlin set out the fundamental nature of negative freedom as "freedom from"—freedom from interference in making choices for oneself: "I am normally said to be free to the degree to which no man or body of men interferes with my activity. Political liberty in this sense is simply the area within which a man can act unobstructed by others."[19] What makes Berlin's account both noteworthy and provocative is his dogged defense of the idea that negative freedom is about the "opportunity for action" rather than action itself:

> If, although I enjoy the right to walk through open doors, I prefer not to do so, but to sit still and vegetate, I am not thereby rendered less free. Freedom is the opportunity to act, not action itself; the possibility of action, not necessarily the dynamic realization of it.[20]

For Berlin, ultimately, negative liberty entails the carving out and preservation of a "'negative' area in which man is not obliged to account for his activities to any man so far as this is compatible with the existence of organized society."[21] In sum, it is a defense of the right not to participate in public affairs.

Dewey's democratic ideal of individual self-realization through participation in public life provides a stark contrast to Berlin's defense of the right to "sit still and vegetate." Dewey's positive conception of liberty holds that "only . . . the man who is realizing his individuality is free in the positive sense of the word."[22] In the defense of positive liberty, one hears echoes of Rousseau's incongruous notion of forcing people to be free. Simply leaving individuals alone is not enough; for Dewey, this would constitute a dereliction of democracy. A toned-down version of Rousseau, Dewey's stance is that a democratic society must create conditions and encourage habits of action and mind that militate in favor of active self-realization through communal life. In keeping with his understanding of democracy as not merely a set of institutions and practices but a moral ideal—a "way of life"—whose values permeate the social environment of a democratic culture, the idea of cordoning off a private region insulated from these deep influences is foreign to Dewey's way of thinking. Though no less aware of the dangers of conformity and the threats to individuality in a democratic society than most liberals, the communitarian strand in Dewey's thought, influenced by a Tocquevillean belief in the power of secondary associations, pulls Dewey in another direction; he never wavered in his faith that the self-development of diverse individuals could be harmonized to further the good of the community as a whole.[23]

In reading Berlin's famous essay, one is struck by the fact that more space is devoted to critiquing positive liberty and offering a warning about the decidedly unfree impulses lurking behind its claims than to defending its negative cousin. Conceptions like Dewey's, which attempt to give content to individual freedom, Berlin argued, do so in the name of particular values valorized by that perspective. As such, these conceptions run the risk of becoming "no better than a specious disguise for brutal tyranny," actually constricting the space of liberty as they claim to defend it. By identifying a "higher" self, a type of character worthy of self-realization, be it more free, original, independent, nonconformist, or more in line with the common good, these accounts authorize coercion in the name of that goal. Here Berlin's villain is Rousseau. Writing against the kind of paternalism that identifies an aim that individuals may not see and that attempts to propel them toward it, Berlin held that such theories treat individuals as if they were not free to choose their own ends, and in fact, "deny their human essence." Programs such as Dewey's, which assume that an ideal, harmonious state of affairs is possible, will succeed only in trampling the liberties of individuals, and, in the worst case scenario, in paving the way to "an authoritarian state obedient to the directives of an *elite* of Platonic guardians."[24]

Following Berlin's reasoning, Rorty agrees that public attempts to mold or encourage individual self-realization will make a mockery of individual liberty. We will consider Rorty's position more fully in a moment, but his defense of a "firm distinction" between public and private rests on a defense of negative liberty attributed to Berlin, and to a certain extent, to Mill. Yet there is an important sense in which Rorty's defense of a private realm is *not* like Berlin's and Mill's; that is to say, Rorty's appeal to their thoughts on this subject rests on a misreading of the ultimate aim of their projects.

There are differences between the positions of Berlin and Mill, but, briefly stated, their advocacy of an inviolable realm of individual liberty amounts to a *public* defense of the private, asserted ultimately in the name of a more democratic, more pluralistic politics. Mill, in particular, was especially attuned to the problem of those who, because of "a low, abject, servile type of character . . . do not desire liberty, and would not avail themselves of it," a condition for which "social support for nonconformity" was required to correct in order to achieve a vibrant democracy.[25] By contrast, Rorty's rationale for detached spheres appears to be, like the romantic liberals, based on a private conception of human flourishing designed to create a space for the free expression of individual creative energies, not as a means of generating a more robust politics, but rather as a program for keeping public life free of them.

A careful reading of Berlin's original essay—and it appears there were not enough of these, since Berlin resorted to providing an unequivocal statement of this in his introduction to the anthology in which it has been immortalized—reveals that "Two Concepts of Liberty" was not meant to be a defense of negative liberty, at least not primarily so. As Berlin recounts in a footnote to his introduction, written eleven years after the original publication, his essay

> was widely taken as an unqualified defense of "negative" against "positive" liberty. This was not my intention. [It] was meant as a defense, indeed, but of a pluralism, based on the perception of incompatibility between the claims of equally ultimate ends, against any ruthless monism which solves such problems by eliminating all but one of the rival elements. . . . I am not offering a blank endorsement of the "negative" concept as opposed to its "positive" twin brother, since this would itself constitute precisely the kind of intolerant monism against which the entire argument is directed.[26]

Indeed, a rereading of the last few pages of the essay confirms this. Adopted as a "more humane ideal" is not just negative freedom pure and simple, but "pluralism, with the measure of 'negative' liberty that it entails." It is "truer" than "the ideal of 'positive' self-mastery by classes, or peoples, or the whole of mankind" because it recognizes the fact that "human goals are many, not all of them commensurable, and in perpetual rivalry with one another." Though indeed most of his essay is negative in stance—Berlin does not actually stipulate a positive vision of what his politics would look like concretely—it is all in the name of this one affirmation: an avowal of a pluralistic politics that does not attempt "to preserve our absolute categories or ideals at the expense of human lives." That is, it is a politics and social arrangement that respects, in a statement that became something of a signature for Berlin, the truth inherent in Kant's remark that "out of the crooked timber of humanity no straight thing was ever made."[27]

There are, then, two aspects of Berlin's ultimate stance: the defense of pluralism with regard to the ends of human life, and his repudiation of single, "true" solutions. Rorty embraces the latter but neglects the full implications of the former; that is, Rorty elides Berlin's crucial emphasis on the irreducible plurality of human ends. The public-private split allows Rorty to maintain a pluralism of individual ends in private while simultaneously authorizing a secure and unchallenged monopoly on liberal ends in public. But this seems to be the kind of "faith in a single criterion" and "single harmonious pattern" that Berlin's work militates against and precisely the "possible danger of the total triumph of any one principle" that he so forcefully repudiates.

RORTY'S POSITION

Although it appears to be a *public* rationale for privacy, since it is understood as protecting the public pursuit of justice from radically individualistic and unshareable sentiments, Rorty, unlike Mill, does not view these endeavors as having anything to offer democratic politics. On the contrary, Rorty's stance is driven by a negative rather than a positive logic. More of an anti-Philosophical, with a capital *p*, curb than the positive corollary of a political theory, it seems to be the result of a philosophical rather than a political dynamic in his thought.[28] If we understand individual projects of self-creation not on the model of the "strong poet," as Rorty does, but instead on that of the self-reliant, democratic individual, it is possible to formulate an alternative view of the relation between public and private that is conceived in the name of politics and yet nonetheless remains consistent with Rorty's stated aims.

Rorty's case for the public-private disjunction relies on two principal arguments. The first grows out of his critique of rationalist philosophy and its foundationalist assumptions. Of a piece with his attempt to sketch a "postmetaphysical" liberal culture where democratic politics can flourish without philosophical justification, this strand of Rorty's thought seeks to purge liberal democratic politics and culture of its "Philosophical" baggage. The remnants of the Enlightenment philosophical worldview that Rorty singles out are the transcendental claim of reason and the essentialist idea of a common human nature. Both notions, which for Rorty are not so much false as simply no longer of much use—his best metaphor for this is a "set of ladders" which liberal democracies have already climbed up—counseled the rightfulness of uniting our public and private strivings in a common, transcendent vision. Here his claim is that these foundationalist presuppositions have become impediments to moral progress, and as such they have no place in a forward-looking, liberal polity.

The second argument theorizes an inherent incompatibility between "self-creation" and "justice," which demands a sharp partition to preserve the integrity of both. This view holds that "the vocabulary of self-creation is necessarily private, unshared, unsuited to argument," while the vocabulary of justice is "necessarily public and shared, a medium for argumentative exchange" (CIS, xiv). At certain points in his thought, the terms of this line of argument shift slightly, where the opposition becomes one of "private perfection" versus "human solidarity." As we shall see, this slippage results from the fact that in Rorty's postmetaphysical polity, social justice, having been stripped of its transcendental claims, boils down to a matter of solidarity. In either case, the proposed remedy is the same: we must ask self-creative individuals "to *privatize* their projects, their attempts at sublimity—to view them

as irrelevant to politics and therefore compatible with the sense of human solidarity which the development of democratic institutions has facilitated"
(CIS, 197). Individual creative energies are granted the space to flourish
within the liberal polity, but with the caveat that they remain within the
boundaries of this nonpolitical realm.

Gauging the merit of Rorty's proposals would seem to require treating him
on the terrain of political theory. To be sure, in the time since the publication
of his *Philosophy and the Mirror of Nature*, there has been a shift in the thrust
of his writing: the radical critique of the foundationalist presuppositions of
the Cartesian-Kantian tradition of Western philosophy has given way to the
more positive task of sketching what a postmetaphysical culture—that is, one
that has given up on the idea that its political practices require philosophical
grounding—might look like. Indeed, the trajectory of Rorty's thought during
the past two decades appears to be, as one reader dubbed it, a "journey from
philosophical diagnosis to political prescription."[29]

There is a recurrent difficulty inherent in the endeavor of reading Rorty as
a political theorist: namely, the difficulty of separating Rorty's anti-Philosophical arguments and negatively driven stances from his positive positions. As is the case with almost all of his positive claims, Rorty's affirmations must be understood against the backdrop of the "Philosophical"
conceptions he is polemicizing against. Bernstein captured this phenomenon
with the keen observation that Rorty himself appears to be obsessed with the
obsessions of philosophers he ostensibly seeks to jettison, and at times he is
unable to let go of them. Arrived at through this negative logic, many of
Rorty's stances are therefore relatively weak as positive affirmations and
must be treated as such.[30]

Yet there is another wrinkle here: while it is generally true that Rorty's political prescriptions remain rooted in his anti-Philosophical stance, as one
traces the development of his thought and the genesis of his ideas about public and private, it becomes clear there is another element at work in his writing since *Mirror* that is political in nature—political in the sense of being an
attempt to advance a particular, partial set of values. Let me explain.

INTERLUDE: RORTY'S
ANTIPOSTMODERN POSTMODERNISM

Part of the immense popularity of *Mirror* and the writings of the 1980s that
propelled Rorty into international renown is attributable to its antifoundational, even subversive, thrust. One must recall that at the time, "deconstruc-

tion" was a buzzword at American universities, where the recently translated works of Foucault and Derrida were being assimilated for the first time. The wide-ranging, radical philosophical critique in *Mirror*, along with his heralding of Wittgenstein, Heidegger, and Dewey as the most influential philosophers of the twentieth century, secured a place for Rorty's antimetaphysical pragmatism as an attractive, homegrown version of American deconstruction.[31] While there is a certain degree of radicalism in the ease with which Rorty declared that long-dominant rationalist assumptions could simply be "shrugged off," his rejection of the idea that there is something called Truth "out there," and his Kuhnian talk of "revolutionary" discourse, when it comes to Rorty's cold-war, liberal politics, nothing could be further from the truth. Despite all the trappings of cutting-edge, radical, postmodernist critique, Rorty by no means understood his "setting aside" of Enlightenment philosophy as a prelude to a radical restructuring of society or an agitated extension of the political into all spheres of life. On the contrary, after jettisoning its philosophical foundations, Rorty envisioned the continuance of liberal politics as usual, if a bit lighter on its feet.

Given this picture, we can entertain the notion that Rorty's emphasis on distinct public and private spheres emerges in part as a way of distancing himself and his pragmatist project from the political implications of the various "postmodern" antifoundationalists with whom he shares so much philosophically, but so little politically.[32] That Rorty's pragmatism occupied a good deal of shared ground with the postmodernists in the first place was an idea that Rorty himself initially promulgated. This emerges in two different essays written in 1980 and collected in his *Consequences of Pragmatism*.

In "Method, Social Science, and Social Hope," Rorty advanced the idea that there was little in Nietzsche or Foucault that could not be found in James and Dewey. Introducing themes that would become a mainstay of his later thought, he argued that the latter's versions of philosophical critique are preferable for being more compatible with "unjustifiable hope" and "human solidarity" (CP, 208).

Similarly, in "Nineteenth-Century Idealism and Twentieth-Century Textualism," Rorty aligned his pragmatism with "textualism," the term he coined for the strand of philosophy and literary criticism of Foucault and Derrida, as well as the Yale school of literary critics including Harold Bloom, Paul de Man, and others. Calling textualism a contemporary version of the idealism of the nineteenth century, he was praised both for an antiscientism that seeks to displace the natural sciences from atop the hierarchy of knowledge and for a critique of metaphysical realism that undermines the correspondence theory of truth. Although Rorty marshals both traditions

Chapter Five

against the idea of philosophy as an epistemologically privileged discipline because they do not rely on metaphysics, he sides with textualism, arguing that it should be understood as an attempt to think through a "thorough-going pragmatism." Here, again, he locates his pragmatism on the same side as the poststructuralists (CP, 150).

After underscoring the common tenets of pragmatism and textualism for a large portion of the essay, however, it becomes clear that Rorty thinks his pragmatism is superior to textualism and wants to distance it from textualism's undesirable political implications. The only grounds for objecting to textualism, though, he argues, having just deflated the epistemological and philosophical objections, are moral.

To be fair, Rorty does acknowledge that the moral objection to textualism he sketches—namely the isolation of the textualists' literary culture from common human concerns—is one which applies to his form of pragmatism as well. However, it turns out that the real villains here are Nietzsche and Foucault. Introducing a further distinction between textualists—a term that has now become interchangeable with "pragmatists"—Rorty argues that while the textualism of Bloom adheres to the spirit of James, the textualism of Foucault follows that of Nietzsche. That is to say, only the former strives to preserve what Rorty calls "our sense of common human finitude" (CP, 158). Yet although he clearly wishes to criticize Foucault's "inhumanism," as he calls it, and to praise Bloom's "sense of our common human lot," Rorty admits that he can offer no argumentation or account of the relevant differences to defend this preference for Jamesian connectedness over Foucauldian detachment. To do so, he continues, "would involve a full-scale discussion of the possibility of combining private fulfillment, self-realization, with public morality, a concern for justice" (CP, 158).

On that note, the essay ends. We are left wondering whether Rorty simply ran out of space or whether such an account is even possible at all. He leaves the question open, perhaps honestly unsure of it himself at that time. But not for long: with the publication of *Contingency, Irony, and Solidarity* in 1989, a book based on two sets of lectures given in 1986 and 1987, Rorty gives us a definitive answer. The first line of the introduction restates the issue at hand, taking up exactly where the 1980 essay left off, and beginning with the topic of "The attempt to fuse the public and the private." Having identified the problem, Rorty proceeds to sketch the issues at stake in the attempt to fuse public and private, and in the third paragraph we get his answer:

> There is no way to bring self-creation together with justice at the level of theory. The vocabulary of self-creation is necessarily private, unshared, unsuited to argument. The vocabulary of justice is necessarily public and shared, a medium for argumentative exchange. (xiv)

And then, more provocatively, he directly identifies the threat:

> The compromise advocated in this book amounts to saying: *Privatize* the Nietzschean-Sartrean-Foucauldian attempt at authenticity and purity, in order to prevent yourself from slipping into a political attitude which will lead you to think that there is some social goal more important than avoiding cruelty. (65)

There is much in these two passages worth pondering. The point I want to underscore is the unquestioned opposition between private perfection and the quest for social justice that has been the cornerstone of Rorty's political vision. As we have seen, this stance rests on one of two logics, both of which are negative: either because to unite public and private is to "relapse into metaphysics," so they therefore must be kept separate in our postmetaphysical polity, or because it is a way of corralling unruly types, like Nietzsche or Foucault, who are insufficiently committed to liberal principles and mores. It does not rest on a positive claim about a fuller conception of justice or a more robust notion of individual self-creation. Although ostensibly part of Rorty's effort to grant priority to democracy over philosophy, neither rationale seeks to expand or enrich democratic politics.

If it turns out that justice and self-creation are not as opposed as Rorty assumes, it may be that they can be combined in an alternative way without betraying Rorty's post-Philosophical principles. This, however, would only take care of part of Rorty's argument for delineating public from private. The objection noted in the second quoted passage above would still remain: namely, that there are certain kinds of individual pursuits that must remain private because they will distract from the guiding principles of public life. We will return to this point below, but it is worth noting that in this context, Rorty's rationale recalls the classical or Arendtian argument we discussed earlier where a clearly circumscribed sphere is required to maintain the sanctity of public pursuits. Like the classical model, Rorty's private realm sometimes appears to be a sort of catchall category in which anything that threatens to disrupt a rather narrow idea of public activities can be dumped, except that instead of necessity and the materialism of household, here it is the potentially illiberal ideas of Nietzsche and Foucault.[33]

MILL, CREATIVE HUMAN ENERGIES, AND SELF-REFORM

For the generation of nineteenth-century liberals that included de Tocqueville and Mill, the distinction between public and private was cast in terms of the individual versus the social collective, and it was driven by the need to protect individual independence of thought from the power of the tyrannical "en masse" or public opinion rather than the power of the tyrannical state. Yet with these thinkers, the rigidity of the public-private split also begins to break down: Tocqueville keenly observed the manifestation of democratic manners in private life, and Mill's defense of negative liberty was not solely for individualism's sake but for the public role of individual ends, as well as the improvement of individual character. The relation between the two spheres of life is understood as more porous and less mutually exclusive: they posit a kind of cross-pollination that is beneficial to both.

In Mill's thought, we see an ideal similar to Berlin's, somewhere between positive and negative liberty—call it "instrumental" liberty. It is instrumental in that the insistence on an inviolable negative area is required, not as some Good in itself but for generating freely chosen individual ends that may vie for public assent as one among many goods. These ends, once secured, provide the engine for politics and the pursuit of justice in public. For Mill, negative liberty and the freedom to choose the ends it makes possible are checks against "the despotism of custom," which threatens to halt the progressive advance of civilization. They are his remedy for "collective mediocrity": "He who does anything because it is the custom makes no choice. . . . He who chooses his plan for himself employs all his faculties."[34]

Mill's *On Liberty* marks the first attempt by a liberal philosopher to theorize a politics firmly grounded in the creative energies of the individual.[35] If we recall the epigraph to the book, Mill's starting point was the fundamental premise articulated by Humboldt in his classic work on *Bildung*: "The grand, leading principle, towards which every argument unfolded in these pages directly converges, is the absolute and essential importance of human development in its richest diversity."[36] Unlike Humboldt, however, in whose political theory individual self-development remained largely irrelevant to politics, and unlike earlier liberals who sought to contain or neuter individual energies, Mill endeavored not only to bring the fruits of individual free choice and self-development into public life, but to posit a conception of politics impelled by their intensity.[37]

Mill located the value of freely chosen individual ends—"pursuing our own good in our own way"—in counteracting what he described in his diagnosis of the "collective mediocrity" of his time as the habit "to desire nothing strongly." The regnant "ideal of character" of his time was in fact "to be without any marked character." As a check and countertendency against this deadening "despotism of custom," Mill sought to ignite "great energies guided by rigorous reason, and strong feelings controlled by a conscientious will."[38] Commenting on the political benefit derived from these ends, Berlin summed it up nicely: "Without the right of protest, and the capacity for it, there is for Mill no justice, there are no ends worth pursuing."[39]

We can begin to see how in Mill's perspective the need for a firm distinction between public and private disappears. Yes, there must remain an inviolable, negative area in which the individual may define and articulate his or her own set of ends. But the boundaries of this realm are not airtight, nor are they meant to constrain the energies nourished by their negative freedom. Yet, as Eldon Eisenach and others rightly argue, a reading of *On Liberty* alone is not sufficient for a full grasp of Mill's position.[40] In his *Autobiography*, Mill suggests that the project of social and political reform of institutions is not enough to address the threats to democracy arising from conformity and the tyranny of public opinion.

One of the primary changes in Mill's thinking that emerges in the wake of his psychological crisis is that he "for the first time, gave its proper place, among the prime necessities of human well-being, to the internal culture of the individual." He continues, "I ceased to attach almost exclusive importance to the ordering of outward circumstances, and the training of the human being for speculation and for action. . . . The cultivation of the feelings became one of the cardinal points in my ethical and philosophical creed." The watershed event is a moment of acute self-reflection in which Mill questions what had until that point been the "object" of his life: "to be a reformer of the world." The question he posed to himself, in a way that anticipates James's pragmatic "test" of our beliefs, was,

> 'Suppose that all your objects in life were realized; that all the changes in institutions and opinions which you are looking forward to, could be completely effected at this very instant: would this be a great joy and happiness to you?' And an irrepressible self-consciousness distinctively answered, 'No!'[41]

In short, public reform without private self-cultivation would fail. Rather than leaving people alone in their private lives, Mill believed that the "culture of feelings" and "sympathetic and imaginative pleasure" activated in him by his reading of Wordsworth were not only "something which could be shared in by all human beings," but something which "would be made richer by every improvement in the physical or social condition of mankind."[42] In *On Liberty*, he attempts to demonstrate that the converse is true as well by linking self-culture to social improvement. While Mill's cultivation of the feelings provides a bridge between public and private, Rorty's sentimental education is understood to affect us only in our public selves.[43]

As he argued in the early essay, "The Spirit of the Age," Mill believed that he was living in "an age of transition of opinions." Influenced by Thomas Carlyle's theory of great individuals as the engine of historical change, Mill thought that a revitalization of individual creative energies—specifically, the production of new ends of life—was required to resist the power of public opinion and propel society into a higher state. This is the role that Mill envisioned his own autobiography as playing, and it is what he hoped to inspire in others, in the spirit of an Emersonian exemplar. As his epigraph to *On Liberty* implies, this understanding of historical change is why everything for Mill is ultimately subordinated to an "art of life" premised on self-culture.[44] Unlike Rorty, who appeals to the weaving of new narratives of our collective past and future as a means of change, but only by severing them from projects of self-redescription, Mill believes that both kinds of narratives are involved in the process of social transformation: narratives of individuals shaping their own selves *and* narratives of social progress and collective reform.

On this reading, what Mill's account suggests is less the need for separate realms than a political argument for overcoming the problematic division of human activity into either a closely cropped, quietistic private existence or the hollow, conformist invocation of ideals in public. Unlike Rorty, who in his recent work has espoused the ideal of "an intricately-textured collage of private narcissism and public pragmatism" (ORT, 210), Mill was not content with an artificially bifurcated solution that ultimately does a disservice to both individual self-development and the pursuit of justice. This is one of the fundamental insights Mill derives from his youthful crisis: improving on the condition of collective mediocrity demands something more. What I read him as at least gesturing toward—albeit in undeveloped, skeletal form—is a concept of intermittent citizenship, propounded most notably by Thoreau, where cultivating the creative passions needed to fuel the public drive to eliminate injustice requires the occasional respite proffered by the untrammeled space of private detachment.[45]

The theme of *On Liberty* that Rorty and Berlin do not take up is the issue of those members of society "who do not desire liberty, and would not avail themselves of it" and who willingly submit themselves to the collective opinion, rather than think for themselves. Taking this problem into account casts Rorty's zeal to leave people alone and even Berlin's defense of the right not to participate in a new light. The problem is not, as it is in Berlin's case, that these citizens of "servile" characters choose not to contribute to public life; on the contrary, Mill's point is that they are incapable of making their own choices at all: "I do not mean that they choose what is customary in preference to what suits their own inclination. It does not occur to them to have any inclination except for what is customary. Thus the mind itself is bowed to the yoke." On this point, Mill is clear: "IIe who docs anything because it is the custom makes no choice."[46]

For Mill, the capacity to make choices is predicated upon the possession of a certain type of character, which in turn requires the ability of each "to use and interpret experience in his own way." The latter is of course an echo of an Emersonian theme that runs throughout the pragmatist tradition, especially in James. The person who can be said to have a "character" is for Mill one "whose desires and impulses are his own—are the expression of his own nature, as it has been developed and modified by his own culture." Thus, the threat to democratic life of collective mediocrity and the tyranny of the majority is not so much, as Tocqueville thought, an excess of individualism, but in Mill's view "not the excess, but the deficiency, of personal impulses and preferences."[47] As Richard Friedman argued in a seminal essay, Mill "appears to think that it is possible to speak of men having choices 'properly their own' only in so far as they call society's standards into question." Liberty can be "lost" through a lack of character or "self-determination" on the part of those "to whom it does not occur (or who submissively declines) to question established social practices in the name of 'his own' beliefs or preferences."[48] At stake here for Mill in the preservation of "the spirit of liberty" was nothing less than "human advancement"; Mill took the contest between "the love of liberty or of improvement" and "the sway of custom" to be "the chief interest of the history of mankind."[49]

The importance of developing beliefs and preferences properly one's own lies in Mill's understanding of freedom as self-reform.[50] In his *System of Logic*, Mill defended the idea that humans are possessed of "a power of self-formation" by which we are "capable of making our own character." Being able to modify our own character—if we in fact wish to, an important caveat—is what enables us to achieve the "moral freedom" inherent in knowing that our "habits and temptations" are not our "masters" but our "own." Recognizing this freedom, he argues, will foster "a much stronger spirit of self-culture."[51] In *On Liberty*, published sixteen years later, this capacity to cultivate one's own character becomes essential for remedying the loss of liberty that occurs through a self-abdication of it to public opinion. Interestingly, while Rorty seems to evince a related notion of freedom as the recognition of the contingency and hence alterability of our beliefs, he does not draw the inference that such self-modification, though of value to "strong poets," is important for public life.

If Mill had only begun to scratch the surface of these ideas' potential, on the other side of the Atlantic their development had begun in the work of Emerson, Thoreau, and Whitman in ways that would influence later pragmatists like James and Dewey, as would Mill. In the thought of these American thinkers, the ideal that Mill was fumbling about for, largely without precursors to guide him—the ideal of democratic individuality—received its fullest expression, and with it the possibility of a democratic polity and social order that does not cave to the pressures of collective mediocrity and subordinate itself to the tyranny of public opinion, but rather seeks to empower the average, everyday citizen and, on her back, raise the entire culture.

RORTY'S CASE FOR PUBLIC AND PRIVATE REVISITED

Once we abandon the "set of ladders" for reaching the "outside" of our minds and our language, the important question becomes "what sort of human being you want to become." For Rorty, this divides into two subquestions: first, "With what communities should you identify, of which should you think of yourself a member?" and second, "What should I do with my aloneness?" The former question deals with your obligations to other human beings, and the latter, your obligation to become who you are, as Rorty puts it borrowing Nietzsche's phrase (ORT, 13).

These two sets of questions correspond respectively to the public and private realms and undergird Rorty's understanding of liberalism more generally as defined by dual priorities: diminishing the causes and effects of pain and cruelty, and providing a space for the individual pursuits of self-creation and self-perfection—in other words, social justice and individual self-realization. The problem with this picture is that Rorty never questions the idea that the activities in these two realms are inherently opposed.

In a sense, this view is not all that surprising, given the sources Rorty draws on in his depiction of individual self-realization. For one, his conception of the kinds of individuals who undertake such projects, what he also calls "becoming autonomous," is modeled on Harold Bloom's idea of the "strong poet"—someone driven by the "horror of finding himself to be only a copy or a replica."[52] Thus, from the outset, Rorty's idea of self-creation takes on a narrowly poetic cast and becomes something of interest only to a select few, where "the aesthetic search for novel experiences and novel language" is paramount (EHO, 159). From there, Rorty borrows from the English poet Philip Larkin the idea of a "blind impress"—the distinctive, but elusive something that "all our behavings bear," which individuals who seek autonomy spend their lives trying to figure out. As a representative example of someone engaged in a project of individual aesthetic self-creation, Rorty cites Vladimir Nabokov's erotically obsessed character Humbert Humbert of *Lolita* fame. Calling our attention to Humbert's "inattentiveness to anything irrelevant to his own obsession"—in particular, the suffering he is inflicting on poor Lolita—Rorty generalizes from this example to make the larger point that the individual pursuit of autonomy—that is, self-realization—must be privatized to keep it from undermining the fundamental directive of liberal politics, namely the reduction of suffering (CIS, 141–68).

Interestingly, Mill's attempt to employ individual energies in the political realm did ultimately rely upon a narrow minority, not unlike Rorty's strong poets, of what he called "persons of genius"—the inevitably more "well-developed human beings." Yet, unlike Rorty—and unlike Nietzsche, as well—Mill keenly felt the need "to show that these developed human beings are of some use to the underdeveloped."[53] At first blush, Mill's conception of the role of intellectuals is remarkably close to Rorty's idea of wide-ranging literary critics who serve as "moral advisers" and help us "reweave" our beliefs and desires by "enlarging our acquaintance" (CIS, 79–82). However, for Rorty, the strong poets rather than the public intellectuals are the ones engaged in a project of self-cultivation. The difference remains that because Rorty conceives of the strong poets so narrowly and radically individualistically, he is unable to posit any sort of role for them in public and is forced to confine them to a free but insular existence in private. By contrast, echoing the idea of an "exemplar" developed by Emerson, Mill asserts that "the first service which originality has to render [those lost in the crowd] is that of opening their eyes: which being once fully done, they would have the chance of being themselves original."[54]

To be fair, Rorty's account is more nuanced than this, developed over the course of the decade of the 1980s, through one book-length work and two substantial collections of essays; I have surely oversimplified here. Nevertheless, Rorty's tendency to view individual aesthetic pursuits as inimical to the other-regarding character of our lives is the result, at least in part, of his reduction of the realm of possible versions of self-realization to that of the "cruel aesthete," the self-absorbed individual totally oblivious to the pain and suffering going on around him, whereas Mill suggests that "to reform the self requires the reform of society and to reform society requires self-reformed men."[55]

The other reason Rorty views private and public pursuits as so opposed is that he makes solidarity and a shared collective identity the sine qua non of social justice. Here, as we have noted, Rorty's communitarianism, for lack of a better word, has not received the attention it warrants; indeed, it occupies a dominant place in his political theory. Forging a democratic moral community is a project which lies behind his recent turn to literature, and it is an essential ingredient in the quest for social justice, understood as a "larger loyalty."[56] For Rorty, justice is a moral ideal, embodying a particular set of liberal beliefs and desires that is exemplified in Judith Shklar's definition of liberals as those who think cruelty is the worst thing we do (CIS, xv). But since universalist or transcendental conceptions of morality are not available to Rorty, following Wilfrid Sellars, he understands morality and moral obligation in terms of "we-intentions." In Sellars's view, the core meaning of immoral behavior is "the sort of thing *we* don't do" (quoted in CIS, 59, 190). Rorty's claim is that our sense of solidarity with others is strongest when we identify with them as being "one of us." Our task, as liberals, is to dedicate ourselves to "extend[ing] our sense of 'we' to people whom we have previously thought of as 'they'" — to "stay on the lookout for marginalized people" and to try to "notice our similarities with them" (CIS, 192–96).

One can see how the solitary individual's attempts to come to terms with the "idiosyncratic contingencies" of which she is a product, if that were all there were to self-realization, would be at odds with the public effort to recognize our shared similarities. On the face of it, Rorty's vision of public life is not unattractive. The question is whether the program of "an intricately-textured collage of private narcissism and public pragmatism" will ultimately get us to there from here (ORT, 210). My contention is that it will not. Counseling us to divide our selves into private and public parts—to be, in alternate moments, "Nietzsche and J. S. Mill"—his view holds that when we enter the sphere of the political, it is appropriate that we leave the best parts of ourselves at home, and that the liberal politics of reducing suffering requires nothing more. Although recent insights into the socially constructed character of human existence were of course not available to Mill, his thinking in this area suggests a rather advanced grasp of the way self-knowledge is political because what is taken inside is the product of outside social forces. To put it another way, he understood that "the social and psychological barriers to self-reform are also barriers to reform in society at large."[57] Rorty, by contrast, who claims socialization indeed "goes all the way down," resists this insight when he insists on an inviolable barrier between private self-cultivation and public justice (CIS, 185).[58] This is especially curious given Rorty's belief in the contingency of human life. To be sure, as Berlin put it, "No man is an island. . . . The social and the individual aspects of human beings often cannot, in practice, be disentangled."[59]

PERFECTIONISM AND THE
BRIDGING OF PUBLIC AND PRIVATE

My main criticism of Rorty's political theory is that its conceptions of politics and public life neither enlist nor require the individual's highest energies or most fully developed selves. This marks a departure from the pragmatist tradition that runs from Emerson to James and Dewey. My claim is not that individual self-realization is incomplete without participation in public life; this is a version of a classical view, expressed by those who rely on a positive conception of liberty, such as Arendt, and to a certain extent, Dewey. Rather, the view I am asserting is that democratic politics is incomplete without the fruits of individual self-realization. Or, to put it another way, rather than asking whether self-realization without involvement in public life is rich enough to fully realize the self, my question asks whether politics without self-realization is rich enough to satisfy the ideals of democracy.[60]

One of the points I want to return to in making my argument is Mill's understanding of the role of individual ends—"pursuing our own good in our own way"—in politics. Mill suggests that in the absence of such ends, democratic public life would be anemic and succumb to the pressures of collective mediocrity because the inner lives of its citizens are so undeveloped. Freely chosen individual ends are predicated upon seeing the world in one's own way; if these ends are absent from public life, for Mill there is no justice to be pursued. What Mill accomplishes in this formulation is to bridge public and private by connecting ethics, or the development of one's character, with the public pursuit of justice. Or, to put it another way, he allies what might be called the "ethics of the self" with the "politics of the other."[61] As Mill puts it in *On Liberty*, "In proportion to the development of his individuality, each person becomes more valuable to himself, and is, therefore, capable of being more valuable to others" (127).

This is an important point. Part of Mill's rationale for the political or social value of self-reform is that it promises a benefit for our relations to others. By contrast, Rorty wants to separate duties to self from our duties to others, arguing that we need to distinguish between the ethical considerations involved with "one's sense of solidarity," and those arising from "one's idiosyncratic attempt to create oneself anew" (CIS, 194). In other words, he makes the kind of individual self-improvement associated with ethical character irrelevant to public life, where it simply matters that we recognize and empathize with the suffering of the other, while at the same time leaving our fundamental ethical orientation unchanged.[62] Or, if you like, he splits ethics off from politics, whereby the latter becomes the realm of a shared collective identity from which individual conceptions of the good life are either excluded altogether or, if admitted, required to be completely uniform—read, liberal.

At risk of painting with too broad a brush, it may be that this problem is part of a larger shortcoming of liberalism more generally that contracts the role of the individual conscience in politics. That is to say, the understanding of conscience in classical liberalism tends to be social rather than individual. For Rorty, this is evidenced most clearly in his understanding of morality in terms of "we-intentions." Here social or political norms are internalized, but so much so that they supplant the independent dictates of conscience.[63]

As a way of remedying this shortcoming, in what follows I suggest two resources on which liberal perspectives may draw in rethinking the political implications of a rigid separation of public and private realms. One is a distinctive conception of democratic individuality, the other, the doctrine of moral perfectionism. Both notions rely on a "moral give and take between political and nonpolitical spheres" and ground their conceptions of politics in a fruitful linkage of the ethics of the self and the politics of the other. Here perfectionism is understood as a demand to reform our society and institutions spurred by individual self-realization, in which the latter need not be expressions of the "longing for total revolution."[64] The key point is that the resources arise out of themes connected with the pragmatist tradition with which Rorty identifies.

Talk of "perfectionism" inevitably means talk of "ends," which in the context of public life tends to disconcert liberals, raising the specter of "teleology"—something regarded as anathema to a tolerant, difference-respecting public sphere, at least since Rawls's *A Theory of Justice*. Yet it may be worth inquiring about the costs of maintaining a public realm free of all individual value commitments.[65] As liberals from Locke to Rawls and Rorty have worked to protect individual freedoms from public or state authority, or vice versa, one of the things that has gotten lost is the way in which the values and institutions of democratic public life infect the goings-on of private, nonpolitical life. Dewey hit upon the nature of this moral or ethical influence when he said that democracy was more than an institutional arrangement: it was a set of habits, a "way of life."[66] More recently, George Kateb has argued eloquently about the "moral distinctiveness" of democracy and called attention to the ways in which the spirit of the public sphere manifests itself in private life.[67]

What these perspectives point to is a more fluid relation of mutual influence, as opposed to Rorty's "equally valid, yet forever incommensurable" view, between public and private spheres (CIS, xv). The picture they paint of private life is not one of radically autonomous, self-interested, and self-regarding individuals pursuing narrowly aesthetic aims. Nor do they see individuals as realized fully only through participation in the lofty affairs of public life, remaining unfulfilled and imperfectly human without it. Recognizing that we are socially constituted beings who may only occasionally realize ourselves politically, they advance the possibility of democratic individuality as a distinctive mode of human existence. Somewhere between the classical liberal and republican theories, they conceive of public citizenship as an activity that is episodic and intermittent, as an expression of their democratically infused individuality. Initiated by the call of conscience, individuals act either to right some wrong or to resist on behalf of less fortunate others.[68] Though they do not conceive it in these terms, the kind of political theory they pave the way for, I want to argue, between liberalism and repub-licanism, is a version of political or moral perfectionism.[69]

Any discussion of democratic individuality must begin, and probably end, with Emerson, Whitman, and Thoreau.[70] This is not the place for a full-scale discussion of their views on individuality; it will suffice for our purposes to underscore several major points of divergence from Rorty's assumptions, drawing on Kateb's work and that of Stanley Cavell. The core disagreement concerns the strength of the boundary between realms.

One of the reasons for Rorty's insistence that we must circumscribe indi-vidual projects of self-realization and insulate public life from their corrosive influence is his assumption that they aim at "a kind of perfection which has nothing to do with relations to other people" (CIS, 142). This may no doubt be true in certain instances—namely, Humbert Humbert—but there is no reason to believe it is true in all cases. Because it provides a way to distinguish be-tween different forms of individuality and individual self-expression, the per-spective of democratic individuality is helpful here. The claim is that democ-racy fundamentally transforms individuality; unlike Romantic versions, which may be aristocratic, solipsistically detached, or antisocial, or even thin liberal conceptions, where individuals are little more than the bearers of abstract rights or self-interested automatons to whom the political is a mere framework for enabling their pursuits (to say nothing of the antidemocratic individualism of Nietzsche), this perspective holds that individuality, in its distinctly demo-cratic form, is inseparable from democratic values and practices.[71]

There is no better illustration of this than Thoreau's two-year withdrawal into the Walden woods. The doctrine of democratic individuality transforms a seemingly antisocial flight from social and political life into the political act of withdrawing one's consent from a government engaged in an unjust war and unwilling to put an end to human enslavement. Thoreau only withdraws, as Cavell once put it, just far enough to still be seen. As Kateb explains, the introspective is qualitatively different than the intimate or narrowly personal, and the cultivated inward self is different from the merely expressive self. Unlike Rorty's narcissistically self-absorbed aesthetes, the democratic indi-vidual seeks detachment or withdrawal—Berlin's "negative area"—as a respite from the sometimes suffocating demands of social life, for the kind of introspection and self-development which make possible the freely chosen ends Mill thought were so crucial, not just to individual self-fulfillment, but to *public* life. Rather than mere inwardness, the dynamic of democratic indi-viduality is one of inwardness and emergence.[72]

The doctrine of democratic individuality also transforms our relations with others. Unlike the unbridgeable chasm Rorty cuts between the individual's "aloneness" and her concern for others, this form of individuality relies on the conviction that "one can make the sense of one's infinitude a bridge to other human beings."[73] As Emerson wrote in one of the bibles of democratic individuality, "To believe your own thought, to believe that what is true for you in your private heart is true for all men,—that is genius." Or as Whitman proclaimed in the opening lines of *Song of Myself*:

> I celebrate myself, and sing myself,
> And what I assume you shall assume,
> For every atom belonging to me as good belongs to you.

While the strong poets of Rorty's liberal utopia preoccupy themselves with overcoming their anxiety of influence, democratic individuals endeavor to create "a poetical relation to reality." This project includes their relations to others; unlike Rorty's strong poets, they seek to redefine these bonds in ways consistent with their (reformed) inner natures, not to eliminate them through the assertion of radical uniqueness. Like Whitman, who in celebrating himself was celebrating the lives of all of his countrymen, the democratic individual sees all individuals in both aesthetic and moral terms—as beautiful, as humans, as fellow sufferers. He encourages us to extend ourselves so as to see from the perspective of another and identify with his suffering, yet without ever losing one's own distinctiveness, for, in the end, "they are not the me myself."[74]

One of the key differences between Rorty and the poetic precursors of his pragmatism, like Emerson, Thoreau, and Whitman, concerns their view of the aesthetic. For Rorty, an absorption in individual aesthetic projects is solipsistic and anathema to a concern for others because he understands the aesthetic in such radically individualistic terms. These earlier thinkers—Whitman, in particular—appreciated the social character of the aesthetic and the ways in which aesthetic experience offers a basis for forging social and communicative ties between individuals based a notion of "moral beauty." This idea cuts across the traditional moral-aesthetic opposition that Rorty's public-private split merely reproduces in another form. This aesthetic strand of pragmatist thought finds its way into the work of James and Dewey.[75] As Alexander Nehamas has argued at a more general level, aesthetic judgments that grow out of one's individuality, because they are judgments of value, implicate one in a web of relationships that includes other people. In an echo of Dewey's language, he claims that they are "neither completely objective nor entirely social nor purely private," but "personal." "Far from closing us off from the world," he argues, aesthetic absorption "often leads further into it."[76] Oddly, Rorty draws on a more narrow literary conception of the aesthetic rather than the richness of the pragmatist tradition itself.

As is well known, these nineteenth-century thinkers' fear of conformity led them to treat collective social projects, like Rorty's conception of justice as a "larger loyalty," with acute suspicion. Perhaps they sometimes err too far on the side of the individual. Yet no one more deeply comprehended the conflicting demands of individuality and human community. Rorty's partitioning of the self and its sphere of existence offers a tidy and convenient, but ultimately unrealistic, solution. For Emerson and company, by contrast, defining the line between public and private was an ethical task for each individual, a practical project.[77] In their skepticism toward robust forms of commonality, what they oppose is not mutuality and relations with others tout court, but merely the strong senses of collective identity and group affiliation that seek uniformity of vision and action at the expense of diversity and disagreement. Only through a continual dynamic of inwardness and emergence, and temporary, instrumental alliances with others, can the individual be active in the social realm while maintaining an integrity of self. Berlin's tribute to Mill provides a fitting creed: "He was loyal to movements, to causes, and to parties, but could not be prevailed upon to support them at the price of saying what he did not think to be true."[78] To put it another way, he lived by a self-constituted inner ideal.

Rorty's greatest fear with regard to self-realization can be traced to the idea that those who attempt autonomy demand that their autonomy be embodied in our institutions: "The search for private perfection . . . is neither trivial nor, in a pluralistic democracy, relevant to public policy" (PSH, 170; CIS, 65). Using one's private convictions as a basis for politics represents for Rorty the cardinal transgressive sin. The concern is not so much that one's private beliefs influence political convictions—"of course they will," he readily admits. The problem is that the "sources" of our moral beliefs are valued for idiosyncratic personal reasons, and they therefore are at odds with the shared character of public democratic consensus. Such private beliefs are "conversation stoppers" in public discourse. For instance, if someone asserts that she holds a political position because it is required by her understanding of God's will, Rorty believes most citizens will respond, "We weren't discussing your private life; we were discussing public policy. Don't bother us with matters that are not our concern." Rorty's solution is that we drop all references to the sources of our beliefs when presenting arguments in defense of our political positions. That way the workings of democratic debate are insulated from all idiosyncratically personal and transcendentally justified premises that are inhospitable to consensus.[79]

Leaving aside the question of whether this is even feasible on a practical level—at the present moment at least, these kinds of sources are continually invoked in debates about abortion, stem cell research, and the like, and show no signs of abating—making one's personal perspective or "temperament" the basis of public policy does not seem to be what Mill, or even Emerson or Whitman, is after. Their claim cuts much deeper: in the absence of what Mill calls "social support for nonconformity" and the active cultivation by individuals themselves of standards, preferences, and inclinations "properly their own," the arguments presented in public will suffer, and the democratic ideal itself will lose its capacity for collective improvement.[80]

By contrast, Rorty's position adopts a laissez-faire approach and simply works with individual standards and preferences as they come, without any regard for the quality of these impulses themselves. Additionally, by separating self-realization from the pursuit of justice, Rorty's account runs the risk of exempting the self, or at least part of it, from the demands of justice. And when this privatized self is combined with its public half, whose participation in the quest for justice merely conforms to the judgments of the "we," it is a rather inadequate conception of the politics of justice. Because his understanding of public life is predicated upon a historicized and nontranscendental consensus—that is, "we-intentions"—he leaves himself no other option than to relegate all ideas that do not fit within the broad outlines of this commonality to "private" status.[81] While I am not suggesting that Rorty drop the emphasis on contingent and historically constituted consensus, a better approach might be to exclude from public only "selfish" forms of life, based on the distinction developed by Nehamas in his reading of Oscar Wilde, rather than all sources of individual idiosyncrasy. Wilde held that

> selfishness is not living as one wishes to live, it is asking others to live as one wishes to live. And unselfishness is letting other people's lives alone, not interfering with them. Selfishness always aims at creating around it an absolute uniformity of type. Unselfishness recognizes an infinite variety of type as a delightful thing, accepts it, acquiesces in it, enjoys it.[82]

In this way, it may be possible to allow the full selves of individuals with all their creative energies into the public realm through social support for the kind of unselfishness that will strengthen an antifoundational and historicist democratic society.

CONCLUSION

Rorty's understanding of politics is increasingly moving toward a "politics of the other." Manifested in his project of "sentimental education" and the idea of justice as a "larger loyalty," the overriding aim of politics is the creation of a democratic moral community by fostering identificatory states of sympathy and compassion. This is done by familiarizing ourselves with the details of the lives of distant others, mostly through what Rorty calls "sad, sentimental stories," but also through the descriptions found in novels like *Uncle Tom's Cabin*, to make us more sensitive and more aware. If we can be brought to see our differences as less important than our shared ability to suffer and feel pain, a kind of moral progress toward a more humane social world can be made.[83]

As attractive an idea as this is, because the private parts of our selves are disconnected from the public pursuit of justice, it allows us "to put ourselves in other people's places without feeling we have to *do* anything about it."[84] This, I want to argue, is the result of Rorty's splitting the ethics of the self from the politics of the other—or, if you like, severing ethics and politics. Here the perspective of moral perfectionism points to some resources not foreign to the pragmatist tradition from which Rorty's account would benefit.[85]

Beginning from the premise of a linked relation between the ethics of the self and the politics of the other, moral perfectionism holds that any change in the outer social realm—say, Rorty's moral progress—that does not entail "a new attainment of the self" will prove inadequate, a hollow invocation of ideals in which fundamental transformation is absent.[86] Rorty's various partitions ensure that there is never enough of ourselves involved in public life for it to be a transformative experience, either for ourselves or for social life. This is of crucial importance when one abandons Rorty's bifurcated view and entertains the possibility that the greatest barriers to a knowledge of the other lie within oneself.[87] On the perfectionist view, we ourselves are implicated in society's failures to achieve justice. It aims to teach how to respond to those failures, and to one's compromise by them, "otherwise than by excuse or withdrawal." Here, "measuring the degree of one's society's distance from strict compliance with the principles of justice is a function of taking the measure of one's sense of compromise with injustice."[88]

Though this is not the place to elaborate a full defense of perfectionism, in recent years a number of contemporary thinkers have articulated versions of it that do not entail a conception of the good that would trump all others and which are not incompatible with a liberal framework.[89] Cavell argues that the brand of Emersonian moral perfectionism he advocates represents not a competing moral theory that conflicts with, say, that of liberals like Rawls, but rather "a dimension of the moral life any theory of it may wish to accommodate." Speaking of the kind of disdain for democratic culture expressed by thinkers like Nietzsche or Heidegger, or even Emerson—the very expressions Rorty seems to fear—Cavell suggests, somewhat provocatively, that they be seen as "an expression of democracy and commitment to it." He continues,

> Only within the possibility of democracy is one committed to *living* with, or against, such culture. This may well produce personal tastes and private choices that are, let us say, exclusive, even esoteric. Then my question is whether this exclusiveness might be not just tolerated but treasured by the friends of democracy.[90]

Democratic individuality, combined with a perfectionist view of justice, suggests a way in which the creative energies of its citizens need not be merely corralled and tolerated by democracy, as Rorty's account asserts, but fully incorporated and channeled in ways that advance rather than neglect its public pursuit of justice. Like Mill's notion of making choices "properly one's own," living against one's culture rests on a self-cultivated capacity to call society's standards into question.

The great poet-theorists of democratic individuality sought to ignite the creative energies of democratic individuals. The work of Emerson, Thoreau, and Whitman abounds with tropes of "sleep-walking" and "slumbering," and the need to wake men from these muted states of existence. Mill too sought to jar individuals from "the deep slumber of a decided opinion" and their tendency "to desire nothing strongly."[91] While Rorty believes that liberal democracy should leave people alone, these thinkers believed a democracy worthy of the name required more character. Simply prescribing such character would be counterproductive; instead, they must be inspired to cultivate their own. These individual energies, they believed, once awakened, could fundamentally alter the culture of democracy, transforming a herd of unthinking sheep into an active, independent-minded citizenry composed of self-reliant souls capable of resisting the tyranny of public opinion and achieving the most distant reaches of the democratic vista.[92]

Because Rorty's public-private divide sequesters these energies within a bounded realm and allows the only influence of private upon public to be "accidental," he severs them from this crucial transformative role (CIS, 37). That such a transformation, "a new degree of culture," would "instantly revolutionize the entire system of human pursuits," as Emerson predicted, remains an open question, as it should, given the open-ended nature of the American "experiment."[93] But who other than Rorty would be more fitted to drumming up the requisite amount of optimism and social hope?

To the extent that Rorty's pragmatism aspires to a transformative politics and to the active pursuit of the changes that the attainment of social justice requires, it need not fear individual creative energies and should abandon the impulse to corral and neuter them. The repudiation of single, true solutions that Rorty shares with the pragmatist tradition and its precursors does not ultimately contain the extent of pluralism of individual ends in public and the emphasis on cultivating impulses and perspectives "properly their own" that are needed to strengthen collective self-improvement in a democracy and avoid the debilitating effects of unchecked conformism. As Mill observed nearly a century and a half ago—a point not lost on James—the greatest threat to the advancement of the democratic project is "not the excess, but the deficiency, of personal impulses and pretenses." Ignoring this advice will ensure that Rorty's vision amounts to "little more than an apologia for the status quo."[94]

NOTES

1. See Walt Whitman, "Democratic Vistas," in *The Portable Whitman*, ed. Mark Van Doren (New York: Penguin Books, 1973), 317–84.

2. Some also have read Rorty as making a salutary contribution to the contemporary theory of cosmopolitanism: Amanda Anderson recently called Rorty "the pragmatist thinker to consider most extensively the relation between the cultivation of ethos or character and larger political goals," highlighting his value for deepening the cosmopolitan ideal, in "Pragmatism and Character," *Critical Inquiry* 29 (Winter 2003): 282–301. Similarly, Jerold Abrams sees Rorty as a bridge between advocates of a positive ethics of self-fashioning, like Foucault, Richard Shusterman, Alexander Nehamas, and Stanley Cavell, and theorists of a democratized global cosmopolitanism, including Rawls, Habermas, Karl-Otto Apel, and Martha Nussbaum. See Abrams, "Aesthetics of Self-Fashioning and Cosmopolitanism: Foucault and Rorty on the Art of Living," *Philosophy Today* 46, no. 2 (Summer 2002): 185–92.

3. See John Stuart Mill, "Autobiography," in *John Stuart Mill: A Selection of His Works*, ed. J. M. Robson (New York: St. Martin's Press, 1966), esp. chap. 5. My reading of Mill here is indebted to Eldon J. Eisenach's thoughtful attempt to integrate Mill's often conflicting Benthamite and Coleridgean impulses in "Self-Reform as Political Reform in the Writings of John Stuart Mill," *Utilitas* (1990); and Richard B. Friedman's trenchant analysis in "A New Exploration of Mill's Essay *On Liberty*," *Political Studies* 14, no. 3 (1966): 281–304. See also Eldon J. Eisenach, "Mill's *Autobiography* as Political Theory." Both of Eisenach's essays appear in Eisenach's recent collection, *Narrative Power and Liberal Truths: Hobbes, Locke, Bentham, and Mill* (New York: Rowman & Littlefield, 2002).

4. See Richard Rorty, "Remarks at MOMA," unpublished manuscript listed on Rorty's homepage: www.stanford.edu/~rrorty/moma.htm. Reflecting on the work of Peter Eisenman and Jacques Derrida, Rorty describes it in this way: "On my reading of him, Derrida is part of a swelling chorus of philosophers who have contributed to a movement of intellectual liberation, a movement of which American pragmatism was one manifestation. This movement is a shift away from the idea that there is something to which human beings are responsible—something like God, Reality, or Truth. It is a movement toward increasing self-reliance on the part of our species, toward the idea that we are responsible only to one another, and not to anything that is neither a human being nor a creation of human beings." And later, "Philosophical anti-representationalism is one of the many forms that this sense of increasing self-reliance has taken in recent times."

5. See Richard Bernstein, "Rorty's Liberal Utopia," in *The New Constellation: The Ethical-Political Horizons of Modernity/Postmodernity* (Cambridge, MA: MIT Press, 1992), 276, 280, passim.

6. James's dedication to his *Pragmatism* lectures reads, "To the memory of John Stuart Mill, from whom I first learned the pragmatic openness of mind and whom my fancy likes to picture as our leader were he alive to-day."

7. For Rorty's interpretation of James as helping us see the opposition between "cooperative endeavors" and "private projects," see his "Religious Faith, Intellectual Responsibility, and Romance," in PSH, 148–67.

8. See Benjamin R. Barber, *Strong Democracy: Participatory Politics for a New Age* (Berkeley: University of California Press, 1984). On the participatory model, see also, among others, Sheldon S. Wolin, *Politics and Vision: Continuity and Innovation in Western Political Thought* (Boston: Little, Brown & Co., 1960). Though I share many of their criticisms of liberalism, I propose different remedies.

9. The idea that liberalism is driven by anxiety and punctuated by fear is not a novel notion. One need only recall the pivotal role played by fear in the constitution of the Hobbesian political order. More than forty years ago, Sheldon Wolin attempted to dispel the misleading view of liberalism as an activist philosophy, the product of a fruitful communion with the individual's creative abilities. On the contrary, the central thrust of the Lockean worldview, one dominant for over two centuries, asserts the limits of human action and depicts man as confined to "a state of mediocrity, incapable of extremes," virtually eliminating the possibility of creative, transformative action. From the correspondence of Locke, quoted in Wolin, *Politics and Vision*, 296–97. On liberalism and anxiety, see pp. 314–25, chap. 9, and passim.

10. See John Stuart Mill, *On Liberty* (New York: Penguin Books, 1974), 140 and epigraph.

11. On this conception of the political, see Wolin, *Politics and Vision*; and Norman Jacobson, *Pride and Solace: The Function and Limits of Political Theory* (New York: Methuen, 1978).

12. Nancy Rosenblum introduces this distinction in her discussion of public and private in chapter 3 of her *Another Liberalism: Romanticism and the Reconstruction of Liberal Thought* (Cambridge, MA: Harvard University Press, 1987), a work I have benefited from greatly. Rosenblum's aim is to achieve a mutual reconciliation between liberalism and romanticism designed to avoid the "cold impersonality" of some liberal thought, on the one hand, and the "unrestrained eruption of personal, expressive impulses," on the other. Though highly valuable for its attempt to bring together two strands of political thought that share more than is commonly recognized, and to broaden some of liberalism's needlessly narrow assumptions about human life, Rosenblum's account suffers from the fact that it never gets beyond a somewhat misleading and overgeneralized rationalist-romantic opposition. As a result of always viewing romantic sensibilities from the vantage of an (implicitly) Enlightenment, rationalist standpoint, Rosenblum never questions her characterization of them as "romantic"; by contrast, the Romantics themselves did not view their expressiveness as a function of romantic longings but rather as fundamentally personal, political, moral, individual, or whatever. For an alternative reading that emphasizes a greater interconnectedness and the Romantics' indebtedness to Kant, see M. H. Abrams, *Natural Supernaturalism: Tradition and Revolution in Romantic Literature* (New York: W. W. Norton & Co., 1971).

13. See Wolin, *Politics and Vision*, 305, chap. 9, passim. Wolin's is the preeminent account of this aspect of liberalism. Much of my thinking in this area is indebted to Wolin's seminal work.

14. For Wilhelm von Humboldt's views, see his *The Sphere and Duties of Government*, as the title was originally translated in 1854. It has been reissued under the title *The Limits of State Action*, trans. J. W. Burrow (Cambridge: Cambridge University Press, 1969).

15. See Hannah Arendt, *The Human Condition* (Chicago: University of Chicago Press, 1958), 22–37.

16. Arendt cites the following report by Xenophon about Sparta, although she describes it as "certainly exaggerated": "Among four thousand people in the market place, a foreigner counted no more than sixty citizens," in *The Human Condition*, 32n.

17. See Richard Shusterman, "Pragmatism and Liberalism between Dewey and Rorty," in *Practicing Philosophy: Pragmatism and the Philosophical Life* (New York: Routledge, 1997), 67–88.

18. Isaiah Berlin, "Two Concepts of Liberty," in *Four Essays on Liberty* (New York: Oxford University Press, 1969), 172. Rorty quotes the same passage in CIS, 46.

19. Berlin, "Two Concepts of Liberty," 122.

20. Berlin, *Four Essays*, xliii.

21. Berlin, *Four Essays*, lx.

22. John Dewey, *The Early Works of John Dewey*, ed. Jo Ann Boydston (Carbondale: Southern Illinois University Press, 1978), 3:344.

23. Dewey was well aware of the forces of what John Stuart Mill called "collective mediocrity" that threatened to suffocate individual self-development. But Dewey identified the crushing power of unquestioned conventions as the offending factor, not anything inherent in the "en masse" quality of the democratic public. Thus, the remedy for Dewey was not to insulate the individual from the democratic collective through the demarcation of distinct spheres, but to encourage the kind of critical intelligence and robust individuality that enabled the democratic individual to exist in the social environment with a minimum of domination. This is of course all prefigured in Emerson's idea of self-reliance. We will return to this point below.

24. Berlin, "Two Concepts," 131–37, 146–52.

25. Mill, *On Liberty*, 114, 128–29, 140. For a discussion of this point, see Friedman, "A New Exploration."

26. Berlin, *Four Essays*, lviii n.

27. See Berlin, "Two Concepts," 170–72. This statement later found its way to the cover of a collection of Berlin's essays. See Isaiah Berlin, *The Crooked Timber of Humanity: Chapters in the History of Ideas*, ed. Henry Hardy (Princeton, NJ: Princeton University Press, 1990).

28. Back in the early 1980s, Rorty distinguished between "philosophy," which he described in terms of Wilfrid Sellars's notion of "an attempt to see how things, in the broadest possible sense of the term, hang together, in the broadest possible sense of the term," and "Philosophy," which is concerned, following Plato and Kant, with "asking questions about the nature of certain normative notions (e.g., 'truth,' 'rationality,' 'goodness') in the hope of better obeying such norms." Rorty aligns himself

with the former endeavor, asserting that for pragmatists, "the best hope for philosophy is not to practice Philosophy" (CP, xiv–xv).

29. The phrase is Ian Shapiro's. See his *Political Criticism* (Berkeley: University of California Press, 1990), esp. chap. 2. Shapiro sees Rorty's work in the decade immediately following the publication of *Philosophy and the Mirror of Nature* as an effort to "describe a politics he thinks we should embrace once we wholeheartedly reject foundationalist presuppositions" (20).

30. See Richard J. Bernstein, *Philosophico-Political Profiles: Essays in a Pragmatic Mode* (Philadelphia: University of Pennsylvania Press, 1986), 47. Bernstein continues, "As one follows the nuances of [Rorty's] arguments, it begins to dawn on the reader that just when he thinks he is getting down to the hard core of these disputes, he discovers that there is no core" (23).

31. This point is made by Rorty in a recent interview. See Derek Nystrom and Kent Puckett, *Against Bosses, Against Oligarchies: A Conversation with Richard Rorty* (Charlottesville, VA: Prickly Pear Pamphlets, 1998). To a question about the interest in his work at the time, Rorty's response was, "Yeah, if you wanted non-foundational sounding stuff, mine was as good as any" (54). They go on to discuss how the vast majority of this influence was among nonphilosophers.

32. I use the term *postmodern* loosely here, as a useful shorthand, acknowledging that most of the major thinkers associated with it—with the exception of Lyotard—shunned the label, including Foucault, Derrida, and after an initial embrace, Rorty. The effort to distance himself from the postmodernists occurred not so much as a result of being lumped in with them by his reading public, but even earlier, based on Rorty's own visceral reaction to the politics he interpreted them as espousing, as opposed to his.

33. Curiously, despite the fact that it is developed at length in *Contingency* and that it appears to be central to the overall coherence of his liberal utopia, in a recent interview Rorty has tried to downplay the significance of his public-private split: "I didn't say everybody had a public/private split, but some people do. . . . My public/private distinction wasn't an explanation of what every human life is like. I was, instead, urging that there was nothing wrong with letting people divide their lives along the public/private line. We don't have a moral responsibility to bring the two together. It was a negative point, not a positive recommendation about how everybody should behave." See Nystrom and Puckett, *Against Bosses*, 61. However, in reading Rorty's texts, one is likely to come across statements that give a different impression of his enterprise. For example, "I want to defend ironism, and the habit of taking literary criticism as the presiding intellectual discipline, against polemics such as Habermas'. My defense turns on making a firm distinction between public and private" (CIS, 83). Or, "The compromise advocated in this book amounts to saying: *Privatize* the Nietzschean-Sartrean-Foucauldian attempt at authenticity and purity, in order to prevent yourself from slipping into a political attitude which will lead you to think that there is some social goal more important than avoiding cruelty" (CIS, 65). Or, again, "We should stop trying to combine self-creation and politics, especially if we are liberals. The part of a liberal ironist's final vocabulary which has to do with public action is

never going to get subsumed under, or subsume, the rest of her final vocabulary" (CIS, 120–21). The reader can make her own judgment.

34. Mill, *On Liberty*, 122–23, 131, 135–136.

35. A recent revisionist book by Frederick Beiser attempts to resituate the thought of the German Romantics in the crucial decade of 1790–1800, making a rather compelling case that the commonly regarded as aesthetic or nonpolitical work of thinkers like Schiller, Schlegel, and Humboldt, among others, was in fact motivated by political ends having to do with preparing the ground for the institution of republican government. See Frederick C. Beiser, *Enlightenment, Revolution, and Romanticism: The Genesis of Modern German Political Thought, 1790–1800* (Cambridge, MA: Harvard University Press, 1992). Mill's generation, which includes Emerson, Thoreau, and Whitman, seems to be the first where the quality of citizens' individuality itself becomes a matter of political import.

36. This is a quote from Humboldt's *The Sphere and Duties of Government*. Although written in 1791–1792, Humboldt's work remained unpublished until 1852, seventeen years after his death. It appeared in English in 1854, just as Mill was writing *On Liberty*. Born of the Romanticism of Herder, Schiller, Humboldt, and Goethe, the notion of *Bildung* or "self-culture" lays claim to a distinguished lineage both within the German tradition and without, having had a marked influence on, among others, the likes of Carlyle, Coleridge, John Stuart Mill, and Matthew Arnold. For a nuanced history of its influence on German politics and culture, see W. H. Bruford, *The German Tradition of Self-Cultivation: 'Bildung' from Humboldt to Thomas Mann* (New York: Cambridge University Press, 1975). Interestingly, Rorty discusses *Bildung* or "self-formation" in the final chapter of *Philosophy and the Mirror of Nature* as the idea we should substitute for the acquisition of knowledge as the highest goal of thinking. But citing the term as "too foreign" and the word *education* as "too flat," he drops *Bildung* and adopts *edification* as the moniker for this new genre of philosophizing— the project of "finding new, better, more interesting, more fruitful ways of speaking" (PMN, 359–60). To the extent that it figures in his more recent work, edification is a private activity severed from its connection to politics and the culture at large. This marks a departure from thinkers like Humboldt and Schiller, who considered it a crucial part of the *political* preparation of individuals through aesthetic education—not believing reason alone had the power to motivate people to act—for republican government. See also Beiser, *Enlightenment, Revolution, and Romanticism*.

37. As I note in footnote 35 above, there is reason to believe Humboldt's view was more complicated than this. See Beiser, *Enlightenment, Revolution, and Romanticism*, chap. 5. Humboldt thought the proper aim of the state was to promote the *Bildung* of its citizens, which was best accomplished through liberty. However, the full development of the individual is realized in private and has nothing to do with public life. Indeed, the entire raison d'etre of the edifice of the state exists in Humboldt's view to promote these individual ends. Thus, while *Bildung* is relevant to the ultimate end of government, there is no sense of an ongoing politics that relies on *Bildung* beyond the securing of the conditions for its development.

38. Mill, *On Liberty*, 135–36.

39. Isaiah Berlin, "John Stuart Mill and the Ends of Life," in *Four Essays*, 197.

40. See, for example, Eisenach, "Mill's *Autobiography* as Political Theory." See also Eldon J. Eisenach, *Two Worlds of Liberalism: Religion and Politics in Hobbes, Locke, and Mill* (Chicago: University of Chicago Press, 1981), 199–205.

41. Mill, *Autobiography*, 88–89, 94–95. It is not coincidental that James dedicated his *Pragmatism* lectures to Mill. See footnote 6 above.

42. Mill, *Autobiography*, 95–96.

43. For Rorty's discussion of sentimental education and "sad, sentimental stories," see "Human Rights, Rationality, and Sentimentality" in TP, 167–85. The goal of this kind of education is to get "people of different kinds sufficiently well-acquainted with one other" to cultivate the sort of sympathy required to expand the purview of who is included in the phrase "people like us." By manipulating sentiments, as he puts it, it may be possible to train people to see differences between humans as morally insignificant and to be able to imagine themselves in the place of the oppressed or less fortunate (TP, 172–79). It is interesting to note that the idea of sentimental education has antecedents in the work of Mill (see Rosenblum, *Another Liberalism*, 129–31). However, while for Rorty this is something which takes place in private, largely through reading literature, for Mill sentimental education is a public activity: it is political institutions and public involvement that generate the kind of sympathy for others that serves as an emendation to private self-concern. For Mill, unlike Rorty, public and private activities are not distinct and irreconcilable, but mutually compensatory.

44. Quoted in Eisenach, "Mill's *Autobiography* as Political Theory," 166. On Mill's understanding of self-culture, which he develops in his *System of Logic* and elsewhere, see also Friedman, "A New Exploration." My argument here relies on both of these lucid and suggestive accounts.

45. On this reading of Thoreau, see George Kateb, *The Inner Ocean: Individualism and Democratic Culture* (Ithaca, NY: Cornell University Press, 1992).

46. Hume, *On Liberty*, 124–26.

47. Hume, *On Liberty*, 122, 124–25.

48. Friedman, "A New Exploration," 290.

49. Hume, *On Liberty*, 136. "The only unfailing and permanent source of improvement," Mill held, "is liberty, since by it there are as many possible independent centers of improvement as there are individuals."

50. Here I am indebted to Friedman, "A New Exploration," 294.

51. John Stuart Mill, *A System of Logic*, bk. 6, chap. 2, sec. 3. Book 6 is published separately as *On the Logic of the Moral Sciences* (New York: The Library of Liberal Arts, 1965). Here the influence of Coleridge is evident, whom Mill had already written on in 1840; the Coleridgean idea of culture, understood as self-cultivation, though socially conservative, is also an affirmation of the individual's self-reflexive capacity to alter itself through "self-education." On this point, see Eisenach, "Self-Reform as Political Reform," 244.

52. For more on Bloom's conception, see his *The Anxiety of Influence* (New York: Oxford University Press, 1973), 80, passim. Rorty's work is peppered with references to this notion, but see in particular CIS, 23–43.

53. Mill, *On Liberty*, 128.

54. Mill, *On Liberty*, 130. Also like Emerson, Mill suggests that genius and originality are best understood as akin to thinking, and as such are quite widely distributed. Cf.: "Whoever thinks at all, thinks to that extent, originally," in Mill, "On Genius," in *Mill's Essays on Literature and Society*, ed. J. B. Schneewind (New York: Collier Books, 1965), 92.

55. Eisenach, "Self-Reform as Political Reform," 250. For a good account of the narrowness of Rorty's conception of the aesthetic and his undue insistence on radical novelty as a criterion of individual self-creation, see Shusterman, *Practicing Philosophy*, 67–88; as well as his *Pragmatist Aesthetics: Living Beauty, Rethinking Art* (Cambridge: Blackwell, 1992), 101–6, 255–58. Shusterman makes a compelling case that Rorty diverges sharply from Dewey's idea of the aesthetic as a central quality of everyday existence.

56. This communitarian thrust emerges a decade before the publication of *Contingency* in his 1979 presidential address to the American Philosophical Association, the speech that unleashed the storm, if you will, on the eve of the publication of *Philosophy and the Mirror of Nature*. For those who search in vain for the actual "consequences" of Rorty's pragmatism, which often appears to be little more than a defense of the liberal status quo, if liberated from its philosophical baggage, the best candidate is this heightened, nonessentialist sense of community. Here it is worth quoting from Rorty's 1979 address: "Our identification with our community—our society, our political tradition, our intellectual heritage—is heightened when we see this community as *ours* rather than *nature's*, *shaped* rather than *found*, one among many which men have made. In the end, the pragmatists tell us, what matters is our loyalty to other human beings clinging together against the dark, not our hope of getting things right" (CP, 166). On Rorty's notion of justice as loyalty, see the essay "Justice as a Larger Loyalty," in *Cosmopolitics*, ed. Pheng Cheah and Bruce Robbins (Minneapolis: University of Minnesota Press, 1998), 45–58. There is a certain irony in the fact that identity has come to play such a central role in Rorty's political vision given his polemics against "cultural politics." See, for example, AOC, 73–107.

57. Eisenach, "Self-Reform as Political Reform," 250.

58. Cf. also: "There is nothing to people except what has been socialized into them" (CIS, 177).

59. Berlin, "John Stuart Mill and the Ends of Life," 191.

60. Here my question differs from Shusterman's, who raises the first question, and following Dewey, answers in the negative. Rorty, by contrast, would say yes—private self-realization can be completely fulfilling without public action; one thing has nothing to do with the other. While Shusterman believes, writing with his own participation in the politics of the 1960s in mind, that cultural politics can "enhance our private perfection," my claim is that private perfection can enhance our politics. See Shusterman, *Practicing Philosophy*, 79–87.

61. I borrow these useful categories from Shusterman, who uses them to characterize Dewey's democratic ideal, which by identifying self-realization with public action for the public good binds the two together. See his *Practicing Philosophy*, 78. Eisenach's conception of self-reform as political reform rests on a similar distinction.

62. Although it may not appear so on my rendering, Rorty's position is actually a very thoughtful and ingenious compromise that is not without a certain power. However, I for one have never been convinced by his claim that people can (and do) divide themselves in such a way that they can be, "in alternate moments, Nietzsche and J. S. Mill" (CIS, 85). More recently, he has curtailed his example somewhat to read, "There is no reason why one cannot be a revolutionary activist on weekdays and a reader of John Ashbery on weekends." See "Duties to the Self and to Others: Comments on a Paper by Alexander Nehamas," *Salmagundi* 111 (Summer 1996): 65. Still, it seems to me that people simply do not work this way, at least to the extent that they have any coherence to their existence. Who, after having read Nietzsche, is able to embrace liberal democratic politics as usual without, at the very least, looking askance at it?

63. Wolin makes this argument about liberalism's "socialized conscience" in *Politics and Vision*, 343–51, linking this point with liberalism's having "so fatally misunderstood the crushing power of social conformity" (346). Rorty distinguishes between "public" and "private" morality, where the latter is something like ethics or "the development of character," in his terms. By contrast, public morality is that which is "codifiable in statutes and maxims" (EHO, 153). Because Rorty understands the ethical in such stridently aesthetic terms—on the model of the strong poet—the only thing with any political relevance is his public morality.

64. Kateb, *The Inner Ocean*, 43–44. The "longing for total revolution" is a phrase Rorty borrows from Bernard Yack for the kinds of individual demands which should be constrained in private (CIS, 65). By assimilating all such demands to this one extreme type, Rorty leaves no room for the perfectionist possibilities.

65. For Rawls, for instance, this means that in his theory of justice the individuals behind the veil of ignorance are kept free of any "ethical motivation." See John Rawls, *A Theory of Justice* (Cambridge, MA: Harvard University Press, 1971), 584. Among alternative views that attempt to include such motivations are Martha Nussbaum's idea of "perceptive equilibrium," developed in her book *Love's Knowledge: Essays on Philosophy and Literature* (New York: Oxford University Press, 1990), chap. 6; and the version of moral perfectionism articulated by Stanley Cavell in his *Conditions Handsome and Unhandsome: The Constitution of Emersonian Perfectionism* (Chicago: University of Chicago Press, 1990), chap. 1. Both authors develop their ideas explicitly as alternatives to Rawls, specifically to his notion of "reflective equilibrium."

66. Dewey made remarks to this effect in many places, but for one, see "Creative Democracy—The Task before Us" in *The Later Works: 1925–1953*, ed. Jo Ann Boydston (Carbondale: Southern Illinois University Press, 1981–90), 14:226–29.

67. See George Kateb, "The Moral Distinctiveness of Representative Democracy," in *The Inner Ocean*, esp. 43–50.

68. On this view of citizenship, see also Dana Villa, "The Philosopher versus the Citizen," *Political Theory* 26, no. 2 (1998): 147–72. Villa affirms the necessity for a politics of individual judgment that is "morally suspicious of strongly held public purposes and the energies they enlist," developing a form of "Socratic citizenship" that possesses the capacity to "rise from the 'we'—not to an Archimidean standpoint, but to the standpoint of a conscientious, nondogmatic, 'I'" (166).

69. Although he does not use this term, Dewey does tend to give teleological priv-
ilege to the individual, making assertions like "growth is the only end," though this is
complicated by the fact that the social environment is always of primary importance
for Dewey as well. Kateb does not mention perfectionism, despite certain affinities
with that position, and seems to think that all of his proposals could be realized within
a liberal framework. John Stuart Mill occasionally moved in this direction, judging
institutions by their capacity to affect individuals internally. See Rosenblum, *Another
Liberalism*, 130–31.

70. I am aware of no better work on this trio, at least from the perspective of political theory, than Kateb's *The Inner Ocean*.

71. See Kateb, *The Inner Ocean*, 77–80. As he puts it, "The meaning of the theory
of democratic individuality is that each moral idea needs the other, both to bring out
its most brilliant potentialities and to avoid the most sinister ones" (79).

72. Kateb, *The Inner Ocean*, 97, 236; Rosenblum, *Another Liberalism*, 83–84.

73. Kateb, *The Inner Ocean*, 34.

74. Ralph Waldo Emerson, "Self-Reliance," in *The Portable Emerson*, ed. Carl
Bode (New York: Penguin Books, 1981), 138; Walt Whitman, "Song of Myself," in
Leaves of Grass (New York: Bantam Books, 1983), 22, sec. 1; Kateb, *The Inner
Ocean*, 93–94, 226; Whitman, "Song of Myself," 25, sec. 4.

75. For an excellent discussion of these linkages and of moral beauty, see Raphael
D. Allison, "Walt Whitman, William James, and Pragmatist Aesthetics," *Walt Whitman Quarterly Review* 20, no. 1 (2002): 19–29. On the narrowness of Rorty's conception of the aesthetic, see Shusterman in footnote 54 above.

76. Alexander Nehamas, "The Art of Being Unselfish," *Daedalus* (Fall 2002):
61–62, 65.

77. See Gerald M. Mara and Susan L. Dovi, "Mill, Nietzsche, and the Identity of
Postmodern Liberalism," *The Journal of Politics* 57, no. 1 (1995): 1–23.

78. Berlin, "John Stuart Mill and the Ends of Life," 203. Rosenblum aptly terms
such short-lived affiliations "shifting involvements." See Rosenblum, *Another Liberalism*, 125–51.

79. See "Religion as a Conversation-Stopper," in PSH, 168–74, Rorty's review of
Stephen L. Carter's *The Culture of Disbelief*.

80. What is noteworthy about the proponents of democratic individuality is their
general distrust of government and their studied reluctance to enter public life. Only
intermittently do their expressions of democratic individuality propel them into public life, often in the name of resistance on behalf of others driven by the dictates of
conscience. Even though they appear consonant with his political aims, on Rorty's
scheme such impulses must be confined to the private realm.

81. The exemplars here for private philosophizing are Derrida and Proust: "Proust
succeeded because he had no public ambitions" (CIS, 118). Similarly, Derrida, at least
on Rorty's reading, succeeded because he limited himself to "private jokes" and wrote
about his "private fantasies," which, although they incidentally were about philosophers, did not try to grant them a public or political relevance. Rorty has in mind here
Derrida's *The Post Card from Socrates to Freud and Beyond*, trans. Alan Bass
(Chicago: University of Chicago Press, 1987). See CIS, chap. 6. He puts this work in

the same category as *Tristram Shandy*, *Finnegan's Wake*, and *Remembrance of Things Past* (127n). Nietzsche and Heidegger, by contrast, err in thinking their thoughts have a wider applicability beyond their personal narratives of self-creation. Despite their presuppositions to the contrary, Rorty thinks liberals should read Nietzsche and Heidegger the same way we read Proust (see CIS, 96–121).

82. Quoted in Nehamas, "The Art of Being Unselfish," 68.

83. Rorty discusses "sad, sentimental stories" in "Human Rights, Rationality, and Sentimentality" in TP, 167–85.

84. Bruce Robbins, "Sad Stories in the International Public Sphere: Richard Rorty on Culture and Human Rights," *Public Culture* 9 (1997): 226–27.

85. Rawls considers the merits of perfectionist theories in his *A Theory of Justice*, sec. 50, and ultimately rejects it, largely on the basis of its teleological emphasis. However, it is only the antidemocratic, Nietzschean version of perfectionism that he considers. For a point-by-point rejoinder to Rawls's objections and a defense of an Emersonian brand of moral perfectionism, see Cavell, *Conditions Handsome and Unhandsome*, xxii–xxxi, 47–51, chap. 1, passim.

86. Cavell, *Conditions Handsome and Unhandsome*, xix, 13. Cf. Emerson's warning in "Self-Reliance": "All men plume themselves on the improvement of society, and no man improves," *The Portable Emerson*, 161.

87. In light of Rorty's claim that his politics of reducing suffering entails merely being made aware of the details of the lives of distant others, this is of the utmost importance.

88. Cavell, *Conditions Handsome and Unhandsome*, xxvii, 18. Interestingly, Mill began to move in this direction in *On Liberty*, though he conceived it more in terms of a collective failure: "If society lets any number of its members grow up mere children, incapable of being acted on by rational consideration of distant motives, society has itself to blame for the consequences" (150).

89. A common thread of these accounts is a kind of teleology of human flourishing. See, for example, Mara and Dovi, "Mill, Nietzsche, and the Identity of Postmodern Liberalism." Nussbaum's version of "political perfectionism" holds that once the emphasis on human flourishing is predicated upon certain necessary material and educational conditions, it generates a radical demand for social and educational change. See her *Love's Knowledge*, 195–219.

90. Cavell, *Conditions Handsome and Unhandsome*, xxxi, 50.

91. Mill, *On Liberty*, 105, 135. Cf. Emerson, in "The American Scholar," speaking of the tendency to seek money and material possessions: "Wake them and they shall quit the false good and leap to the true, and leave governments to clerks and desks. This revolution is to be wrought by the gradual domestication of the idea of Culture," in *The Portable Emerson*, 66.

92. In one of his most recent works, Rorty refers to this as "achieving our country," a phrase he borrows from James Baldwin's *The Fire Next Time*. See AOC. I remain unconvinced that this kind of achievement is possible given the (limited) resources of Rorty's liberalism. On Baldwin's understanding, this political project is predicated upon a kind of deep self-reflection and self-remaking, particularly on the part of

whites, insofar as their identities rest on a "forgetting" of the more unsavory parts of America's history, that Rorty's public-private split would seem to militate against.

93. Emerson made similar sweeping claims in several of his essays regarding the transformative effects of a greater, more widespread self-reliance. This is from "Circles," in *The Portable Emerson*, 233.

94. Bernstein uses this phrase to describe Rorty's pragmatism in contrast to Dewey's more transformative version. See his "One Step Forward, Two Steps Backward: Richard Rorty on Liberal Democracy and Philosophy," in *The New Constellation*, 233. Similarly, Shusterman characterizes Rorty's liberalism as merely providing "the necessary stable framework of social organization for us to pursue in peace and comfort our individual aesthetic goals." See his *Pragmatist Aesthetics*, 239.

Chapter Six

America as the Greatest Poem

Any honest examination of the national life proves how far we are from the standard of human freedom with which we began. The recovery of this standard demands of everyone who loves this country a hard look at himself, for the greatest achievements must begin somewhere, and they always begin with the person.

—James Baldwin, "Nobody Knows My Name"

Fostering the "Emersonian combination of self-reliance and patriotism found in James and Dewey" has become a key political aim of Rorty's pragmatism. His recent work—most notably *Achieving Our Country* and the essays collected in *Philosophy and Social Hope*—weds an Emersonian affirmation of the creative power of individuals to imagine new possibilities to the cultivation of a national identity, a project that Rorty identifies with Whitman's ideal of the United States themselves as "essentially the greatest poem." Tempering Emerson's individualism with the "quasi-communitarian rhetoric" of Whitman, Dewey, and James Baldwin, Rorty evinces a thoughtful conception of democratic politics as "Emersonian self-creation on a communal scale." This will enable us, in a phrase he borrows from Baldwin, to "achieve our country"—to realize the enduring promise of America's highest ideals (EHO, 2; AOC, 8, 22; PSH, 34).

Casting the imagination as "the cutting edge of cultural evolution," the source of "new conceptions of possible communities" and "new ways of being human," brings Rorty's project in line not only with Emerson's, but with other purveyors of a poetic pragmatism, like W. E. B. Du Bois, who, in Cornel West's words, sought to create "new visions and vocabularies for the moral enhancement of humanity."[1]

Yet Rorty's pragmatism departs from that of Emerson, Whitman, and neglected pragmatists like Du Bois and Alain Locke on an important point. These thinkers, to varying degrees, saw flaws in the national character and looked to literature, poetry, and art in general to alter it. The value of this poetic strand of pragmatist thought is that its affirmations of American culture are partial; what is affirmed is then turned against some aspect of the culture itself—for example, its racism, imperialism, or excessive materialism—in the name of moving it to a higher level. Importantly, these partial or detached affirmations did not preclude an ongoing commitment to the project of improving America.

Rorty's conception of self-reliance on a communal scale raises a number of key issues for political theorists, including how to balance the tension that makes democratic collective self-renewal possible between a diversity of individual perspectives and communal ties, the question of the degree of connectedness of the social critic, how a democracy should best deal with a past about which it cannot be proud, and the relation of self-criticism to social criticism. I argue that the sentiment that binds Whitman to his country, like Baldwin, is love, not, *pace* Rorty, pride. Unlike pride, the bonds of love are strong enough to permit the kind of sometimes antagonistic relationship inherent in Baldwin's famous remark, "I love America more than any other country in the world, and, exactly for this reason, I insist on the right to criticize her perpetually." Only against the background of a relation of love can what Baldwin called "the gravest questions of the self" be addressed.[2]

The task of achieving our country and moving it to a higher level involves striking a balance between creative visions that we must attain and a communal bond to keep us together along the way. Too much of either, and the transformative project degenerates into detached radicalism or a static celebration of past glories and vague possibilities. Despite his affirmations in an Emersonian spirit of the need for "new conceptions of possible communities" and "new ways of being human," Rorty ultimately capitulates to one pole of the combination of self-reliance and patriotism (PSH, 87–88). As a result, while he retains the sense of attachment inherent in the projects of Whitman and Baldwin, he elides their self-expressed criticisms. In Rorty's vision of how best to "achieve" America, it is no longer possible, to paraphrase Stanley Cavell, to express one's commitment to democracy by living in some measure *against* its culture.[3]

ACHIEVING RORTY'S COUNTRY

The idea of America as an ongoing project, a work in progress whose greatness remains to be achieved, has been a recurrent way of thinking about the

American experiment, from the original Puritan "errand into the wilderness" to its secularized version in Emerson and Whitman of America as a poem whose greatness is as yet unsung, and to Baldwin's exhortation to Americans, both white and black, to "end the racial nightmare" and "make America what America must become."[4] It rests in each of its guises on an implicit political theory and an implicit vision of political life. This vision is forward-looking—the political order is viewed not as it is but as it might be, in terms of imagined possibilities projected into a distant, unrealized but attainable moment—and transformative, inasmuch as it is committed to lessening the distance between an imagined possibility and current conditions.[5]

Whitman opens the second paragraph of the original preface to *Leaves of Grass* with the assertion, "The Americans of all nations at any time upon the earth have probably the fullest poetical nature. The United States themselves are essentially the greatest poem." He would spend the remaining four decades of his life attempting to convey the full meaning of this declaration. Rewritten and rearranged over the course of at least a dozen editions, *Leaves of Grass* grew from twelve poems to over three hundred as he tried to come to terms with the curious admixture of diverse parts and a single whole at the heart of this poetical nature, through a brutal civil war, the emancipation of its slaves, and his own becoming. Rorty glosses this passage in the following way:

> Whitman thought that we Americans have the most poetical nature because we are the first thoroughgoing experiment in national self-creation: the first nation-state with nobody but itself to please—not even God. We are the greatest poem because we put ourselves in the place of God: our essence is our existence, and our existence is in the future. Other nations thought of themselves as hymns to the glory of God. We define God as our future selves. (AOC, 22)

Noting that Whitman's view, like James's and Dewey's, is "more secular and more communal" than its precursor in Emerson, Rorty quotes West's description of Emerson's conception of "the individual *as* America," an "ideological projection of the first new nation in terms of a mythic self" that has appropriated God-like power for use in transforming the world.[6]

Rorty emphasizes the secularist dimension of Whitman's vision because it leads him to the two points he wants to underscore in order to assimilate Whitman to his pragmatic project, which by the mid-1990s explicitly links the pragmatist philosophy he used to critique the Cartesian-Kantian tradition in *Philosophy and the Mirror of Nature* to an affirmative take on American politics.[7] First, he focuses on Whitman's remark in *Democratic Vistas* that America "counts . . . for her justification and success . . . almost entirely upon the future," which he nicely connects to his larger pragmatist stance: "If there is anything distinctive about pragmatism it is that it substitutes the notion of a better future for the notions of 'reality,' 'reason,' and 'nature.'" Second, he interprets the substitution of our future selves for God as a recognition of the historical rootedness and fallibility of all human endeavor. This paves the way for Rorty's argument that we substitute hope for transcendental knowledge: "Whereas Marx and Spencer claim to know what was bound to happen, Whitman and Dewey denied such knowledge in order to make room for pure, joyous hope" (PSH, 23–27).

In Rorty's version of this project, hope, pride, and a forward-looking optimism dominate, as do the imagination and a sense of unrealized possibilities. His political vision rests on the principle that "national pride" is "a necessary condition for self-improvement." In the absence of such pride and a recognition of America's past achievements, majoritarian politics will lack the emotional component necessary for lively, imaginative, and committed public debate and collective action. This is the cornerstone of his political theory: "A shared sense of national identity" is "an absolutely essential component of citizenship" (AOC, 3–4, 32). Rorty does not seek a "simpleminded militaristic chauvinism"; he readily admits that there are abhorrent episodes in America's past that surely are cause for a chastening of our pride. Yet for a nation to achieve itself, it is crucial that "pride outweighs shame" (PSH, 253).

On at least one front, Rorty makes an important and much-needed point. The contemporary left has indeed lost significant ground to the right in the larger conversation about America as a result of its failure to articulate a coherent vision of what America should be that touches the sources of national identity and patriotism. Yet by casting this problem in terms that pit "the politics of difference" against national identity, and multiculturalism against patriotic attachments, Rorty does more to entrench these antagonisms than to alleviate them. A return to a nationalistic, state-centered politics is surely a nonstarter; some third way is needed—a point we will return to below (PSH, 252–53).[8]

Rorty's position holds that "a nation cannot reform itself unless it takes pride in itself—unless it has an identity, rejoices in it, reflects upon it and tries to live up to it." This is an echo of Whitman's assertion that "two or three really original poets" are needed to deepen the democratic commitment by giving "more compaction and more moral identity (the quality most needed) to these States."[9] However, Rorty tends to conflate pride and identity; identifying with one's country as one's own is not the same thing as taking pride in it. To be fair, he does allow that an identification with America does not preclude shame at "the greed, the intolerance, and the indifference to suffering" that are also present. Indeed, when Rorty asserts that "you can feel shame over your country's behaviour only to the extent to which you feel it is your country," I think he is on stronger ground than when he equates identification with pride and suggests that "a left that refuses to take pride in its country will have no impact on that country's politics" (PSH, 253–54).

Rorty's rebukes of the "unpatriotic," "postmodern," "cultural" left for "refusing to rejoice in the country it inhabits" have become familiar (PSH, 252). In these instances, he parts company with the Whitman of *Democratic Vistas*, whose pride had been chastened by the persistent shortfall of moral and religious character in relation to America's material success. By contrast, Rorty seems interested in getting people to be proud of America in the present and to celebrate her past—that is, for what she *has* become, rather than for what she *will* or *may* become. This is precisely his beef with people like Foucault and Heidegger—namely, that they refuse to take pride in what their civilization has already achieved. What ignites Rorty's ire is that "readers of Foucault may often come away believing that no shackles have been broken in the past two hundred years" (AOC, 7). In these moments Rorty's project abdicates the critical function so crucial to both Whitman and Baldwin and becomes merely an effort to redeem America's past rather than to improve its present.

To be sure, Rorty is right to criticize leftist intellectuals guilty of the sort of forgetting that elides the fact that America is *their* country, no matter how much disdain they harbor for particular aspects of her culture. This forgetting may account for the failure of certain leftist stances to resonate with the American citizenry. As Whitman knew, democracy must get "a hold in men's hearts, emotions and belief" if it is to succeed.[10] But never losing sight of the fact that she is your country is not the same thing as taking pride in it. For Rorty, the problem with postmodern, "cultural" leftists, then, is not simply that they refuse to identify with America, but that they refuse to take pride in her achievements and credit her advances. Put another way, while Whitman's pride in America's future was a way of remaining committed to the project of correcting present failures, which in his view were nothing to be proud of, Rorty seems to insist that we be proud of America's past and present while we are attempting to reform it—something I believe limits the transformative power of his project.

Cultivating a national identity and the emotion of national pride is for Rorty the work of narrative and stories: "inspiring stories" about "what a nation has been and should try to be" that incite a nation to self-improvement (AOC, 3, 15). It is a job for literature—for the novel, in particular, which he has called "the characteristic genre of democracy" (EHO, 68). He links this narrative project to his philosophical critique by arguing that "stories about what a nation has been and should try to be are not attempts at accurate representation, but rather attempts to forge a moral identity" (AOC, 13).

While this would appear to place Rorty in the tradition of Whitman's call for a "national literature" in *Democratic Vistas*, an echo of Emerson's search for a bard to sing the as-yet-unsung song of America in "The Poet," Rorty's view of literature as a "civic religion" is more Arnoldian than Emersonian. Rather than "liberating gods" who "unlock our chains and admit us to a new scene," Rorty envisions a "religion of literature" capable of inspiring and generating hope (AOC, 136). Only on this basis can the kind of moral community united by a shared national identity that he believes is necessary for a meliorative politics be forged. That is, he wants to assimilate individuals to a preexisting national identity rather than provoke them to generate a new one by following their own muse. For Emerson, by contrast, hope is only transformative when linked to the innovative power of "genius," to the creative capacity of ordinary individuals. Rorty's exaltation of hope without an embrace of individual creativity severs a linkage that was crucial for Emerson, and for Whitman as well, who held that "a nation like ours . . . is not served by the best men only but sometimes more by those that provoke it— by the combats they arouse." Whitman's ideal of a "truly grand nationality," which he attributes to John Stuart Mill, entails not only "a large variety of character," but "full play for human nature to expand itself in numberless and conflicting directions."[11]

PRIDE VS. LOVE

Ironically, it is the very figures whom Rorty invokes who have done the most to gesture toward some third way, beyond simply accepting or rejecting "America." Whitman, in particular, was acutely attuned to the tension between diversity and union, between "Individualism" and "Patriotism," in America:

> Must not the virtue of modern Individualism, continually enlarging, usurping all, seriously affect, perhaps keep down entirely, in America, the like of the ancient virtue of Patriotism, the fervid and absorbing love of general country? I have no doubt myself that the two will merge, and will mutually profit and brace each other, and that from them a greater product, a third, will arise. But I feel that at present they and their oppositions form a serious problem and paradox in the United States.[12]

Whitman thought this a question "which time only can answer," and was merely suggestive about the form of this reconciliation, insisting only that it was "our task to reconcile them." Yet to what extent is such a reconciliation possible at all?

To be sure, this passage from his *Democratic Vistas* admits of a certain faith. Although the tone and message of *Vistas*, written a decade and a half later, differs from the untempered optimism of his original 1855 preface to *Leaves of Grass*, in 1871, Whitman was still with "as yet unshaken faith" in America and its democratic experiment. Clearly, the Whitman of *Vistas* is more aware of the flaws in the American moral character—for instance, the "hollowness of heart" and the "atmosphere of hypocrisy throughout"—and has a keener sense of the darker underside of America's material and productive successes. Somewhat disillusioned, Whitman conveys a sense that there is much work still to be done. As one reader put it, "He has not lost his faith in the future, but the future is the only thing which gives him hope. . . . It is simply that he must imagine a golden age to come rather than hail one that is here."[13]

This is a significant point when it comes to Rorty's approach. *Vistas* has been called a "chastisement" by one of America's "best lovers." Indeed, the operative sentiment that binds Whitman to his country is love, not pride. Only the mode of a lover's chastisement enables Whitman to criticize America while remaining committed to the project of achieving a better future. As we have seen, Rorty quotes with praise Whitman's notion that America "counts . . . for her justification and success . . . almost entirely upon the future" (PSH, 26–27). But he glosses it as a pragmatist critique of representationalism rather than as a political stance. As a result, he elides the critical implication of Whitman's stance: Whitman transferred all questions of America's justification to the future because he found little in the present to be proud of. I want to argue that substituting love for pride will greatly improve Rorty's vision.

Though he remained cryptic, Whitman's notions of "adhesiveness" and "amativeness," conceptions of forms of attachment—a social bond—held in place through friendship, fraternity, and sexual love, suggest the contours of the potential third way to which he alluded.[14] As he suggests in the above passage, "love" of country is, literally, the key element. But it must be tempered or chastened in some way by "Individuality" or, in another parlance, by difference, for America to move itself to a higher state.[15]

Baldwin strikes a similar chord in his vision of how America might achieve its promise. He believed that the "relatively conscious" whites and blacks to whom this task fell must, "*like lovers*, insist on and create, the consciousness of others." Love occupies an important place in Baldwin's vision of how America is to be achieved. As a complex, many-sided, but enduring bond, only love is potent and tenacious enough to sustain the paradoxical relationship of African Americans to their country. This relationship, Baldwin argued, writing in 1951, is not simply one of "oppressed to oppressor, of master to slave," nor is it "motivated merely by hatred." Settling merely for hatred was the error common to Elijah Muhammad and the Nation of Islam, as well as

Richard Wright's portrayal of Bigger Thomas in *Native Son*. The conceit of this hatred is that it betrayed the fact that the relationship of blacks to America was "literally and morally, a *blood* relationship." Unlocking the "altogether savage paradox of the American Negro's situation" would be impossible "until we accept how very much it contains of the force and anguish and terror of love."[16]

For Baldwin, we might say, love is the condition of growth. "Love," he said, "does not begin and end the way we seem to think it does. Love is a battle, love is a war; love is a growing up." A familiar refrain in Baldwin's writings on race and America is the idea that at some level "a failure to look reality in the face," either by America collectively, as a nation, or individually, was somehow at the root of racial problems. Bringing America to see itself "as it really is," and getting whites to see not only blacks as they really are but to accept themselves as they really are, becomes the sine qua non of achieving our country. Love is essential to this kind of self-acceptance, both individually and collectively: "Love takes off the masks that we fear we cannot live without and know we cannot live within." He continues, "I use the word 'love' here not merely in the personal sense but as a state of being, or a state of grace—not in the infantile American sense of being made happy but in the tough and universal sense of quest and daring and growth."[17]

Although Baldwin occasionally waxed romantic and spoke of "a freedom that was close to love" and made remarks like, "if love will not swing wide the gates [to the acceptance of blacks], no other power will or can," he was by no means quixotic in his embrace of love. Rejecting Christian love as "a mask for hatred and self-hatred and despair," he was acutely aware that "power *is* real, and many things, including, very often love, cannot be achieved without it." He noted, reflecting on the 1954 Supreme Court decision outlawing segregation, that "had it been a matter of love or justice" and not of "the realities of power in this difficult era," the decision "would surely have occurred sooner."[18]

For Baldwin, almost incredibly, love is the name for the connection between both blacks and whites, and between blacks and the country that brutally enslaved their forebears. On the first count, this is exemplified by his repeated insistence that "Whether I like it or not, or whether you like it or not, we are bound together forever. We are part of each other. What is happening to every Negro in the country at any time is also happening to you." On the second, it is evidenced in the resoluteness of his belief, in the face of his own seething hatred, that "I am not a ward of America; I am one of the first Americans to arrive on these shores." The key point is that love means accepting America, warts and all, and making it one's own through a commitment to seeing through the project of making it a better place. Any effort at achieving our country must begin from a full embrace of where we now are and who we are now, not merely who we want to become.[19]

In the end, the importance of love resides in the fact that "the question of this color, especially in this country," involved, inescapably, "the graver questions of the self," a point we will discuss further below. The racial tensions in America, Baldwin believed, were "rooted in the very same depths as those from which love springs, or murder." He could easily have used the word "loved" rather than "liked" when he asserted that "no one, after all, can be liked whose human weight and complexity cannot be, or has not been, admitted."[20] The implication remains that in the absence of love, and in the absence of attention to the "graver questions of the self," which in my view are indeed absent in Rorty's merely public assertions of a "we" consciousness, any connection that is forged will lack a fundamental recognition of the other's full humanity.

COMMUNITY, INNOVATION, AND DEMOCRATIC SELF-RENEWAL

The notion of achieving our country is a claim about democratic self-renewal, about the capacity of a collectivity to transform itself from within. At bottom, it rests on a deep tension dramatized by Rorty's notion of self-reliance on a communal scale. This tension is inherent in the interplay between individualism and patriotism at the heart of Whitman's affirmation of America's "poetical nature." The individual generation of "new conceptions of possible communities" and "new ways of being human" that Rorty embraces in both an Emersonian and Whitmanian vein conflicts with the need to recognize what we have in common with others, which is a precondition of collective identity, and thus of political agency.[21]

This tension surfaces in Rorty's work in the form of a thinly veiled fear. It is a fear, oddly enough, that Rorty shares with Sheldon Wolin. Rorty, like Wolin, fears that an excessive emphasis on the recognition of differences will erode the communal prerequisites of political action.[22] While for both thinkers there is a certain amount of quasi-ideological antipostmodernist bias animating these fears, they also express a fundamental problem at the heart of their commitments to democratic collective self-transformation: the tension between community and innovation, between "discovering the common and creating new commonalities, respecting old boundaries and installing new ones."[23]

Wolin's vision of politics is sustained by a distinction between the mundane, everyday functioning of democratic procedures and the rarer, more "fugitive" moments of genuine democracy marked by the collective expression of the will of the *demos*. His understanding of the transformative power of democracy rests on a quintessentially Emersonian insight about the creativity of ordinary individuals. But, given his strong commitment to the *demos* as a collective, a commitment Emerson was much more guarded about, Wolin must harmonize this innovative capacity with the collective preconditions of democratic action: "The possibility of renewal draws on a simple fact that ordinary individuals are capable of creating new cultural patterns of commonality at any moment."[24]

Rorty, similarly, wishes to affirm both the creative or imaginative capacity of individuals, which he describes as a matter of generating new metaphors, and the collective or communal bases of shared identification that enable collective agency. This is particularly germane to his affirmation of Whitman's poetic ideal. As Rorty puts it, "Nations rely on artists and intellectuals to create images of, and to tell stories about, the national past" (AOC, 4). Yet, because rooted in individual aesthetic visions of the world, not only will there be a plurality of different stories, but the individualistic nature of these stories may undermine the unity of vision inherent in patriotism or national pride. As I noted earlier, this tension is inherent in the complex form of national attachment that Whitman posits in *Vistas*, with its origins in Mill's Humboldtian stress on the diversity of character. Rorty insightfully perceives the roots of Whitman's "truly grand nationality" and traces it back to the epigraph to Mill's *On Liberty*, which quotes Humboldt on "the absolute and essential importance of human development in its richest diversity." However, Rorty interprets Mill and Humboldt's "richest diversity" and Whitman's "full play" as antitranscendentalist claims against the idea of an "authoritative guide [e.g., "Plato's or even Christ's] to human conduct." He then contrasts this "romance of endless diversity" with contemporary multiculturalism and affirms a Whitmanesque notion of public life as a "poetic agon, in which jarring dialectical discords would be resolved in previously unheard harmonies"—a very attractive ideal, to be sure, but one that would seem at odds with Rorty's arguments for a public realm guided by a shared liberal "we" consciousness. To put it another way, Whitman's ideal of variety in unity is a far cry from a public sphere defined by a "firm distinction" between public and private that ensures that individual forms of life remain outside the political realm rather than providing an arena where "jarring discords" collide (AOC, 22–25).[25]

The tension between individual creative energies and the terms of collective attachment is not so easily disposed of. When push comes to shove and the two conflict, Rorty, like Wolin, will always be more inclined to sacrifice individuality to preserve commonality. (For Emerson, by contrast, it was the reverse.) Nevertheless, Rorty insists that there is no incompatibility between "respect for cultural differences" and the brand of "American patriotism" he advocates. It seems to me that he is genuine in this commitment and is not an adherent of what he calls an "arrogant, bellicose nationalism." Because he limits the terms of this commonality to the exclusively affirmative stance of national pride, however, he must reject most expressions of difference or individuality for "refusing to rejoice in the country it inhabits" (PSH, 252–53). Put differently, because he does not adequately differentiate between pride and identification, it becomes impossible to engage with one's country by continually arguing with it—that is, by refusing to rejoice in it lest we neglect the work that remains to be done.

The larger issue at stake in Rorty's appropriation of Baldwin and his criticisms of postmodern difference politics concerns the degree of attachment of the social critic to her society. Here the tension between innovation and community is brought into bold relief. Rorty's appropriation of Baldwin's stance tends to emphasize the communal or connected side at the expense of the creative or innovative side. Baldwin is an exemplar for Rorty because of his ability to combine "a continued unwillingness to forgive [America for its racial crimes] with a continuing identification with the country that brought over his ancestors in chains (AOC, 12)."[26] From Rorty's vantage, the strength of Baldwin's stance is twofold: first, for all his criticisms of America, he never stops thinking of it as *his* country, and second, because he refuses to allow his disgust with the racist side of the American character to lead to a resignationist withdrawal from the project of collective self-improvement.

For Rorty, both a claim about attachment or identification with one's country and a claim about moral or political agency are at stake. As we have seen, Rorty argues that the refusal of the postmodern or "cultural" left to identify with America has contributed to a "detached" and "spectatorial" malaise that permits the right to dominate national politics. But he does not stop there: the problem with the postmoderns is not simply that they refuse to identify with America—this in my view is a more warranted criticism—it is, Rorty asserts, that they refuse to take pride in her achievements and credit her advances.

Rorty's stance sets him against the idea that social criticism requires radical detachment and makes him an advocate of what Michael Walzer has called "connected criticism." The connected critic, Walzer holds, is neither emotionally nor intellectually detached from the society she inhabits. A "local judge," the connected critic is "one of us" who appeals to local principles, proffering social criticism from within. For Walzer, social criticism is a byproduct of a larger activity that he calls "cultural elaboration and affirmation"—the work of "priests and prophets; teachers and sages; storytellers, poets, historians, and writers generally."[27]

Rorty conceives a similar process when he speaks of social criticism as the work of "cultural reweaving." The point is that criticism must take place in and through a set of values shared with one's fellow citizens. We become critics "naturally," as Walzer tells it, not through detachment—that is, not through either transcendence or estrangement—but through engagement: "by elaborating on existing moralities and telling stories about a society more just than, though never entirely different from, our own."[28]

Stories—that is, nontranscendental, contextualized narratives of self-understanding—about "what a nation has been and should try to become" are likewise a part of Rorty's project of achieving our country. Both Walzer and Rorty uphold a pragmatist understanding of beliefs as linked to plans of action: stories are more than a matter of setting out where we are and how we got here; they are crucial to the process of "deciding what we will do next" and "what we will try to become." Like Walzer, who sees cultural elaboration as "intended to set people in motion," Rorty argues that stories are the key ingredient in "persuading a nation to exert itself."[29]

But can a "connected" critic really be critical? Rorty never really addresses this issue and tends to skim over it when he casts the only available options as "piecemeal reformism" or "total revolution." Walzer explicitly addresses it, but the tension between community and innovation, between connectedness and criticism, emerges here as well. One of the aims of the connected critic is to "create a new awareness among his own people of what is being done in their name." In the case of South African poet Breyten Breytenbach, the topic of an insightful chapter of Walzer's, this is a matter of "creating a new Afrikaner consciousness" to supplant the one on which the subjugation of blacks rested. But if the critic is to generate this new consciousness, to what is he to remain connected? Walzer gets around this problem by mitigating the degree of newness of the critic's vision. It is less the creation of a new consciousness, he argues, than "a change in the relative weight" of the emphases of the old consciousness. "The new culture is never wholly new; it is in large part a rearrangement of ideas already present in the old."[30]

I mention this case because the creation of a new consciousness is an essential part of Baldwin's program of achieving our country. Rorty appropriates Baldwin's emphasis on both identification and political agency, but he neglects the crucial role of this novel consciousness. Both "a new black man" and "a new white man" are needed, Baldwin thought, if we are to reach the point where we recognize that "this world is white no longer, and it will never be white again." As we have seen, Rorty too celebrates the creative production of "new conceptions of possible communities." But this commitment amounts to little more than lip service because of Rorty's insistence on a singular "we" identity in public. Visions of new possibilities do certainly grow out of elements that are already present and not de novo. But Baldwin's "love" for America is strong enough to withstand his novel vision of what America must become without tempering the force of its innovativeness and inherent criticism. Integration, on Baldwin's novel view, means "that we, with love, shall force our [white] brothers to see themselves as they are, to cease fleeing from reality and begin to change it."[31] This surely is connected criticism. But, importantly, the terms of the connection are different.

TOWARD A DETACHED ATTACHMENT

The traditional defense of detached social criticism makes critical vision de- pendent on the critic's radically detaching herself from the everyday, shared world to ascend to some Archimedean standpoint to either invent the truth (the romantic model), to discover it (the natural law model), or to receive it through divine revelation (the religious model). What these perspectives share is the assumption that critical or moral principles are only available when one steps back from one's social position and local attachments. Both Walzer and Rorty reject this transcendental assumption and argue for a kind of connected criticism articulated both through and from the realm of our parochial attachments. But not all detachment is radical and transcendental. This is a possibility I want to consider in this section—the possibility of a "detached attachment," in George Kateb's paraphrase of Whitman, as the cru- cial element in democratic self-renewal.[32]

A key difference between Walzer's and Rorty's accounts of connected crit- icism is that while Walzer insists no less firmly than Rorty on the attachment of the critic to the shared beliefs and values of her fellow citizens, he allows for the possibility that this relation may be an ambiguous or "antagonistic" connection. Walzer's evocative metaphor for the functioning of connected criticism is "Hamlet's glass"—a mirror "where you may see the inmost part of you," as Hamlet puts it. Quoting Breytenbach, Walzer suggests that the critic "holds his words up to us like mirrors." What makes this a critical ac- tivity, Walzer holds, is that we are not happy with what we see in the mirror: "The point of holding up the mirror is to demonstrate that the ideal order is not here, or that we're not there. The stories that we tell ourselves about the realization of freedom and equality are untrue: one has only to look in the glass and see."[33]

Both philosophers identify a dual function of "culture criticism," in Rorty's phrase, as a matter of, first, "elaboration" (Walzer) or "reweaving" (Rorty) of current beliefs and values, and, second, of expressing the culture's hopes and aspired-to ideals. Much less strident in his critique of philosophy's metaphysical presuppositions, Walzer has no problem asserting that the critic "shows us to ourselves as we really are" and "exposes the false appearances of his society." Rorty would likely object to the "mirroring" metaphor in Walzer's statement that "the critic elaborates the hopes, interprets the ideals, and holds both against his mirror image of social reality." Yet accurate representations of current conditions are, on Walzer's scheme, essential; without the contrast between the way things are now and our aspirations of how they should be, the critical enterprise loses its bite.[34]

This leads to a major difference between Rorty and Walzer on the critic's relation to present conditions, and on the question of pride. Because his antirepresentationalist position rules out any claims about the nature of "reality," Rorty's connected critic must stop at the portrayal of our ideals, the "dream country" for which we hope, and eschew "the one to which [we] wake up every morning." From this move, it follows that the attitude most appropriate to our ideals and aspirations is one of prideful optimism toward the future rather than the disgust or betrayal evoked by present failures. On this point, Rorty is explicit: while an emotional involvement with one's country may naturally take the form of either "intense shame" or "glowing pride," politics will not be "imaginative and productive" unless "pride outweighs shame" (AOC, 3, 101).

The point of the critic's holding a mirror up to society on Walzer's account is the revelation that we don't like what we see in the reflection. Thus, criticism only has a grip on those "who are uneasy with the mirror image," which Walzer believes will be a large majority. By contrast, Rorty's insistence that pride must outweigh shame ensures that a felt sense of compromise on the part of society's members for its shortcomings is never experienced.[35]

This sense of one's self being compromised by the shortcomings of one's society, I want to argue, rather than pride, is a prerequisite of democratic self-renewal. In other words, to modify Rorty's phrase, *shame* is a condition of growth. Such compromise is only possible, paradoxically, under a kind of connection that admits of some detachment. Or, better, the kind of alienation from one's society or disgust with it inherent in shame can only be a condition of growth when expressed in the form of a continued commitment to changing it. What Kateb calls detached attachment is another name for the kind of agonized relation to democracy that Stanley Cavell has eloquently described in the context of Emersonian moral perfectionism as the uniquely democratic possibility of "*living* with, and against" one's culture, and for the possibility that Walzer seems to allow for when he speaks of an ambiguous or "antagonistic" form of connectedness.[36]

There are two points I wish to make in the remainder of this chapter about the notion of detached attachment that underscore its relevance to the project of democratic self-renewal expressed in achieving our country. The first involves demonstrating that the idea of a detached attachment is compatible with the forms of connectedness that both Walzer and Rorty seek and does not violate their concerns about radical or transcendental detachment. The second is to try to outline what makes detached attachment central to Baldwin's understanding of how we are to achieve our country. Briefly put, it has to do with making self-transformation a critical component of collective transformation—something that Rorty's notion of "Emersonian self-creation on a communal scale" suggests but never realizes.

As to the first point, the version of moral perfectionism that Cavell adduces from Emerson's writings is understood, first and foremost, as something "essential to the criticism of democracy from within." What makes perfectionism "necessary" to democracy is its aim of not "excusing democracy for its inevitable failures, or looking to rise above them, but in teaching how to respond to those failures, and to one's compromise by them, otherwise than by excuse or withdrawal." Detached attachment, a notion Kateb discerns in both Emerson and Whitman, is similarly a way of engaging thoughtfully with one's world. Although it involves a "partial but studied disengagement," it is not a call for solipsistic withdrawal. Instead, it seeks to establish a "poetical attachment to things and beings" in order to enable what Emerson called "an original relation" to reality, but also to cultivate a greater openness toward others.[37]

A poetical attachment to things means, on this Whitmanesque reading, "to become attached with unreserved love." Such a relation is only possible by becoming detached from oneself and the immediate attachments of one's everyday world, but "without, of course, pretending to be able or wanting to abandon them." Even though Whitman's idea of "adhesive love" is "unrelated to tight collectivity," Kateb nevertheless thinks that "adhesiveness" is not the best model for understanding this democratic connectedness because it undermines the individualism Whitman sought to promote and, most importantly, because "it serves the sinister project of nationalism." Instead of adhesiveness, Kateb argues, democratic connectedness is a matter of "receptivity or responsiveness" to others.[38]

Interestingly, both Walzer and Rorty offer George Orwell as an exemplar of connected social criticism.[39] Both emphasize his connectedness; the "mainstream" (Walzer) tenor of his social criticism; his steadfast resistance to pat, ideological solutions; and the fact that he never sacrificed the suffering of flesh-and-blood individuals in the name of abstract principles. In an insightful and original essay, Walzer does better than the standard accounts that attribute this simply to Orwell's "ordinary decency." He accounts for Orwell's virtues by noting that "Orwell was faithful to what he was. . . . His success has something to do with his ability, on all his journeys, physical and intellectual, to take himself along."[40]

I think this remark captures something fundamental, not just about Orwell and connected criticism, but about politics more broadly that both Cavell and Kateb are trying to convey—namely, that the full force of our selves or our character must be present in all our commitments. Baldwin makes the similar point that white Americans, if they are to change, must overcome the "individual uncertainty," the "inability to renew themselves at the fountain of their own lives," so that they can "be *present* in all that one does." This insight is also central to Walzer's conception of connected criticism in that the "hopes and ideals" we glimpse in the critic's mirror, he argues, "have an actual location—in our 'souls,' in our everyday consciousness of the moral world." This, I want to argue, is a marked improvement on Rorty's understanding of achieving our country, which, by contrast, involves only the "public" parts of our selves, leaving our "souls," if you will, at home when we enter public life.[41]

However, the problem with Walzer's account is that it assumes a static conception of "soul" or self. He praises Orwell because, throughout the different experiences and provocations of his life, he was always able to stay "faithful to what he was," and he always "managed to connect his old self and his new politics." It is important for Walzer to insist on this static self because the only alternative, as he casts it, is the kind of detached or disconnected criticism that he identifies in Jean-Paul Sartre and Simone de Beauvoir. On this latter model, which Walzer is writing against, the critic must first "escape his own condition" and "universalize" himself before he joins a political struggle, so that "he transforms himself even as he transforms the world." Now severed from all particularistic ties, this detached critic is more likely to take the kind of abstract view that places critical principles ahead of one's fellow citizens— precisely Rorty's critique of the postmoderns. What keeps Orwell connected, by contrast, is, in a phrase of Baldwin's, his "moral center." The lesson of what I have been calling detached attachment is that this moral center must not be understood statically.[42]

Detachment need not mean a radical cutting off from society and membership; this is the fundamental point that Cavell and Kateb make via their readings of Emerson and Whitman. Nor must it translate into a groundless abstraction from all concrete others. Because he takes Orwell's self-constancy as a standard, Walzer rejects Sartre's approach to criticism because, on the Sartrean view, the critic must "invent himself as a social critic" and create "a new life." The "failures" of Sartre's and Beauvoir's social criticism in the context of the Algerian war can thus be attributed to "the radical character of their self-criticism." However, in rejecting the idea that the critic transforms herself as she transforms the world, even though he does it for good reasons, Walzer needlessly rules out the possibility of detachment and self-criticism tout court.[43]

The tension that causes Walzer to insist on a static, particularist self to which the critic can remain connected is the same tension that causes Rorty to privatize the creative energies of the self—namely, the tension between community and innovation, and the tendency for the latter to undermine the former. Emersonian moral perfectionism and the detached attachment it entails allow the critic both to offer a new vision of the world—as a higher, unattained but attainable state of current conditions—and to avoid the radical detachment that both Walzer and Rorty find pernicious because it understands these visions as a function of the self's becoming. And, since the critic remains connected to her particular values as well as to the values of her world, the vacuity of the abstract, universalist conception is avoided.

The most eloquent and compelling statements of the position I want to affirm are Cavell ruminating on Emerson. Elaborating the relation to democratic life of the kind of detached attachment we have been discussing, he explains that the "training and character and friendship Emerson requires" should be understood as

> preparation to withstand not its rigors but its failures, [the] character to keep the democratic hope alive in the face of disappointment with it. . . . The distance of any actual society from justice is a matter for each of us to access for ourselves. I will speak of this as our being compromised by the democratic demand for consent, so that the human individual meant to be created and preserved in democracy is apt to be undone by it.[44]

The self-transformation or becoming implied in this last line is the key. Cavell further describes this as "an expression of disgust with or a disdain for the present state of things so complete as to require not merely reform, but a call for a transformation of things, and before all a transformation of self." The possibility that this entails—and the one which is squeezed out of existence in both Rorty and Walzer—is the possibility of a democratic collective self-transformation driven neither by a "longing for total revolution" nor by merely "giving voice to the common complaints of the people."[45]

The cultivation of "a new mode of human being, of being human," which Rorty invokes in his Emersonian moments, is on this view not something that "comes later than justice but that is essential in pursuing the justice of sharing another's fate." As I intimated above, the cardinal requirement of Emersonian perfectionism is "that we become ashamed in a particular way of ourselves, of our present stance," not as a prelude to detachment and spectatorship, as shame is understood by Rorty, but as "a sign of consecration to the next self." Perfectionism, at bottom, is a way of relating to the world that enables us to see not only ourselves but, simultaneously and inevitably, the possibilities of our world "in a transformed light."[46] Anything less, I want to assert, will be inadequate to Baldwin's program for achieving our country.

ACHIEVING OUR SELVES:
SELF-CRITICISM AS SOCIAL CRITICISM

In this final section, I will try to link the particular relation to the world of detached attachment that I have outlined to Baldwin's project of democratic self-renewal. The promise of Rorty's argument in *Achieving Our Country* is that it goes beyond providing a conception of social criticism by addressing the crucial phase of transformation and actual change that follows the critical moment. "Philosophy," he has argued, in one of his more suggestive ideas for what should come after metaphysics, "should stop trying to provide reassurance and instead encourage what Emerson called 'self-reliance'" (PSH, 34). In other words, philosophy should give up on the quest for certainty, as Dewey called it, and instead foster imagination, "thinking up interesting alternatives to one's present beliefs." Indeed, Rorty has recently suggested that we understand his pragmatism precisely as "an attempt to alter our self-image" (PSH, 72).

I welcome the appearance of these themes in Rorty's thought, and I believe that he is on the right track here. On the most sympathetic reading, changing the way we describe ourselves—what he calls "self-redescription"—is in important ways a prelude to actually changing ourselves, and by extension, transforming our world. The question is whether his effort to wed the work of self-transformation to a patriotic orientation in a bifurcated way—namely, via his "firm distinction" between public and private, what he has called "a collage of private narcissism and public pragmatism"—is adequate to the task of achieving our country (ORT, 210).

Specifically, my central criticism of Rorty's approach is that it divorces self-criticism from social criticism so as to betray both Baldwin's fundamental insight that the politics of race in America "has everything to do with ourselves" and the creative ambiguity inherent in the idea of "the individual as America." Although he values individual projects of self-creation and makes the necessary space for such projects a priority in his "liberal utopia," by casting self-examination as an inherently private matter of no bearing on public life, Rorty renders the kind of deep introspection Baldwin thought essential to achieving our country superfluous to politics. In the end, Rorty's conjunction of distinct modes of private self-creation and public moralism proves in-adequate when juxtaposed to Baldwin's engagement with a community *and* his demand that people change themselves.[47]

Part of the problem has to do with their divergent understandings of our re-lation to the past. Rorty's appeal to Emersonian self-reliance is part of the proj-ect of extricating ourselves from unhelpful, past—mostly transcendental—ways of looking at the world. Once we have been "unfitted" for "listening to transcendental stories," Rorty holds, it will be possible to substitute the idea of creating a better future for the attempt to escape time and history, and for philosophy to take up what Dewey called the social and moral strifes of the day (PSH, 68–69). Yet the phrase "self-reliance" merely serves as a proxy for hope in Rorty's scheme. The independent spirit of Emerson's "The American Scholar" that Rorty evokes here turns out to be merely a way of scoring anti-Philosophical, with a capital *p*, points. On Rorty's reading, one of the reasons behind Dewey's evasion of representationalism was that it had become an im-pediment to developing a sense of self-reliance (ORT, 17). Changing the pic-ture we have of ourselves is indeed for Rorty an important way of freeing our-selves from outmoded philosophical vocabularies of the past. When it comes to politics, however, his attitude toward the past is very different; we must tell "inspiring stories about episodes and figures in the nation's past" if we are to produce the kind of optimism about the future that will keep citizens engaged (AOC, 3).

Baldwin once said that "an invented past can never be used." There is a sense in which he is wrong about this: an invented past can be both effective and dangerous as a political force. But what I think he meant is that, to the extent that we still cling to "chimeras" and do not face certain unseemly facts about ourselves and our country, we preclude the possibility of change. By "change," he meant not change "on the surface but in the depths . . . change in the sense of renewal." Americans, he believed, are still "trapped in a his-tory which they do not understand." Until this past is not only understood but faced and confronted, America will remain captive to it and barred from meaningful change. This is why self-examination is needed: "The great force of history comes from the fact that we carry it within us, are unconsciously controlled by it in many ways, so history is literally *present* in all that we do." If we are not capable of this self-reflection, Baldwin warned, we "may yet become one of the most distinguished and monumental failures in the his-tory of nations"—an echo of Whitman's belief that "the United States are des-tined either to surmount the gorgeous history of feudalism, or else prove the most tremendous failure of time."[48]

There are occasions in Rorty's writing where he leaves the door open for a method of identifying with one's country not grounded in pride. For example, at times it seems only necessary to "derive our moral identity, at least in part, from our citizenship in a democratic nation-state, and from leftist attempts to fulfill the promise of the nation" (AOC, 97). Indeed, he has asserted that "we should face up to unpleasant truths about ourselves," but with the caveat that "we should not take those truths to be the last word about our chances for happiness, or about our national character" (AOC, 106). Yet the "idea of a national identity" and "the emotion of national pride" remain for Rorty in a complementary relationship and constitute the critical force behind political involvement. His statement about confronting past wrongs is followed by a reaffirmation of his call for "shared utopian dreams." Not taking pride and "rejoicing" in one's country becomes synonymous with admitting that one's country is incapable of reform and abandoning the project of achieving our country (PSH, 252). Perhaps when it comes to a certain species of postmodernist, this assertion holds. But Baldwin provides a perfect counterexample where it does not. Rorty, however, mistakes the nature of Baldwin's connection to America to be one of pride rather than love.[49]

To be fair, it also should be pointed out that Rorty intends the "episodes and figures" of the past to serve as ideals or exemplars to which the country should then endeavor to "remain true," as hopes that the country would have to transform itself to fulfill (AOC, 3–4, 8). Yet while Rorty's projection of hopes and ideals to spur collective change appears to echo the Emersonian idea of an unattained yet attainable self that pulls us out of our current state onto the plane of becoming, it fails to accommodate the necessary concomitant that "in criticizing my society for its relative disadvantages I am in effect criticizing myself." The crucial point about perceiving the shortfall of one's society in terms of its own ideals is that one feels that the "compromised state of society, since it is mine, compromises me." This same insight lies behind Walzer's mirror and Baldwin's idea that whites' estrangement from blacks is a measure of their estrangement from themselves. The "story of the Negro is the story of America—or, more precisely," he adds, "the story of Americans," because of this fact: "What we really feel about him is involved with all that we feel about everything, about everyone, about ourselves."[50]

What makes Rorty's pragmatism potentially so suited to Baldwin's reading of American racial politics is that Baldwin's idea of achieving our country is in large measure a matter of changing the self-descriptions of whites—that is, of altering their self-image. Baldwin argued that only once whites had abandoned the self-descriptions that rest on the assumption of black inferiority would "the Negro problem" cease to be "needed." Here, existing "models of how to live" would not be sufficient, particularly those proffered by whites; "new standards" would be required, standards which will arise only from a "fruitful communion with the depths of [their] own being." This is the Emersonian theme of innovation through self-creation. Such ongoing transformation of our self-descriptions needs to be an integral part of the ongoing project of achieving our country.[51]

But if the process of democratic self-renewal is an ongoing one, what becomes of the theme of commonality? For Baldwin, like Rorty, the idea of achieving our country entails a common identity. But for Baldwin, this identity can only come about through a continued confrontation with the past, not a prideful affirmation of some "dream country," and through the arduous work of critical self-examination necessary for becoming who we are as Americans. It is worth noting that Baldwin, like Rorty, did think it important to recognize that "the history of the American Negro problem is not merely shameful," but it is also "something of an achievement."[52] But to the extent that this recognition becomes a shield for taking refuge from the past and not a goad to continued struggle, it is an obstacle rather than a stimulus to achieving our country. The crucial difference is that the need to achieve an identity and to become who we are, to adapt a phrase of Nietzsche's, is what binds us together, not the identity that has already been achieved itself. In other words, it is precisely a commitment to the (unfinished) American experiment that makes this project ongoing and gives rise to the continual possibility of democratic renewal, not a commitment to a static identity.

Baldwin never tired of pointing out what was wrong with the portrayal of the black condition depicted in Wright's *Native Son*. Part of the reason it fails for Baldwin is that both Bigger Thomas and the well-meaning liberal whites in the story, like Jan and Bigger's attorney, Max, never get beyond categories of identity and self-description that still "need" the problem of race. Wright's depiction of Bigger's all-consuming anger and hatred, and the pride endemic to the liberal hope of redeeming it, are two sides of the same coin of the denial of Bigger's "human weight and complexity." This is exemplified in Max's summation at the end of Bigger's trial. His address, Baldwin argues,

> seems to say that, though there are whites and blacks among us who hate each other, we will not; there are those who are betrayed by greed, by guilt, by blood lust, but not we; we will set our faces against them and join hands and walk together into that dazzling future when there will be no white or black.[53]

Baldwin describes this as "the dream of all liberal men, a dream not at all dishonorable, but, nevertheless, a dream." The problem with an identification with this "dazzling future" is that it locates the work that needs to be done elsewhere than with us ourselves. This is the problem with Rorty's appeal to a future "dream country" as well. Severing democratic renewal from renewal at the level of our selves ensures that there will be no renewal, only reentrenchment in a different form. The work that needs to be done resides precisely "in the heat and horror and pain of life itself where all men are betrayed by greed and guilt and blood lust and where no one's hands are clean." Love, the "torment and necessity" of love, is the only bond capable of seeing us through this work.[54]

CONCLUSION

I concur with Rorty's assertion that "we have to work out from the networks we are, from the communities with which we presently identify" (ORT, 202). In his essays of the 1980s, this was for Rorty largely a negative claim, a way of scoring points against transcendental and foundationalist approaches. More recently, it has become the basis for the positive political program of achieving our country where an inclusive, nonessentialist collective identity of "we liberals" serves as the nonfoundationalist ground of a transformative pragmatism. Yet too strong an attachment to "the communities with which we presently identify" can become a recipe for self-protective stagnation rather than collective self-improvement. "New conceptions of possible communities" and "new ways of being human" must be created, though without disrupting the forms of attachment that make a transition from the present state to some improved future condition possible.

This is the most sympathetic reading of Rorty's notion of "Emersonian self-creation on a communal scale." Its greatest virtue resides in its commitment to starting where we are now, rather than transcending it in the name of some abstract principle. So often in contemporary life, criticism of America from both the left and the right is expressed in a spirit of self-disgust that is quick to distance itself from the present state of affairs. What postmodern leftists who participate in the "America Sucks Sweepstakes" share with reactionary voices of perpetual moral indignation like William Bennett and the late Allan Bloom is this sense of deep revulsion to all or some part of where and who we are now. Their criticisms are articulated not in terms of a transformed vision of current conditions but some foreign set of values, whether it is a Continental radicalism that is alien to the American spirit or some version of man's timeless truths. The important point that Rorty gleans from Baldwin's model of social criticism is that one needs to embrace one's culture as it is now, warts and all, in order to transform it. A commitment to achieving our country is a commitment to what William James called the project of "raising the tone of democracy," a project that can only be fulfilled through values generated from within. Rorty's problem is that rather than starting from where we are now, he seeks to ground this project in a romanticized past and who we want to become instead.[55]

The question that remains is whether this kind of connectedness is best expressed in terms of a relation of prideful affirmation or one of a lover's chastisement. As I have argued, only the latter enables the kind of detached attachment necessary for a truly transformative critique of democracy's shortcomings from within. To be sure, *pace* Rorty, the category of identity is indeed operative here. But Baldwin's insight, which echoes Whitman's *Democratic Vistas*, is that we need to remain connected, not to a particular vision of America, or to the terms of a particular identity, but to the project of transforming it. The actual form this vision will ultimately take cannot be worked out in advance, nor will it ever be permanently resolved; it must continually be defined and redefined as the struggle for its achievement among many different voices proceeds. After all, the image that Whitman so eloquently evoked is one of democratic *vistas*, in the plural. And the particular vista championed by Rorty—his liberal utopia—represents only one way, and not necessarily the best way, to "achieve our country."

NOTES

1. Rorty, PSH, 87–88; Cornel West, *The American Evasion of Philosophy: A Genealogy of Pragmatism* (Madison: University of Wisconsin Press, 1989), 142.

2. James Baldwin, *Notes of a Native Son* (Boston: Beacon Press, 1955), 6.

3. On this point, see Stanley Cavell, *Conditions Handsome and Unhandsome: The Constitution of Emersonian Perfectionism* (Chicago: University of Chicago Press, 1990), 50, passim.

4. On the Puritan errand, see Perry Miller, *Errand into the Wilderness* (Cambridge, MA: Harvard University Press, 1956). See also Ralph Waldo Emerson, "The Poet," *Essays: First and Second Series* (New York: Vintage Books, 1990); Walt Whitman, 1855 preface to *Leaves of Grass* and *Democratic Vistas*, both in Mark Van Doren (ed.), *The Portable Walt Whitman* (New York: Penguin Books, 1973); and James Baldwin, *The Fire Next Time* (1963; New York: Vintage International, 1993).

5. On this conception of political theory in general, see Sheldon Wolin, *Politics and Vision: Continuity and Innovation in Western Political Thought* (Boston: Little, Brown & Co., 1960). He discusses the "imaginative reordering of political life" as "a necessary complement to action" (8–11, 17–27).

6. See West, *The American Evasion of Philosophy*, 12–13. Quoted in Rorty, PSH, 26.

7. Daniel S. Malachuk argues that the end of the Cold War marks the point at which Rorty begins to recognize that there is still in fact work to be done in the liberal public sphere. Prior to this, it was enough in Rorty's view to simply "cherish liberal institutions in the face of Soviet imperialism." Since the fall of communism, Rorty increasingly sees pragmatism as a progressive force and relies more heavily on James

and on Whitman to make his case. See Daniel S. Malachuk, "Walt Whitman and the Culture of Pragmatism," *Walt Whitman Quarterly Review* 17, nos. 1–2 (1999): 65–67.

8. For a lucid discussion of Rorty's narrative of the left's demise and many of these issues more generally to which I am indebted, see George Shulman, "Hope and American Politics," *Raritan* 21, no. 3 (2002): 1–19.

9. Walt Whitman, *Democratic Vistas*, in *The Portable Walt Whitman*, ed. Mark Van Doren (New York: Penguin Books, 1973), 323.

10. Whitman, *Democratic Vistas*, 323.

11. Whitman, *Democratic Vistas*, 317. Cf. Emerson: "The book, the college, the school of art, the institution of any kind, stop with some past utterance of genius. This is good, say they,—let us hold by this. They pin me down. They look backward and not forward. But genius looks forward: the eyes of man are set in his forehead, not in his hindhead: man hopes: genius creates," in "The American Scholar," in *The Portable Emerson*, ed. Carl Bode (New York: Penguin Books, 1981), 56.

12. Whitman, *Democratic Vistas*, 329n.

13. Mark Van Doren, editor's note to *Democratic Vistas*, in *The Portable Walt Whitman*, 315.

14. Justin Kaplan traces these terms to Whitman's lifelong interest in phrenology. Whitman's copy of Orson Fowler's *Practical Phrenology* defined *amativeness* as "sexual love" and *adhesiveness* as "Friendship; attachment; fraternal love" symbolized by "two women embracing each other." Kaplan notes that the "two women" became for Whitman "two men." See Justin Kaplan, *Walt Whitman: A Life* (New York: Simon & Schuster, 1980), 146–56, 233–34.

15. By contrast, Rorty has asserted that the "liberal ironist," an embodiment of lived, pragmatist individuality, "thinks that recognition of a common susceptibility to humiliation is the *only* social bond that is needed" (CIS, 91). The problem here is that the ironist's individuality never impacts the shared terrain.

16. Baldwin, *The Fire Next Time*, 105 (emphasis added); "Many Thousands Gone," in *Notes of a Native Son*, 33. For Baldwin's recounting of his experiences with Elijah Muhammad and the Nation of Islam, see *The Fire Next Time*, 47–82.

17. James Baldwin, "Nobody Knows My Name," in *Nobody Knows My Name: More Notes of a Native Son* (New York: Laurel Books, 1961), 113; "In Search of a Majority," in *Nobody Knows My Name*, 99; *The Fire Next Time*, 22, 94–95.

18. Baldwin, *The Fire Next Time*, 30, 39, 41, 72–73, 87.

19. Baldwin, "Nobody Knows My Name," 114; *The Fire Next Time*, 98; "Stranger in the Village," in *Notes of a Native Son*, 111.

20. Baldwin, *Nobody Knows My Name*, 12; *The Fire Next Time*, 95–96; "Stranger in the Village," 137.

21. William Connolly calls attention to this "ambiguity of the common" in the work of Sheldon Wolin. See Connolly's "Politics and Vision" in *Democracy and Vision: Sheldon Wolin and the Vicissitudes of the Political*, ed. Aryeh Botwinick and William Connolly (Princeton, NJ: Princeton University Press, 2001), 15–18.

22. See, for example, AOC, 101; PSH, 252. For Wolin's views, see his "Fugitive Democracy," in *Democracy and Difference: Contesting the Boundaries of the Political*, ed. Seyla Benhabib (Princeton, NJ: Princeton University Press, 1996), 31–45.

23. Connolly, "Politics and Vision," 15.

24. Wolin, "Fugitive Democracy," 43. He continues, "Individuals who concert their powers for low income housing, worker ownership of factories, better schools, better health care, safer water . . . and a thousand other common concerns of ordinary lives are experiencing a democratic moment."

25. Rorty understands multiculturalism as suggesting a "morality of live-and-let-live, a politics of side-by-side development in which members of distinct cultures preserve and protect their own culture against the incursions of other cultures" (AOC 24).

26. Interestingly, Rorty often adopts the language of "forgiveness" in this context and accuses the postmoderns for believing that America has "sinned" beyond redemption. For a discussion of Rorty's views on sin, see Shulman, "Hope and American Politics." Shulman argues that for Rorty, sin signifies the past and its power, something that jeopardizes the hope and promise of a better American future.

27. Michael Walzer, *Interpretation and Social Criticism* (Cambridge, MA: Harvard University Press, 1987), 36–40. See also his *The Company of Critics: Social Criticism and Political Commentary in the Twentieth Century* (New York: Basic Books, 1988). In Walzer's scheme, like Rorty's, social criticism should follow the model of Orwell rather than Foucault.

28. Rorty, CIS, 82–85, passim; Walzer, *Interpretation and Social Criticism*, 52, 64–65.

29. Rorty, AOC, 3–4, 11–13. Walzer describes them in this way: "The argument is about ourselves; the meaning of our way of life is what is at issue. The general question we finally answer is not quite the one we asked at first. It has a crucial addition: what is the right thing *for us* to do?" in *Interpretation and Social Criticism*, 23.

30. Walzer, *The Company of Critics*, 99, 222.

31. Baldwin, "Stranger in the Village," 111–12; *The Fire Next Time*, 9–10.

32. George Kateb, *The Inner Ocean: Individuality and Democratic Culture* (Ithaca, NY: Cornell University Press, 1992), 166–67. For a discussion of these models of social criticism, see Walzer, *Interpretation and Social Criticism*, 1–32.

33. Walzer, *The Company of Critics*, 22, 230–31.

34. Walzer, *The Company of Critics*, 231–33.

35. Walzer, *The Company of Critics*, 231n. I should point out that there are a few places where Rorty mentions that reading certain novels can "unsettle" readers—see, for example, TP, 323. However, in these instances, there is no mention of pride, which is precisely my point.

36. Cavell, *Conditions Handsome and Unhandsome*, 50.

37. Cavell, *Conditions Handsome and Unhandsome*, 3, 18; Kateb, *The Inner Ocean*, 165–68.

38. Kateb, *The Inner Ocean*, 96, 165–66, 242, 252, 259–60. There is one exception to this where Whitman describes adhesiveness as a matter of "momentary intensities." See, esp. George Kateb, "Whitman and the Culture of Democracy," in *The Inner Ocean*, whose subtlety and insight I have not even begun to capture in this brief space. For a contrasting view of Whitman which focuses on his unique understanding of nationhood, see Samuel H. Beer, "Liberty and Union: Walt Whitman's Idea of the Nation," *Political Theory* 12, no. 3 (1984): 361–86.

39. See Walzer's chapter on Orwell in *The Company of Critics*; Rorty's chapter on Orwell in *Contingency*; and his essay "Heidegger, Kundera, and Dickens," where Rorty reads Dickens through Orwell and praises both for their connectedness as social critics.

40. Walzer, *The Company of Critics*, 121–22.

41. Baldwin, *The Fire Next Time*, 43–44; Walzer, *The Company of Critics*, 231. For Rorty's view, see chaps. 4 and 5 of *Contingency*. Charles Molesworth makes a similar point in his gloss on Whitman's line that "personal force is behind everything . . . the self is always present in what we see and desire and project, and that any politics that does not address the powers of selfhood is doomed to distortion." See "Whitman's Political Vision," *Raritan* 12, no. 1 (1992): 102. A similar sentiment can be found in Stanley Fish, *The Trouble with Principle* (Cambridge, MA: Harvard University Press, 1999): "No part of the self (deliberative reason, reflective self-consciousness) [exists] abstracted from substantive commitments" (14).

42. Walzer, *The Company of Critics*, 121–21, 140–41; Baldwin, *Notes of a Native Son*, 6. Interestingly, Baldwin made a similar observation when he said he distrusted Richard Wright's association with "the French intellectuals, Sartre, de Beauvoir, and company" because "ideas were somewhat more real to them than people." See Baldwin, "Alas, Poor Richard," in *Nobody Knows My Name*, 148.

43. Walzer, *The Company of Critics*, 140–41.

44. Cavell, *Conditions Handsome and Unhandsome*, 56–57.

45. Cavell, *Conditions Handsome and Unhandsome*, 46. The "longing for total revolution" is a phrase Rorty borrows from Bernard Yack (see Yack's book by the same title). Rorty discerns it in anyone not willing to reconcile his or her political aspirations to his Deweyan "piecemeal reformism." The last phrase is from Walzer, *The Company of Critics*, 16. I am suggesting that his view of social criticism as merely "evoking the core values of his audience in a powerful and plausible way" is not enough to achieve the kind of transformation that Baldwin's achieving our country requires. Walzer, *Interpretation and Social Criticism*, 89.

46. Cavell, *Conditions Handsome and Unhandsome*, xix, 16, 25.

47. Baldwin, "In Search of a Majority," 112. Shulman makes this point about Baldwin in "Hope and American Politics," 18–19.

48. Baldwin, *The Fire Next Time*, 8, 81, 92; "White Man's Guilt," quoted in Shulman, "Hope and American Politics," 12; "Nobody Knows My Name," in *Nobody Knows My Name*, 99. Whitman, *Democratic Vistas*, 318. On our relation to the past more generally, see David Bromwich, *A Choice of Inheritance: Self and Community from Edmund Burke to Robert Frost* (Cambridge, MA: Harvard University Press, 1989).

49. On at least one occasion, Rorty does evince a kind of political theory of love, although he does not relate it to the nation as such. He argues that "the moral tasks of liberal democracy" are divided between the "agents of love" and the "agents of justice." We can think of the former as "connoisseurs of diversity" who endeavor to have society recognize the differences of all its members, and the latter as "guardians of universality" who make sure people who have been admitted as citizens are treated equally. "It is well for society," he continues, that most of the time "justice has to be enough." Still, the goal, which takes the form of his familiar partitioned stance, is "the

ultimate synthesis of love and justice . . . an intricately-textured collage of private narcissism and public pragmatism." The recognition of difference thus becomes a private
matter with no necessary connection to public life. See ORT, 205–10.

50. See Cavell, *Conditions Handsome and Unhandsome*, 28; and Baldwin, "Many
Thousands Gone," 18; see also *The Fire Next Time*, 44.

51. Baldwin, *The Fire Next Time*, 22, 96–97. One of the engines of this ongoing
self-transformation is the "self-decentering" involved in our responses to the demands
of the other. On this point, see Fred Dallmayr, "Beyond Fugitive Democracy: Some
Modern and Postmodern Reflections," in *Democracy and Vision*, 72–75. This may be
what Baldwin had in mind when he remarked that "the only way [the white man] can
be released from the Negro's tyrannical power over him is to consent, in effect, to become black himself," in *The Fire Next Time*, 96.

52. Baldwin, "Stranger in the Village," 149.

53. Baldwin, "Many Thousands Gone," in *Notes of a Native Son*, 35.

54. Baldwin, "Many Thousands Gone," 35; *The Fire Next Time*, 85–86.

55. William James, "The Social Value of the College Bred," in *William James:
Writings, 1902–1910*, ed. Bruce Kuklick (New York: Library of America, 1987),
1248. Though he admitted that *tone* was "a terribly vague word to use," James held
that "by their tone are all things human either lost or saved. If democracy is to be
saved it must catch the higher, healthier tone." For Rorty's discussion of Jonathan
Yardley's phrase "the America Sucks Sweepstakes" and why he has borne the brunt
of criticism from both the left and the right, see PSH, 3–22.

Conclusion

Rorty and Thesis Eleven

Though often misunderstood, the tradition of American pragmatism, at its best, has been a program for change. Shot through with Romantic notions about the power of imaginative thought to transform the world, it nevertheless retains an empiricist bent, responding to social and cultural crises via thoughtful and critical assessments of what American democracy is and must strive to become. As Cornel West has eloquently argued, we should see pragmatism as "an attempt to reinvigorate our moribund academic life, our lethargic political life, our decadent cultural life, and our chaotic personal lives for the flowering of many-sided personalities and the flourishing of more democracy and freedom."[1]

Understood in this context, Rorty's notion of "redescription" is a claim about the power of words, about the transformative power of imaginative language. The strongest case for its value to political theory is that Rortyan redescription heeds the admonition of Marx's eleventh thesis on Feuerbach: "The philosophers have only *interpreted* the world, in various ways; the point, however, is to *change* it."[2] However, Rorty's stance responds to Marx's thesis by refuting it. Reinterpreting the world, or to use Rorty's term, redescribing it, contra Marx, *is* a way of changing it. Redescriptions have the power to change minds because seeing our world in a transformed light is part and parcel of action to transform it. As Rorty puts it,

> We are no longer trying to understand the world, in the sense in which both Aristotle and Hegel understood "understand." It is not that we think the world unintelligible, but rather that we view redescription of it as a tool for social or individual change, rather than as an attempt to grasp intrinsic features of the real. . . . Contexts provided by theories are tools for effecting change. (PSH, 220–21)

183

Whether we seek to interpret it or change it, for Marx there existed a real world "out there" behind appearances, whose truth, through our language and categories of thought, we are capable of apprehending. Rorty rejects the assumptions on which this view rests as untenable anachronisms of a rationalist worldview that unduly privileged philosophy: not only is there no reason to believe that a reality independent of our perspective exists, but if it did, we would be unable to know it in any definitive sense. Language simply does not work that way.

Yet this denial of our linguistic capacity to grasp the real need not mark an erosion of the power of thought. On the contrary, the loss in our ability to accurately describe reality spells a gain in our power to imaginatively portray it. Each new perspective on reality, though partial and incomplete, can illuminate some aspect of it in a novel way and suggest new possibilities for how that reality might be transformed. For Rorty, then, to interpret the world is indeed on some level to change it.[3]

Having displaced the dichotomy inherent in Marx's eleventh thesis, however, Rorty introduces one of his own. The tough choice we face now, he argues, is not between either interpreting the world or changing it but "between trying to change the world or change ourselves" (PSH, 220). As Rorty recounts it, after several generations of Marxists and neo-Marxists digested Marx's thesis, an odd distortion took place. The conviction emerged among a certain group of intellectuals that if, at the level of theory, one's interpretations of the world were sophisticated and critical enough, the mere articulation of them would suffice as a way of changing it. This is the view Rorty is writing against. Because of the power of this distorted belief, Rorty feels it necessary to persuade these intellectuals and their followers—Derrida, for instance—that coming up with elaborate theories is not a way of changing the world, but only part of their own private work of changing themselves. This bifurcated view of public and private projects is characteristic of Rorty's writing since the mid-1980s. For Rorty, then, not all redescriptions are automatically candidates for changing the world, only the ones deemed "public." The choice is between undertaking the private effort of changing oneself or embarking on the public task of changing the world.

This formulation raises a number of issues that need to be addressed. To name just two, who makes this choice? And who determines what will count as a "public" rather than a "private" redescription? On the second count, Rorty presents us with a set of criteria that distinguishes accounts working within metaphysical or rationalist assumptions that seek transcendental solutions from those that recognize the contingency of their vocabularies and point us back to concrete practices and a pragmatic attention to "real" problems, like the reduction of suffering. Yet one cannot help thinking that the decision of what should count as a public solution or be excluded from public consideration might be something better left to the public itself rather than determined beforehand.[4] The first issue is complicated by the fact that the choice does not seem one that can be left to participants themselves, since some who have believed their projects to be of public relevance—for example, Heidegger—at least on Rorty's own reckoning, have been mistaken.

After attempting to frame Rorty's thought in a way that makes it of moment to political theorists, I have offered two principal redescriptions of his project in this book that contextualize the "choice" Rorty proffers. Like all redescriptions, neither claims to have gotten Rorty right, only to offer a vantage that, though admittedly partial, casts certain aspects of his thought in a useful and productive light. In Rorty's parlance, it aims "to see differently rather than deeply." On one redescription, Rorty's rationale for why we must divide public and private can be seen as a kind of ex post facto defense of a preexisting commitment to a particular version of liberalism, and the result of a sense of anxiety about what would become of the priority of diminishing suffering if certain "private" perspectives were allowed to enter the public realm. The other redescription foregrounds Rorty's claims about the transformative power of imaginative writing and reads his recent statements of his political project in light of a conception of democratic criticism from within that originates in Emerson and Whitman and has resonances in Dewey. In the rest of this conclusion, I will revisit each of these perspectives, taking the second redescription first.

From this view, Rorty presents us with a false choice. Changing ourselves appears distinct from changing the world only because his understanding of language divorces words from the selves who use them. In his discussion of the individual's "final vocabulary"—the "here I stand" beyond which there is "no noncircular argumentative recourse," only "resort to force"—in *Contingency, Irony, and Solidarity*, Rorty asserts that "all human beings carry about a set of words which they employ to justify their actions, their beliefs, and their lives" (10, 73). Because he rejects the idea of an essentialist core self to which these words correspond—rightly, in my view—along with the idea of correspondence to reality, these words or vocabularies are all we have. Or better, these linguistic "webs of belief and desire" are all that we are (85). Yet because these words are not understood as immersed in the Jamesian "stream of experience" that helps define our "temperament" and original vision of the world, the "here I stand" is reduced to a "here I say," with no self to back our words up.

To put it another way, if redescribing the world can indeed be posited as a way of changing it, it is only because seeing the world in a new light entails seeing ourselves in a new light, and hence changing ourselves in the process of changing the world. This is why redescription comports so well with a pragmatist conception of belief change rather than a rationalist one, which was the argument of the first chapter. This type of change in perception fits what Stanley Cavell has called Emersonian perfectionism: a change in perception where we come to see ourselves, and hence the possibilities of our world, in a transformed light. But it also resonates with the refrain in Rorty's recent work that describes the pragmatist shift away from nonhuman authorities like God, Reality, or Truth in terms of "a movement toward increasing self-reliance on the part of our species."[5]

While the relation of this perfectionist perspective to pragmatism is by no means straightforward, James seems to underscore its main element—the importance of a new attainment of self—when he asserts that on the pragmatic method, "theories thus become instruments, not answers to enigmas, in which we can rest. We don't lie back upon them, we move forward, and, on occasion, make nature over again by their aid." Speaking of the "illuminating" or "power-bringing" words sought by the metaphysical tradition—like *God*, *Reason*, or *the Absolute*—he appears to have linked working out our personal visions and changing reality when he wrote,

> But if you follow the pragmatic method, you cannot look upon any such word as closing your quest. You must bring out of each word its practical cash-value, set it at work within the stream of your experience. It appears less as a solution, then, than as a program for more work, and more particularly as an indication of the ways in which existing realities may be *changed*.[6]

Leaving aside James's infamous phrase "practical cash-value," the point is that words that are detached from personal experience cannot serve as instruments, or in one of Rorty's better metaphors, as "levers," for change because in the absence of their connection to our temperament, we cannot know whether or not they "work," pragmatically speaking. This question is for James a matter of "consistency" or "fit" with our experience. When competing theories seem equally compatible, "we choose between them for subjective reasons. We choose the kind of theory to which we are already partial."[7]

To be sure, Rorty's position continues to evolve, as his recent, more explicit turn to Emerson and Whitman attests. To some extent, then, the jury is still out. Yet insofar as Rorty is, as Richard Bernstein once observed, still obsessed with the obsessions of philosophers and unable to let go of them, Rorty often interprets pragmatist claims abstractly, as merely antiepistemological claims, and thus obscures their fundamental reliance on personal vision.[8] For instance, because Rorty's understanding of philosophy tends to be shorn of its origins in what James called temperament, he interprets James's claims about individual existence as germane only to abstract philosophical arguments.[9]

The upshot of all this is that, severed from the effort to alter ourselves, re-description will prove unable to change the world. The transformative power of imaginative language hinges on the connection of words to the selves who use them, and, just as importantly, on the connection of these selves to the world around them, including—especially—the public realm. In his famous tract, "Politics and the English Language," one of Rorty's heroes, George Or-well, keenly discerned the connection between the proliferation of lifeless, stale abstractions at the level of language and political conformity in public life. At its best, Rortyan redescription promises a source of fresh metaphors and new angles of vision that will shatter the insipid slogans that underpin such conformity. However, as Orwell knew, the power of words is a function of the extent to which words express one's "private opinions" rather than echo the public beliefs of the day.[10]

No one was more aware of this than Dewey. Dewey asserted that "democ-racy is a *personal* way of individual life" that "signifies the possession and continual use of certain attitudes, forming personal character and determining desire and purpose in all the relations of life."[11] In a way that recalls James's writing on temperament, he stated that we should learn to think of our insti-tutions as "expressions, projections and extensions of habitually dominant personal attitudes." Dewey summed up his view in a passage worth quoting at length:

> Democracy as a personal, an individual, way of life involves nothing funda-mentally new. . . . Put into effect it signifies that powerful present enemies of de-mocracy can be successfully met only by the creation of personal attitudes in in-dividual human beings; that we must get over our tendency to think that its defense can be found in any external means whatever, whether military or civil, if they are separated from individual attitudes so deep-seated as to constitute personal character.[12]

Dewey had faith—perhaps too much faith—that "even when needs and ends or consequences are different for each individual," a "habit of amica-ble cooperation" would prevail in public life to reconcile them. Rorty, for his part, is much less convinced. He insists that when we enter political life, we abandon our right "to believe what we like" because "when so engaged it is necessary to reconcile our beliefs, our habits of action, with those of oth-ers."[13] This is quite true. But it all comes down to how we "reconcile" those beliefs. And here what Whitman referred to as giving "full play for human nature to expand itself in numberless and even conflicting directions"— what Rorty himself in *Achieving Our Country* called "a poetic agon"— would seem a more attractive possibility than leaving our personal visions at home (24).[14]

I now turn to my first redescription. Taken seriously, the idea that anything can be made to look good or bad by redescription is powerful and unsettling. Rorty has been read as not recoiling from the consequences of this claim. Indeed, there is a dark side to his liberal hope: "the acute awareness that there is nothing we can rely on to determine which scenario will be our future."[15] In my view, Rorty does indeed retreat from the consequences of the radical contingency and uncertainty he preaches. Never far below the surface in his work is the fear that liberalism itself may someday be redescribed in terms that make it look unattractive, that an infelicitous redescription may in fact do what Marx wanted done and change the world—but change in a way that supplants liberalism. Historically, such redescriptions have in fact occurred, and overwhelming numbers of people were persuaded that eliminating or enslaving another race of humans was permissible as a result. Despite accusations of a lack of moral seriousness in his work, there are traces of moralism in Rorty; he is deeply offended and affected by the tragedies of the twentieth century and the evils of America's past, so much so that he cannot help but try to prevent their reoccurrence, even at the cost of occasionally betraying his own pragmatism.

If we are indeed to take Rorty's pragmatism seriously and accept his assertion that philosophy can be of no help in dealing with Nazis and other bullies, which I think we should, we must be able to face the frightening, potentially tragic uncertainty that accepting the contingency of our beliefs entails. Even liberalism itself is contingent and subject to future redescription. Because his liberal utopia is designed to preclude the possibility that its citizens would place anything above avoiding cruelty, as noble as this position is, granting this priority a privileged status beyond redescription marks a retreat from our contingent fate.

"We should stop trying to combine self-creation and politics, especially if we are liberals," Rorty has argued: "The part of a liberal ironist's final vocabulary which has to do with public action is never going to get subsumed under, or subsume, the rest of her final vocabulary" (CIS, 120–21). That they should not be combined in individual final vocabularies is a qualitatively different argument than not combining them at the level of theory, and it is here that Rorty's account becomes problematic.[16]

In my view, this apparently needless extension of his prohibition of uniting public and private to individual lives can be accounted for if we recognize that, like James, Rorty does, after all, on some level believe that our philosophies and our commitments are a matter of personal vision. Discussing Nietzsche and Heidegger in *Contingency*, Rorty seems to make the point that their philosophies are indeed, in James's phrase, "accidents more or less of personal vision" and that they are better recognized as such, rather than misleadingly believed to be incarnations of some ahistorical Truth. The problem with Nietzsche and Heidegger is that they take their philosophizing to be of some greater relevance than merely an expression of a personal aesthetic pursuit or James's "accident of personal vision."[17]

The two figures whom Rorty identifies as, by contrast, fully accepting the personal origins of their thinking are Proust and Derrida. In an interesting choice of language, Rorty states that rather than attempting "to create a new self by writing a bildungsroman about our old self"—which is what Proust did—Heidegger tried to "write a bildungsroman about a character called 'Europe,'" which involved "affiliating" himself with something larger than his own "personal canon."[18] On this view, Heidegger failed where Proust succeeded because, unlike Heidegger, Proust "had no public ambitions" and sought no larger "affiliation" for his view beyond relevance for his own life (CIS, 117–19, 103–4).

The reason Rorty adduces for why we must insist on the division between public and private vocabularies is that it allows him to differentiate the thinkers who in his own estimation are relevant to developing a new private final vocabulary—like Plato, Nietzsche, Heidegger, Proust, and Nabokov—from those pertinent to public final vocabularies, like Dickens, Mill, Dewey, Orwell, Rawls, and Habermas. Another way he puts this distinction is that writers in the latter category have something to teach us about politics, while those in the former group do not (even though some of them mistakenly believed they did). The question we seek to answer in articulating our private final vocabularies—"what shall I become?"—must not be allowed to trump the public question of "what sorts of things about what sorts of people do I need to notice?" (CIS, 143–45). Perhaps this is true. But I have tried to argue—in chapters 5 and 6, and in my reading of Rorty's autobiographical essay "Trotsky and the Wild Orchids" in chapter 1—that cultivating our commitments toward others and toward social justice may very well be an inseparable part of answering the ethical question, "what shall I become?"

Rorty introduces a further distinction that cuts across the one between "the pursuit of private perfection" and "serving human liberty" just described. Nabokov (private perfection), he argues, can be "reconciled" with Orwell (serving human liberty) because, even though they fall in opposite categories, both were "political liberals" because "they both met Judith Shklar's criterion of a liberal: somebody who believes that cruelty is the worst thing we do" (CIS, 1456). These liberal thinkers, then, are the only ones capable of doing through redescription "what Marx wanted done—change the world." Nietzsche and Heidegger, though ironists, are not *liberal* ironists, and therefore their personal visions must be barred from the public realm. This, rather than a rejection of personal vision in toto, appears to lie behind the need for a "firm distinction" between public and private.

At the end of the day, however, a minimal degree of public-private exchange must be allowed in order for Rorty's argument about the novel as the primary vehicle of moral reflection in a democracy to fly. After all, the invention of new metaphors necessary for redescription is primarily a function of the (private) work of composing novels and poems. Given his strictures on the public and private, Rorty must be careful here; the closest he comes to an affirmation of the personal origins of our public commitments is to say that "poetic, artistic, philosophical, scientific, or political progress results from the accidental coincidence of a private obsession with a public need" (CIS, 37). If we cast our private visions merely as "obsessions," excluding them from public life may indeed seem like a good idea. As I argued in chapter 5, there is no reason to interpret them this narrowly and to exclude them from the struggle for social justice. In the end, what for James was the "accidental" quality of all our commitments, in Rorty's formulation seems to become the accidental quality of only our private beliefs. The temperamental origins of Rorty's commitment to liberalism are thus obscured, his autobiographical defense of this "preference" notwithstanding. This commitment ultimately takes on a quality that seems anything but personal or accidental; instead, it is automatically asserted as what "we" believe.[19]

As I have argued, the strongest evidence against his claim that a single thinker cannot combine private irony and a public passion for justice is Rorty himself. To the extent that Rorty adheres to his own division, he makes it impossible to commit himself fully to either irony or justice. When he is willing to cast doubt upon his most cherished beliefs and is yet unable to defend them passionately with his whole self, Rorty's stance suggests apologism or conformism. Without the weight of our selves to back them up, redescriptions are mere words that lack transformative force. When it detaches redescription from self-creation, the stance of private irony and public moralism limits the power of redescription such that our personal vision and temperament—what James called "the potentest of all our premises"—fits neatly and unproblematically within Rorty's liberal framework.

The irony here is that, as Bernstein has observed, the main reason Rorty insulates his commitment to liberalism from the contingency of the ironist is to preserve the "fundamental premise" of his pragmatism that contingent, historicized beliefs can inspire action and be worth dying for. For Bernstein, this contradiction reveals the fatal inadequacy of Rorty's stance: "Rorty's ironist may in fact think that some beliefs are 'worth dying for,' but she has nothing to say about why *her* beliefs are worth dying for rather than the strongly held beliefs of the fanatic or the fundamentalist." The implication is that Rorty should abandon his "fundamental premise," even though without it "his entire project falls apart."[20]

I have tried to argue that this need not occur. Within the resources of the rich tradition of American pragmatism, in all its guises, lie what is required for Rorty to retain his fundamental pragmatism premise *and* retain the coherency of his project. The question is whether he will elect to do so. In the end, it comes down to a question of self-reliance and whether Rorty's own project of self-creation can attain the higher, unattained but attainable self that remains to be forged so that he can move his project to the next level. I can think of no better words on which to end than Dewey's, in one of his most Emersonian moments:

> Surrender of what is possessed, disowning of what supports one in secure ease, is involved in all inquiry and discovery; the latter implicate an individual still to make, with all the risks implied therein. For to arrive at new truth and vision is to alter. The old self is put off and the new self is only forming, and the form it finally takes will depend upon the unforeseeable result of an adventure.[21]

NOTES

1. Cornel West, *The American Evasion of Philosophy: A Genealogy of Pragmatism* (Madison: University of Wisconsin Press, 1989), 4.

2. Karl Marx, "Theses on Feuerbach," in *The Marx-Engels Reader*, Robert C. Tucker, 2nd ed. (New York: W. W. Norton & Co., 1978), 145. The tradition of political theory, on one view, rests on the assumption common to Rortyan redescription that being persuaded to adopt a particular perspective on the world and to see it in a different light can spark change. I make this case in chapter 2.

3. Here Rorty's notion of redescription resonates with Sheldon Wolin's understanding of "vision," a claim I try to defend in chapter 2. Even though the "picture of society given by political theorists is not a 'real' or literal one . . . precisely because political theory pictured society in an exaggerated, 'unreal' way, it was a necessary complement to action." See Wolin, *Politics and Vision: Continuity and Innovation in Western Political Thought* (Boston: Little, Brown & Co., 1960), 17–21.

4. On this point, it should be said that Rorty is presenting his view of how things would work in his "liberal utopia," and thus in some sense is offering them up for public scrutiny. But I think the point that it is a rather "top-down" view still holds.

5. See "Remarks at MOMA," unpublished manuscript on Rorty's homepage, www.stanford.edu/~rrorty/moma.htm. Cf. also: "Answers to this question ["what sorts of people are there in the world, and how do they fare?"] are provided by novels like Steinbeck's, Zola's, and Stowe's—novels that tell you about the wretchedly poor. They are also provided by novels like James' and Proust's that tell you about rich people expanding their horizons. Reading either sort of novel may help the reader to transcend the parents, teachers, customs, and institutions that have blinkered her imagination, and thereby permit her to achieve greater individuality and

greater self-reliance," in Rorty, "Redemption from Egotism: James and Proust as Spiritual Exercises," *Telos* 3, no. 3 (2001): 244. On perfectionism, see Stanley Cavell, *Conditions Handsome and Unhandsome: The Constitution of Emersonian Perfectionism* (Chicago: University of Chicago Press, 1990), xviii–xix. I discuss these issues in chapters 3 and 5.

6. William James, *Pragmatism*, in *William James: Writings, 1902–1910*, ed. Bruce Kuklick (New York: Library of America, 1987), 509–10.

7. James, *Pragmatism*, 580–81. Somewhat paradoxically, James believed theories that "work" would "mediate" between "all previous truths" *and* our "new experiences." This mediating function of his pragmatism has been adeptly criticized by Cornel West. The central difference between Jamesian pragmatism and Emersonian perfectionism is that where James sought to reconcile new experiences with past truths, Emerson saw such novelty as drawing us beyond our old selves toward some higher, unattained but attainable self. On Rorty's "lever" metaphor, see CIS, 174–75.

8. See Richard J. Bernstein, *Philosophico-Political Profiles: Essays in a Pragmatic Mode* (Philadelphia: University of Pennsylvania Press, 1986), 47.

9. See, for example, Rorty's reading of James in "Religious Faith, Intellectual Responsibility, and Romance," in PSH. To take just one point, rather than advocating a wholesale rejection of the idea of correspondence, as Rorty suggests, James believed that pragmatism's "concreteness and closeness to facts . . . converts the absolutely empty notion of 'correspondence' between our minds and reality, into that of a rich and active commerce . . . between particular thoughts of ours, and the great universe of other experiences," *Pragmatism*, 517. Here I find apropos Bernstein's observation that for all his Deweyan talk about making philosophy relevant to political problems rather than the problems of professionalized academics, Rorty "tends to leave us with empty abstractions," in Bernstein, "Rorty's Liberal Utopia," 283–84. Amanda Anderson makes a related point by suggesting that Rorty does not adequately attend to "the distinction between epistemological and ethico-political virtue." See her "Pragmatism and Character," *Critical Inquiry* 29 (Winter 2003): 300.

10. George Orwell, "Politics and the English Language," in *The Collected Essays, Journalism, and Letters of George Orwell*, ed. Sonia Orwell and Ian Angus, vol. 4 (New York: Penguin Books, 1970): 156–69. Jerold Abrams has compellingly argued that Rorty need not exclude the imaginative experimentation in the private realm from public life: "Experimenting with vocabularies and somatic experiences in the private sphere is precisely the tool which will keep political discourse from going stale, and will keep citizens fresh for articulating new social concerns and new areas of human need." See Jerold J. Abrams, "Aesthetics of Self-Fashioning and Cosmopolitanism: Foucault and Rorty on the Art of Living," *Philosophy Today* 46, no. 2 (2002): 190.

11. John Dewey, "Creative Democracy—The Task Ahead of Us," in *The Later Works of John Dewey*, ed. Jo Ann Boydston, vol. 14 (Carbondale: Southern Illinois University Press, 1986), 226 (italics in original).

12. Dewey, "Creative Democracy," 226.

13. Dewey, "Creative Democracy," 228. Richard Rorty, "Pragmatism as Romantic Polytheism," in *The Revival of Pragmatism: New Essays on Social Thought, Law, and Culture*, ed. Morris Dickstein (Durham, NC: Duke University Press, 1997), 30.

Rorty and Thesis Eleven   193

14. Walt Whitman, *Democratic Vistas*, in *The Portable Walt Whitman*, ed. Mark Van Doren (New York: Penguin Books, 1973), 317. Here Whitman is paraphrasing Mill in *On Liberty*.

15. Richard J. Bernstein, "Rorty's Liberal Utopia," in *The New Constellation: The Ethical-Political Horizons of Modernity/Postmodernity* (Cambridge, MA: MIT Press, 1992), 274–75.

16. In a recent interview, Rorty has retreated somewhat from this stance: "I didn't say everybody had a public/private split, but some people do. . . . My public/private distinction wasn't an explanation of what every human life is like. I was, instead, urging that there was nothing wrong with letting people divide their lives along the public/private line. We don't have a moral responsibility to bring the two together. It was a negative point, not a positive recommendation about how everybody should behave." See Derek Nystrom and Kent Puckett, *Against Bosses, Against Oligarchies: A Conversation with Richard Rorty* (Charlottesville, VA: Prickly Pear Pamphlets, 1998), 61. However, I agree with Bernstein that the distinction between public and private is "the central thesis of his book [*Contingency*]" and that the coherence of his position collapses without it. He also points out that it is "curious" that Rorty, "who shows us that most distinctions are fuzzy, vague, and subject to historical contingencies, should rely on such a fixed, rigid, ahistorical dichotomy." See Bernstein, "Rorty's Liberal Utopia," 264, 286.

17. Rorty develops this argument in "Self-Creation and Affiliation: Proust, Nietzsche, and Heidegger," in CIS, 96–121.

18. On this idea see Christopher Voparil, "On the Idea of Philosophy as *Bildungsroman*: Rorty and His Critics," *Contemporary Pragmatism* 2, no. 1 (2005): 115–33.

19. For Rorty's argument about the novel as "the characteristic genre of democracy," see "Heidegger, Kundera, and Dickens," in EHO, 66–82. I examine this claim in depth in chapter 3.

20. Bernstein, "Rorty's Liberal Utopia," 280–81.

21. John Dewey, *Experience and Nature* (New York: Dover Publications, 1958), 245–46.

Index

Aeschylus, 85n35, 93
aesthetics, 1, 21, 29n13, 32n45, 45, 56n20, 72, 75, 80, 92, 132, 149n55, 192n10; and democracy, 105, 111n49, 113n49, 136, 138, 143n2, 147n35, 151n75, 153n94, 164, 189; and political theory, 5, 42–44, 150n63
agélaste, 70, 84n23
Anderson, Amanda, 6n5, 13, 18, 143n2
Arendt, Hannah, 118, 127, 134
argumentation, 9–11, 13, 24, 28n1, 28n4, 35–36, 42, 45–46, 54n1, 54n4, 55n8, 92, 94, 123
Arnold, Matthew, 67–68, 73, 147n36, 160

Baier, Annette, 93, 98–100, 109n24
Baldwin, James, 3, 5, 52–53, 63, 78–79, 152n92, 155–57, 159, 161–63, 165–67, 172–76
Barber, Benjamin, 144n8
Beauvoir, Simone de, 170, 180n42
Beiser, Frederick, 147n35
Beer, Samuel, 179n38
Bennett, William, 67, 79, 176
Bentham, Jeremy, 143n3
Berlin, Isaiah, 4, 120–22, 128, 134, 139, 145n27; influence on Rorty, 114, 119, 121–22, 130, 137

Bernstein, Richard, 1, 5n1, 6n4, 30n23, 33n52; on Rorty, 2, 9, 13, 16, 28n1, 29n12, 54n4, 107n9, 115, 124, 146n30, 153n94, 186, 190, 192n9, 193n16
Bildung, 118, 128, 147, 189
Bloom, Allan, 176
Bloom, Harold, 37, 48, 125–26, 132, 148n52
Booth, Wayne, 73, 77
Breytenbach, Breyten, 166–67
Bromwich, David, 67, 180n48
Brown, Charles Brockden, 84n28
Bruford, W. H., 147n36
Burrows, Jo, 66, 82n10
Butler, Judith, 110n39

Carlyle, Thomas, 129
Carnap, Rudolph, 55n11
Cavell, Stanley, 5, 15, 29n6, 32n42, 81, 88n52, 137, 141, 150n65, 152n85, 168, 170–71, 186. *See also* perfectionism
Cervantes, Miguel, 69
Christianity, 22, 26, 43, 73, 86n39, 162
Coleridge, Samuel Taylor, 143n3, 148
community, 50–51, 57n30, 68, 76, 91, 99, 111n48, 120; Rorty on, 3–4, 6n8, 37, 42–43, 46, 56n18, 57n23, 61–62,

72–76, 78, 81, 82n3, 86n38, 89–90,
92–94, 103, 115, 132, 139–40,
155–60, 163–66, 169, 171, 173, 176
communitarianism, 114, 120, 155;
Rorty's, 48, 57n28, 63–66, 72, 91,
133, 149n56, 166, 176
Connolly, William, 110n39, 178n21
Constant, Benjamin, 117
contingency, 13, 19, 32n41, 42, 63–64,
67, 69–74, 79, 131, 134, 184, 188,
190
Cooper, James Fenimore, 84n28

Dallmayr, Fred, 88n52, 181n51
Darwin, Charles, 26,
democracy, 5, 15–16, 19, 33n52, 61–65,
116–17, 135, 141, 144n8, 156, 159,
163–67, 169, 176–77, 183; and
character, 27, 120–22, 129; and
individuality, 113–14, 134–43,
151n80, 171; and pragmatism,
30n26, 33n52, 50, 70, 86n38, 105,
127, 180n49; and the novel, 40, 61,
65, 69, 70–72, 76–81, 83n18, 107n9,
159, 165–67, 190; as a way of life, 5,
18, 27, 81, 120, 136, 186–87;
deliberative, 57n30
Deneen, Patrick, 57n29
Dennett, Daniel, 43
Derrida, Jacques, 1, 125, 143n4,
146n32, 151n81, 184, 189
Descartes, Rene, 50, 69
Dewey, John, 6n7, 15–16, 39, 43, 53,
54n3, 56n20, 57n29, 93, 95, 113,
131, 134, 138, 149, 172–73, 189,
191; and John Stuart Mill, 145n23,
151n69; and Rorty, 4–5, 22, 35–37,
47–49, 51–52, 58n36, 64, 68, 79,
86n38, 105–6, 111n51, 125, 155,
157–58; *Art as Experience,* 46–47,
58n36, 68, 78, 105; on democracy,
16, 18, 26–27, 30n26, 113, 119–21,
136, 186; *Reconstruction in
Philosophy,* 51–52. *See also*
democracy as a way of life

Dickens, Charles, 61–63, 65, 70, 74, 93,
105, 180n39, 189
Dolan, Frederick, 56n22
Du Bois, W. E. B., 155–56
Dworkin, Ronald, 28n3

edification, 66, 73, 75, 147n36, 192
Eisenach, Eldon, 129, 143n3
Eliot, T. S., 22
Emerson, Ralph Waldo, 81, 117, 130,
133, 145n23, 147n35, 149n59,
152n85, 168–71, 178n11, 191; and
pragmatism, 2–5, 6n6, 13, 16, 30n26,
39, 115, 131, 134, 138, 192n7; and
Rorty, 3–4, 6n8, 27–28, 33n48, 39,
44, 53, 86n38, 105, 111n48, 134,
155–60, 163–64, 171–76, 185–86.
See also self–reliance
empiricism; radical, 16

Feuerbach, Ludwig, 183
Fish, Stanley, 6n7, 12, 15–16, 19–20,
26–28, 29n12, 30n26, 180n41
Flaubert, Gustave, 72, 92
Foucault, Michel, 29n13, 31n34, 93,
125–27, 143n2, 146n32, 159,
179n27, 192n10
foundationalism, 2, 16, 18–20, 24, 27,
28n1, 29n12, 40, 42, 48, 53, 59n40,
64, 66, 69, 82n3, 84n19, 89, 92,
111n50, 115, 123–25, 140, 146n29,
146n31, 176
Fraser, Nancy, 58n33
Freud, Sigmund, 53, 56n21, 66, 87n44
Friedman, Richard, 131

Goodman, Russell, 6n6, 55n15
Gunn, Giles, 6n6, 16

Habermas, Jurgen, 2, 9, 56n22, 95,
143n2, 146n33, 189; and Rorty,
45–47, 100 1, 109n36
Havel, Vaclav, 57n29
Hegel, Friedrich, 13, 25, 33n48, 66,
108n23

116, 119, 134, 143, 156, 161, 185.
See also political theory

Walzer, Michael, 165–72, 174, 179
Warner, Susan, 73, 85n37
West, Cornel, 1, 6n6, 16, 30n18, 52,
    105, 155, 157, 183
Westbrook, Robert, 111n51
Whitman, Walt, 30n26, 105, 111n49,
    113, 117–18, , 131, 137, 147n35,
    160–61, 163, 167, 169–71, 173,
    178n14, 179n38, 180n40; and Rorty,
    3–5, 6n8, 26–27, 36, 49, 85n37,
    115–16, 138–40, 142, 155–60, 164,
    177, 185–87; *Democratic Vistas,*
    157–61, 177; *Leaves of Grass,*
    157–58, 161
Wilde, Oscar, 140

Williams, Bernard, 85n36
Wittgenstein, Ludwig, 37, 40, 56n20,
    125
Wolin, Sheldon, 3, 6n7, 57n30, 81,
    88n52, 107n5, 117, 144n8, 144n9,
    150n63, 177n5, 179n24; and Rorty,
    36–40, 44, 47–50, 52–54, 55n11,
    87n46, 163–64, 191n3
Wordsworth, William, 21, 32n43,
    129
Wright, Richard, 65, 93, 162, 175,
    180n42

Yack, Bernard, 150n64
Yardley, Jonathan, 32n46, 181n55
Yeats, William Butler, 21

Zola, Emile, 65, 93, 191n5

About the Author

Christopher J. Voparil is assistant professor and chair of the Department of Humanities at Lynn University in Boca Raton, Florida, where he teaches philosophy and political theory. He received his PhD from the New School for Social Research in New York City and is the author of articles in *Contemporary Pragmatism* and *Philosophy and Social Criticism*. He is currently working on a book on Emerson and Tocqueville.